NorthStar 5

Listening and Speaking

THIRD EDITION

AUTHOR
Sherry Preiss

SERIES EDITORS
Frances Boyd
Carol Numrich

PEARSON
Longman

NorthStar: Listening and Speaking Level 5, Third Edition

Pearson Education, 10 Bank Street, White Plains, NY 10606

Contributor credit: Linda Lane, American Language Program at Columbia University, authored and edited PRONUNCIATION material for ***NorthStar: Listening and Speaking Levels 1–5, Third Edition.***

Staff credits: The people who made up the ***NorthStar: Listening and Speaking Level 5, Third Edition*** team, representing editorial, production, design, and manufacturing, are Aerin Csigay, Dave Dickey, Christine Edmonds, Ann France, Shelley Gazes, Gosia Jaros-White, Melissa Leyva, Martha McGaughey, Sherry Preiss, Robert Ruvo, Debbie Sistino, Paula Van Ells, and Mykan White.

Cover art: Silvia Rojas/Getty Images
Text composition: ElectraGraphics, Inc.
Text font: 11.5/13 Minion
Reviewers: See page 288
Credits: See page 289

Library of Congress Cataloging-in-Publication Data

Northstar. Listening and speaking. — 3rd ed.
4 v. ; cm.
Rev. ed. of: Northstar / Robin Mills and Helen Solórzano, 2nd. ed. 2004.
The third edition of the Northstar series has been expanded to 4 separate volumes. Each level is in a separate volume with different contributing authors.
Includes bibliographical references.
Contents: Level 2: Basic Low Intermediate /Laurie Frazier, Robin Mills — Level 3: Intermediate / Helen Solórzano, Jennifer P.L. Schmidt — Level 4: High Intermediate / Tess Ferree, Kim Sanabria — Level 5: Advanced / Sherry Preiss.
ISBN-13: 978-0-13-240988-9 (pbk. : student text bk. level 2 : alk. paper)
ISBN-10: 0-13-240988-7 (pbk. : student text bk. level 2 : alk. paper)
ISBN-13: 978-0-13-613313-1 (pbk. : student text bk. level 3 : alk. paper)
ISBN-10: 0-13-613313-4 (pbk. : student text bk. level 3 : alk. paper)
[etc.]
1. English language—Textbooks for foreign speakers. 2. English language—Spoken English—Problems, exercises, etc. 3. Listening—Problems, exercises, etc. I. Mills, Robin, 1964– Northstar. II. Title: Listening and speaking.
PE1128.N674 2008
428.2'4—dc22

2008024491

ISBN-10: 0-13-233674-X
ISBN-13: 978-0-13-233674-1

Printed in the United States of America
3 4 5 6 7 8 9 10—CRK—13 12 11 10 09

CONTENTS

WELCOME TO NORTHSTAR

THIRD EDITION

NorthStar, now in its third edition, motivates students to succeed in their **academic** as well as **personal** language goals.

For each of the five levels, the two strands—*Reading and Writing* and *Listening and Speaking*—provide a fully integrated approach for students and teachers.

WHAT IS SPECIAL ABOUT THE THIRD EDITION?

NEW THEMES

New themes and **updated content**—presented in a **variety of genres**, including literature and lectures, and in **authentic reading and listening selections**—challenge students intellectually.

ACADEMIC SKILLS

More purposeful **integration of critical thinking** and an enhanced focus on **academic skills** such as inferencing, synthesizing, note taking, and test taking help students develop strategies for **success** in the **classroom** and on **standardized tests.** A **culminating productive task** galvanizes content, language, and **critical thinking skills**.

➢ In the *Listening and Speaking* strand, a **structured approach** gives students opportunities for **more extended and creative oral practice**, for example, presentations, simulations, debates, case studies, and public service announcements.

➢ In the *Reading and Writing* strand, a new, **fully integrated writing section** leads students through the **writing process** with engaging writing assignments focusing on various rhetorical modes.

NEW DESIGN

Full **color pages** with more **photos**, **illustrations, and graphic organizers** foster student engagement and make the content and activities come alive.

MyNorthStarLab

MyNorthStarLab, an easy-to-use **online learning and assessment program**, offers:

➢ Unlimited access to reading and listening selections and DVD segments.

➢ Focused test preparation to help students succeed on international exams such as TOEFL® and IELTS®. Pre- and post-unit assessments improve results by providing individualized instruction, instant feedback, and personalized study plans.

➢ Original activities that support and extend the *NorthStar* program. These include pronunciation practice using voice recording tools, and activities to build note taking skills and academic vocabulary.

➢ Tools that save time. These include a flexible gradebook and authoring features that give teachers control of content and help them track student progress.

THE NORTHSTAR APPROACH

The *NorthStar* series is based on **current research in language acquisition** and on the **experiences of teachers and curriculum designers**. Five principles guide the *NorthStar* approach.

PRINCIPLES

1 **The more profoundly students are stimulated intellectually and emotionally, the more language they will use and retain.**

The thematic organization of *NorthStar* promotes intellectual and emotional stimulation. The 50 sophisticated themes in *NorthStar* present intriguing topics such as recycled fashion, restorative justice, personal carbon footprints, and microfinance. The authentic content engages students, links them to language use outside of the classroom, and encourages personal expression and critical thinking.

2 **Students can learn both the form and content of the language.**

Grammar, vocabulary, and culture are inextricably woven into the units, providing students with systematic and multiple exposures to language forms in a variety of contexts. As the theme is developed, students can express complex thoughts using a higher level of language.

3 **Successful students are active learners.**

Tasks are designed to be creative, active, and varied. Topics are interesting and up-to-date. Together these tasks and topics (1) allow teachers to bring the outside world into the classroom and (2) motivate students to apply their classroom learning in the outside world.

4 **Students need feedback.**

This feedback comes naturally when students work together practicing language and participating in open-ended opinion and inference tasks. Whole class activities invite teachers' feedback on the spot or via audio/video recordings or notes. The innovative new MyNorthStarLab gives students immediate feedback as they complete computer-graded language activities online; it also gives students the opportunity to submit writing or speaking assignments electronically to their instructor for feedback later.

5 **The quality of relationships in the language classroom is important because students are asked to express themselves on issues and ideas.**

The information and activities in *NorthStar* promote genuine interaction, acceptance of differences, and authentic communication. By building skills and exploring ideas, the exercises help students participate in discussions and write essays of an increasingly complex and sophisticated nature.

THE NORTHSTAR UNIT

1 FOCUS ON THE TOPIC

This section introduces students to the unifying theme of the listening selections.

PREDICT and **SHARE INFORMATION** foster interest in the unit topic and help students develop a personal connection to it.

BACKGROUND AND VOCABULARY activities provide students with tools for understanding the first listening selection. Later in the unit, students review this vocabulary and learn related idioms, collocations, and word forms. This helps them explore content and expand their written and spoken language.

UNIT 7

Workplace Privacy

1 FOCUS ON THE TOPIC

A PREDICT

1. Look at the cartoon. It shows employees arriving at their offices. The man says he is willing to give up civil liberties in order to gain security. However, he is worried that doing so might mean there will be few civil liberties left. Can you guess what he means by "civil liberties" and "security"?
2. What do you think of when you hear the word *privacy*? What does it mean to you? Brainstorm topics or words that may come up when discussing this issue, such as *snooping, confidential,* and *wiretapping.*

147

B SHARE INFORMATION

In a small group, discuss your answers to the questions.

1. Our ability to enjoy privacy often depends on the physical nature of the space we inhabit. Think about the home you grew up in and the home you are living in now. How does your sense of privacy compare in the two places? What factors make it easy or difficult to find privacy?
2. Think of different cultures you are familiar with. Comment on how the sense of privacy may differ. Think of home, school, and workplace. How much privacy do people expect? How is privacy protected?
3. When do you feel your privacy is being invaded? For example, would you feel your privacy was being invaded if _____?
   a. an employer opened and read your office mail or e-mail
   b. a colleague looked through your files, either on paper or on a computer
   c. someone you just met asked your age, marital status, or salary

C BACKGROUND AND VOCABULARY

To keep up-to-date on workplace privacy and other important issues, many professionals write and read blogs (web logs) on the Internet. The following blog is a composite of information and opinion based on real blogs. On the blog, interested people bring up various aspects of workplace privacy, answering and raising questions. Readers then add their responses in order to conduct a public discussion.

CD 2 *Read and listen to the blog and then match the boldfaced vocabulary with the definitions and synonyms that follow.*

148 UNIT 7

2 FOCUS ON LISTENING

This section focuses on understanding two contrasting listening selections.

LISTENING ONE is a radio report, interview, lecture, or other genre that addresses the unit topic. In levels 1 to 3, listenings are based on authentic materials. In levels 4 and 5, all the listenings are authentic.

LISTEN FOR MAIN IDEAS and **LISTEN FOR DETAILS** are comprehension activities that lead students to an understanding and appreciation of the first selection.

The **MAKE INFERENCES** activity prompts students to "listen between the lines," move beyond the literal meaning, exercise critical thinking skills, and understand the listening on a more academic level. Students follow up with pair or group work to discuss topics in the **EXPRESS OPINIONS** section.

2 FOCUS ON LISTENING

A LISTENING ONE: Interview with an Internet Addiction Counselor

Because so many students overuse the Internet, some university health services offer help with the problem. Dr. Jonathan Kandell, a psychologist from the University of Maryland in the United States, was interviewed by Ira Flatow, host of *Science Friday* from NPR® (National Public Radio). Dr. Kandell discusses his approach to students with symptoms of Internet addiction.

Work with a partner. Listen to the first 35 seconds of the interview. Write down three questions that you think Ira Flatow might ask Dr. Kandell, the counselor.

1. ______________________
2. ______________________
3. ______________________

LISTEN FOR MAIN IDEAS

Look at the chart. Listen to the interview and take notes on the main ideas. Use a separate piece of paper if necessary. (You will note details later.) Work with a partner to compare and revise your notes.

MAIN IDEAS	DETAILS
Focus of interview unusual or "other" addictions	Examples of addictions gambling, . . .
Kandell's view of Internet addiction	Evidence for this view
Chief symptoms/warning signs of Internet addiction	Other symptoms/warning signs
Possible treatment	Reasons this treatment is helpful

LISTEN FOR DETAILS

Read the chart again. Fill in as many details as possible to support the main ideas. Then listen to the interview again to check your work. Work with a partner to compare and revise your notes.

MAKE INFERENCES

When you are listening, making inferences means understanding something that is not literally stated, but which you believe is true based on the intention, attitude, voice, pausing, and choice of words of the speakers.

Read the questions. Then listen to each excerpt from the interview. Write your answers and then discuss them with a partner. Give reasons for your choices. Each question has more than one possible answer.

Excerpt One

A *groupie* usually refers to someone, especially a young woman, who likes a musician, movie star, or sports star and follows this person around hoping to meet the star. Why does Ira Flatow, the host, use the word *groupie* when he advises the radio audience to listen carefully? What does the word *groupie* imply in this context?

____

Excerpt Two

Dr. Kandell doesn't answer Flatow's question directly. What expressions show his hesitation? Why doesn't he answer Flatow directly?

____

Excerpt Three

How does Flatow feel about this topic at this point in the interview? How do you know? What words and tone of voice does he use to indicate his attitude?

____

EXPRESS OPINIONS

Discuss the questions with the class. Give your opinions and give reasons for them.

1. Do you know people who overuse the Internet? Do you overuse it? What are the warning signs? What treatment would you recommend for Internet addicts?
2. Dr. Kandell runs a support group for Internet addicts at his university. Do you think that universities should have this service? How helpful can such a support group be? Explain. What other support groups do you know of? Would you ever join one? Why or why not?
3. Anne Lamott, author of a book of essays called *Bird by Bird*, writes, "Getting all of one's addictions under control is a little like putting an octopus to bed." What does she mean? How do you feel about her analogy? Explain.

LISTENING TWO offers another perspective on the topic and is usually another genre. Again, in levels 1 to 3, the listenings are based on authentic materials and in levels 4 and 5, they are authentic. This second listening is followed by an activity that challenges students to question ideas they formed about the first listening, and to use appropriate language skills to analyze and explain their ideas.

INTEGRATE LISTENINGS ONE AND TWO presents culminating activities. Students are challenged to take what they have learned, organize the information, and synthesize it in a meaningful way. Students practice skills that are essential for success in authentic academic settings and on standardized tests.

B LISTENING TWO: Interview with a Microfinance Director

Listen to a microfinance expert, Will Bullard, tell the story of a woman in a village in Honduras, Central America. This real story illustrates how a local lending organization, or "assembly," works—the benefits and pitfalls.

Part One: Maria Jose's Story

Check (✓) the true statements. Correct the false statements.

____ 1. Maria Jose Perona had nine children, all of whom were malnourished.

____ 2. The women in the assembly decide who gets the loan.

____ 3. The women did not vote to grant Maria Jose Perona the loan because they thought she would spend the loan on food, not on the business.

____ 4. The women finally agreed and gave her a loan of 25 dollars.

____ 5. Maria Jose Perona had to take a test to get the 25 dollars.

____ 6. Maria Jose Perona bought flour and cooking supplies with her loan.

____ 7. She created a small meat pie business in front of the school.

____ 8. Although she paid her friend back, she was not allowed into the assembly.

____ 9. She finally became successful and was then allowed into the assembly.

____ 10. She built a concrete house and became president of the assembly.

Part Two: Non-Monetary Benefits of Microfinance

Check (✓) the non-monetary benefits (other benefits not related to money) that the speaker mentions or implies.

____ 11. sales and marketing skills

____ 12. education

____ 13. confidence

____ 14. risk-taking ability

Part Three: Business Training

Check (✓) the phrases that complete the statement accurately.

The speaker believes that business training is important because the women ____.

____ 15. find the loans too small

____ 16. don't know how to manage their money carefully

____ 17. sell very similar things

____ 18. should sell things that bring them more money

Microfinance: Changing Lives $50 at a Time 235

C INTEGRATE LISTENINGS ONE AND TWO

STEP 1: Organize

Review Listenings One and Two. In each listening, speakers refer to three major benefits of microfinance. Work with a partner. Complete the chart by identifying specific examples of these benefits from each listening.

BENEFITS OF MICROFINANCE	EXAMPLES: LISTENING ONE	EXAMPLES: LISTENING TWO
Financial changes		
Non-monetary changes		
Sustainability		

STEP 2: Synthesize

Work in groups of three. Each person will choose one of the benefits listed in the chart above. Review the related examples from Listening One and Listening Two. After two minutes, close your book and present a one-minute summary to the group. Use examples.

3 FOCUS ON SPEAKING

A VOCABULARY

REVIEW

A journalist for *Economic Daily,* Pedro Martinez, broadcast an "audio postcard" about his recent trip to La Ceiba, Honduras.

236 UNIT 10

3 FOCUS ON SPEAKING

This section emphasizes development of productive skills for speaking. It includes sections on vocabulary, grammar, pronunciation, functional language, and an extended speaking task.

The **VOCABULARY** section leads students from reviewing the unit vocabulary, to practicing and expanding their use of it, and then working with it—using it creatively in both this section and in the final speaking task.

Students learn useful structures for speaking in the **GRAMMAR** section, which offers a concise presentation and targeted practice. Vocabulary items are recycled here, providing multiple exposures leading to mastery. For additional practice with the grammar presented, students and teachers can consult the GRAMMAR BOOK REFERENCES at the end of the book for corresponding material in the *Focus on Grammar* and Azar series.

1 *Read the transcript of Martinez's report. Fill in the blanks with the appropriate word or expression from the list. Use the phrases under the blanks to help you.*

anecdote	had faith in	panacea	took a hit
compelling	hit a ceiling	pitfalls	wiped out
diminish	kicker	sustainable	the world over
elaborate	malnourished		

www.Transformationinternational.org

Greetings from La Ceiba, Honduras. First, I must tell you that this little speck on Earth is just unbelievably gorgeous—beautiful, lush, with breathtaking cloud formations hugging spectacular green mountains.

Still, on the drive from the airport to my lodge I witnessed the pervasive poverty we see ______________ (1. in every area of the world): skinny, ______________ (2. sick or weak due to lack of food) children standing next to houses and shops still not rebuilt since Hurricane Mitch ______________ (3. destroyed) much of the country in 1988. Already the second poorest country in Latin America, Honduras ______________ (4. was negatively affected) and never recovered. To research my article, I set out to visit microfinance institutions as well as meet the microcredit client to whom I had lent money from my laptop in Mexico City, where I live.

Kiva.org is a nonprofit microcredit organization that allows individuals with access to the Internet to fight global poverty in a ______________ (5. able to continue long-term) way by making a direct personal loan to poor entrepreneurs anywhere in the world. On the Kiva website I came across the ______________ (6. so interesting or exciting that you have to pay attention) photo and story of Julia Marta Mendez, a fascinating Honduran widow in her late thirties with six children, to whom I

Microfinance: Changing Lives $50 at a Time **237**

B **GRAMMAR: Count and Non-Count Nouns and Their Quantifiers**

1 *Work with a partner. Examine the statements, and discuss the questions that follow.*

- Very few spiritual **journeys** can compare to visiting the monasteries on Mt. Athos.
- With 20 monasteries and a limit of four days, it took Claassen quite a bit of **effort** to see more than six monasteries on one trip.
- Some monks are concerned about the growing number of **pilgrimages** to Mt. Athos these days.
- It takes a great deal of **discipline** to fast for a month.

1. Categorize the boldfaced nouns into count and non-count nouns.
2. What do the underlined expressions of quantity tell us?

COUNT AND NON-COUNT NOUNS

All nouns in English can be divided into two groups: count nouns and non-count nouns. **Count nouns** are those that can be counted and made plural (*monasteries, monks*). In contrast, **non-count nouns** can be considered as a mass and cannot be made plural (*spirituality, air*). Non-count nouns may refer to categories made up of different things (*money, furniture*), phenomena that occur in nature (*darkness, weather*), or abstractions (*violence, greed, honesty*).

Certain expressions of quantity, called **quantifiers**, state the amount of the noun. Some quantifiers are used with count nouns, and others are used with non-count nouns.

Quantifiers before Count Nouns	Quantifiers before Non-Count Nouns
a lot of	a lot of
many / a great many	a great deal of
quite a few	quite a bit of
a bunch of	a large amount of
a (large) number of	
certain	
not many	not much
very few (just a few / only a few)	very little (just a little / only a little)
a few / few	a little / little
fewer	less

GRAMMAR TIP: Notice the change in meaning when the indefinite article *a* is placed before *few* and *little*.

Few / Little

- negative meaning
- similar to *not much* and *not many*

A few / A little

- positive meaning
- similar to *some* (when talking about a small quantity)

Compare:

- *Few* people can fast more than three days in a row.
- *A few* people from our group decided to return to the monastery for another visit.

136 UNIT 6

The **PRONUNCIATION** section presents both controlled and freer, communicative practice of the sounds and patterns of English. Models from the listening selections reinforce content and vocabulary. This is followed by the **FUNCTION** section where students are exposed to functional language that prepares them to express ideas on a higher level. Examples have been chosen based on frequency, variety, and usefulness for the final speaking task.

The **PRODUCTION** section gives students an opportunity to integrate the ideas, vocabulary, grammar, pronunciation, and function presented in the unit. This final speaking task is the culminating activity of the unit and gets students to exchange ideas and express opinions in sustained speaking contexts. Activities are presented in a sequence that builds confidence and fluency, and allows for more than one "try" at expression. When appropriate, students practice some presentation skills: audience analysis, organization, eye contact, or use of visuals.

C SPEAKING

PRONUNCIATION: Vowel Alternation

In some pairs of related English words, the vowel sounds shift or alternate. These words are pronounced quite differently.

1 *Listen to the difference between the underlined vowels in these pairs of words.*

divine–divinity	grateful–gratitude	compete–competitiveness
/ay/ /ɪ/	/ey/ /æ/	/iy/ /ɛ/

2 *Listen to the pairs of words, and repeat them.*

1. a. divine — divinity
   b. rite — ritual
   c. decide — decision
   d. write — written
2. a. grateful — gratitude
   b. explain — explanatory
   c. Spain — Spanish
   d. nation — national
3. a. compete — competitiveness
   b. keep — kept
   c. steal — stealth
   d. please — pleasure

3 *Work with a partner. Say the pairs of words. Circle only the pairs that have different vowel sounds. Say the circled pairs again. Write* **1** *if they alternate like* divine–divinity; *write* **2** *if the alternation is like* grateful–gratitude; *and write* **3** *if the alternation is like* compete–competitiveness.

____ 1. deal–dealt ____ 7. advise–advisor
____ 2. race–racial ____ 8. sleep–slept
____ 3. line–linear ____ 9. divide–division
____ 4. pervade–pervasive ____ 10. danger–dangerous
____ 5. life–live ____ 11. sane–sanity
____ 6. nature–natural ____ 12. faith–faithful

FUNCTION: Telling an Anecdote

Everyone loves to hear a good anecdote, or short story. Storytelling is one of the oldest, most basic methods for sharing information, knowledge, and experiences. In this short excerpt, the interviewer skillfully encourages William Claassen to share a few of his experiences visiting monasteries around the world.

Spiritual Renewal **141**

PRODUCTION: Group Discussion

In this activity, you will ***conduct a group discussion*** to debate the pros and cons of business expansion for a monastery. Try to use the vocabulary, grammar, pronunciation, and language for telling a story that you learned in the unit.*

Work in a small group. Read the information and case study, which are based on a real story. Then work in a small group, and follow the directions for the speaking activity.

Background

Mepkin Abbey, located in the southeastern state of South Carolina, sits on 3,000 acres of beautiful country property. Since 1949, life there has been dedicated to the Trappist monastic traditions of solitude, prayer, work, and community. People who go on retreat to Mepkin learn the daily routine of the 45 monks who live there. However, retreats are not enough to keep the abbey financially stable. Economic renewal is proposed for the abbey–but are these plans at odds with a centuries-old way of ascetic life?

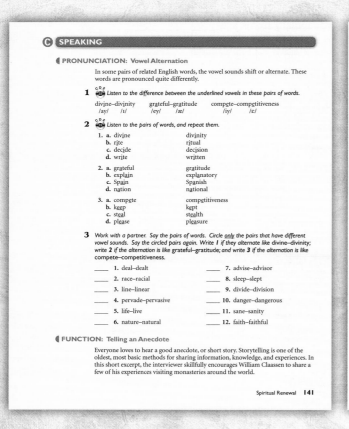

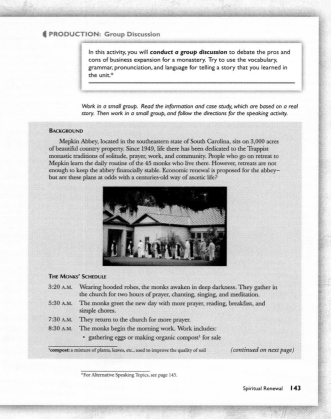

The Monks' Schedule

3:20 A.M. Wearing hooded robes, the monks awaken in deep darkness. They gather in the church for two hours of prayer, chanting, singing, and meditation.
5:30 A.M. The monks greet the new day with more prayer, reading, breakfast, and simple chores.
7:30 A.M. They return to the church for more prayer.
8:30 A.M. The monks begin the morning work. Work includes:
- gathering eggs or making organic compost[1] for sale

[1]**compost:** a mixture of plants, leaves, etc., used to improve the quality of soil

(continued on next page)

*For Alternative Speaking Topics, see page 145.

Spiritual Renewal **143**

ALTERNATIVE SPEAKING TOPICS are provided at the end of the unit. They can be used as *alternatives* to the final speaking task, or as *additional* assignments. RESEARCH TOPICS tied to the theme of the unit are organized in a special section at the back of the book.

COMPONENTS

TEACHER'S MANUAL AND ACHIEVEMENT TESTS

Each level and strand of *NorthStar* has an accompanying Teacher's Manual with step-by-step **teaching suggestions**, including unique guidance for using *NorthStar* in secondary classes. The manuals include time guidelines, expansion activities, and techniques and instructions for using MyNorthStarLab. Also included are reproducible unit-by-unit achievement **tests** of **receptive** and **productive** skills, **answer keys** to both the student book and tests, and a unit-by-unit **vocabulary** list.

EXAMVIEW

NorthStar ExamView is a stand-alone CD-ROM that allows teachers to **create and customize** their own *NorthStar* tests.

DVD

The *NorthStar* DVD has **engaging, authentic video clips**, including animation, documentaries, interviews, and biographies, that correspond to the themes in *NorthStar*. Each theme contains a three- to five-minute segment that can be used with either the *Reading and Writing* strand or the *Listening and Speaking* strand. The video clips can also be viewed in MyNorthStarLab.

COMPANION WEBSITE

The companion website, www.longman.com/northstar, includes resources for teachers, such as the **scope and sequence**, **correlations** to other Longman products and to state standards, and **podcasts** from the *NorthStar* authors and series editors.

MyNorthStarLab

PEARSON LONGMAN mynorthstarlab | AVAILABLE WITH the new edition of ***NORTHSTAR***

NorthStar is now available with **MyNorthStarLab**—an easy-to-use **online** program **for students and teachers** that saves time and improves results.

- **STUDENTS** receive **personalized instruction** and **practice** in all four skills. Audio, video, and test preparation are all in **one** place—available **anywhere, anytime**.
- **TEACHERS** can take advantage of many resources including online **assessments**, a flexible **gradebook**, and **tools for monitoring student progress**.

CHECK IT OUT! GO TO www.mynorthstarlab.com FOR A PREVIEW!

TURN THE PAGE TO SEE KEY FEATURES OF **MyNorthStarLab**.

MyNorthStarLab

MyNorthStarLab supports students with **individualized instruction**, **feedback**, and **extra help**. A wide array of resources, including a flexible **gradebook**, helps teachers manage student progress.

The MyNorthStarLab **WELCOME** page **organizes assignments and grades**, and **facilitates communication** between students and teachers.

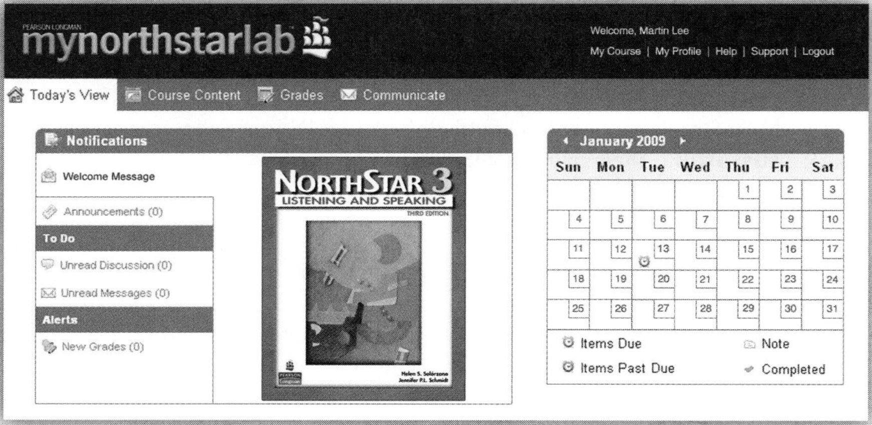

For each unit, MyNorthStarLab provides a **READINESS CHECK**.

➢ Activities **assess** student knowledge **before** beginning the unit and **follow up** with individualized instruction.

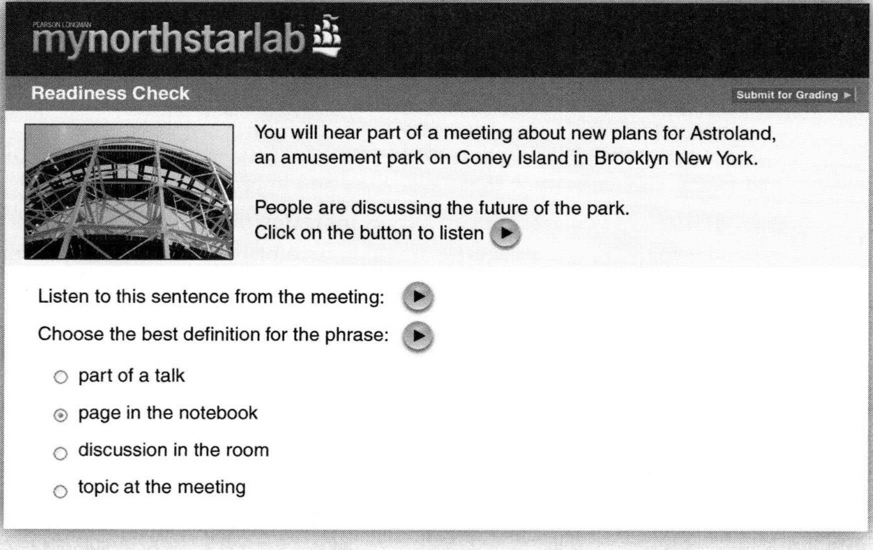

Student book material and **new** practice activities are available to students online.

- Students benefit from virtually unlimited **practice anywhere, anytime**.

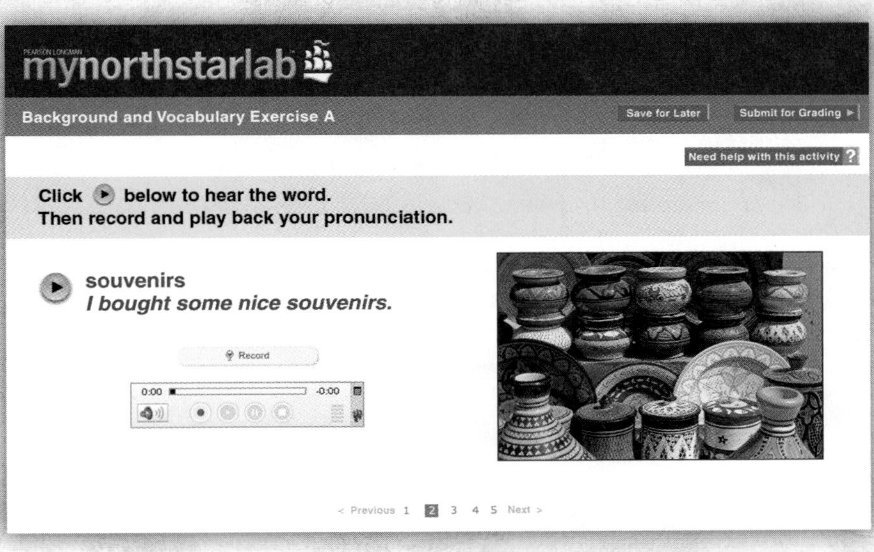

Interaction with **Internet** and **video** materials will:

- Expand students' knowledge of the topic.
- Help students practice new vocabulary and grammar.

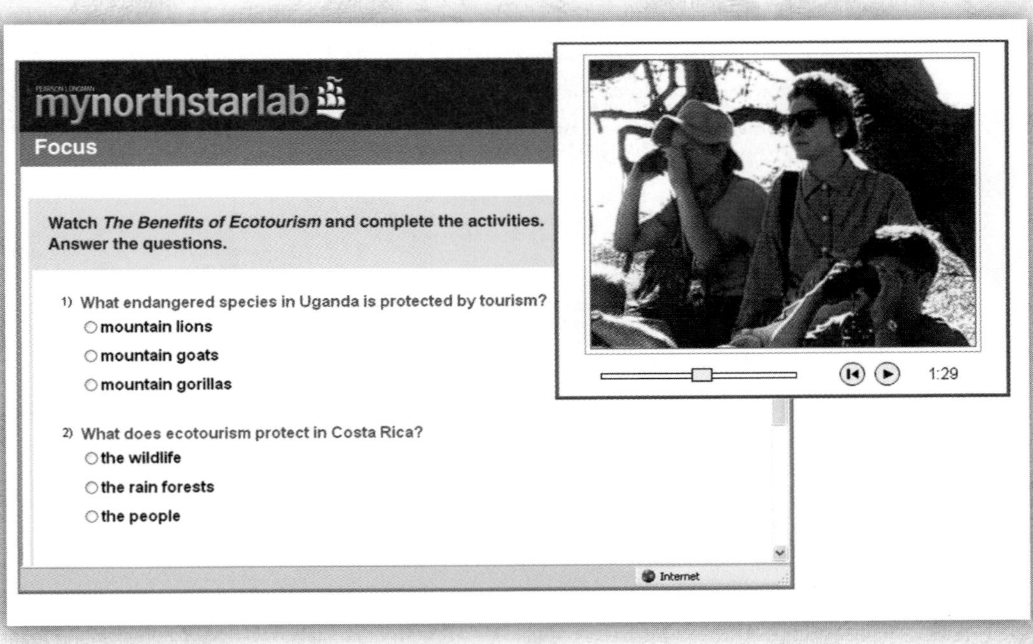

INTEGRATED SKILL ACTIVITIES in MyNorthStarLab challenge students to bring together the **language skills** and **critical thinking skills** that they have practiced throughout the unit.

PEARSON LONGMAN
mynorthstarlab

Integrated Task - Read, Listen, Write

Submit for Grading ▶

THE ADVENTURE OF A LIFETIME

We at the Antarctic Travel Society encourage you to consider an excited guided tour of Antarctica for your next vacation.

The Antarctic Travel society carefully plans and operates tours of the Antarctic by ship. There are three trips per day leaving from ports in South America and Australia. Each ship carries only about 100 passengers at a time. Tours run from November through March to the ice-free areas along the coast of Antarctica.

In addition to touring the coast, our ships stop for on-land visits, which generally last for about three hours. Activities include guided sightseeing, mountain climbing, camping, kayaking, and scuba diving. For a longer stay, camping trips can also be arranged.

Our tours will give you an opportunity to experience the richness of Antarctica, including its wildlife, history, active research stations, and, most of all, its natural beauty.

Tours are supervised by the ship's staff. The staff generally includes experts in animal and sea life and other Antarctica specialists. There is generally one staff member for every 10 to 20 passengers. Theses trained and responsible individuals will help to make your visit to Antarctica safe, educational, and unforgettable.

READ, LISTEN AND WRITE ABOUT TOURISM IN ANTARCTICA

Read.
Read the text. Then answer the question.

According to the text, how can tourism benefit the Antartic?

Listen.
Click on the Play button and listen to the passage.
Use the outline to take notes as you listen.

Main idea:

Seven things that scientists study:

The effects of tourism:

Write.
Write about the potential and risks in Antarctica.
Follow the steps to prepare.

Step 1
- Review the text and your outline from the listening task.
- Write notes about the benefits and risks of tourism.

Step 2
Write for 20 minutes. Leave 5 minutes to edit your work.

The MyNorthStarLab **ASSESSMENT** tools allow instructors to customize and deliver achievement tests online.

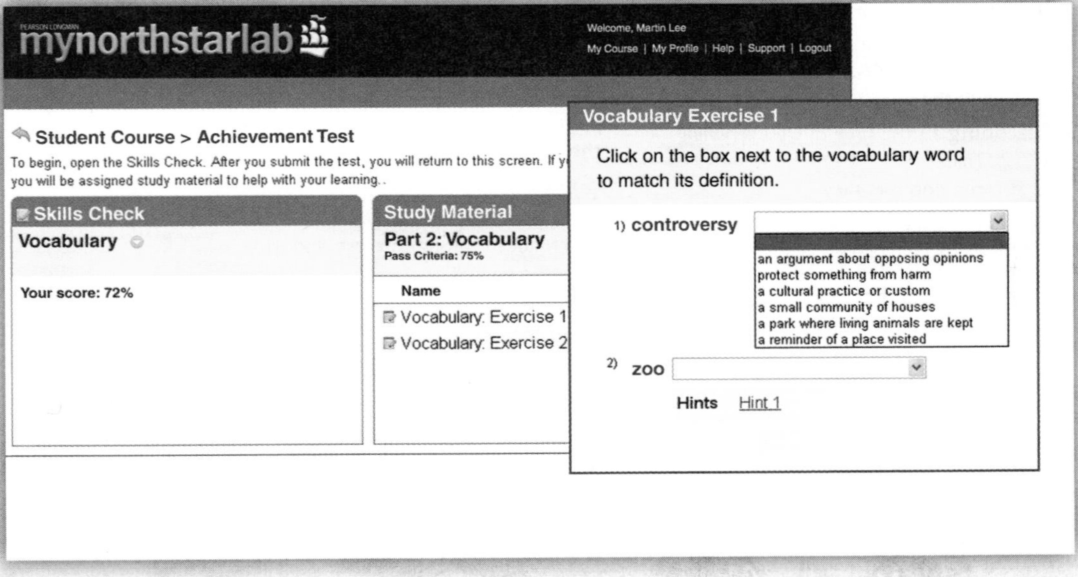

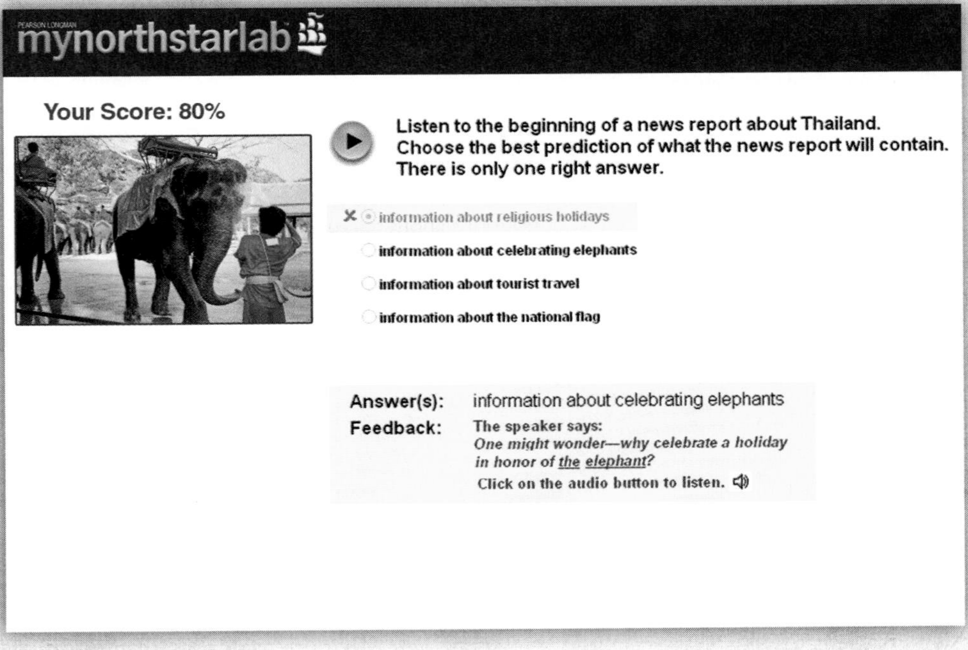

SCOPE AND SEQUENCE

UNIT	CRITICAL THINKING	LISTENING
1 The Internet and Other Addictions **Theme:** Addiction **Listening One:** *Interview with an Internet Addiction Counselor* A radio interview **Listening Two:** *Time to Do Everything Except Think* A radio commentary	Infer word meaning from context Recognize personal assumptions about technology Infer information not explicit in the interviews Compare and contrast differing viewpoints Support opinions with information from the interviews Hypothesize another's point of view	Make predictions Listen for main ideas Listen for details Make inferences Relate listenings to personal experiences and values Organize and synthesize information from the listenings
2 Honesty Is the Best Policy **Theme:** Lying **Listening One:** *Interview with a Psychiatrist* A radio interview **Listening Two:** *Family Secrets* An interview	Clarify values relating to truth and lying Infer word meaning from context Consider the effects of mistrust Investigate motivations for keeping secrets, and exposing the lies of others Investigate multiple sides to an ethical issue	Make predictions Listen for main ideas Listen for details Make inferences based on tone, pace, and vocabulary Relate listenings to personal experiences and values Organize and synthesize information from the listenings
3 The Bold and the Bashful **Theme:** Personality **Listening One:** *Americans Are Getting Shyer* A radio interview **Listening Two:** *The Pollyanna Syndrome* A radio commentary	Infer word meaning from context Analyze the impact of shyness on one's life Infer information not explicit in the interviews Categorize and apply descriptive vocabulary Support opinions with information from the interviews Draw conclusions about personality types and roles	Listen for main ideas Listen for details Make inferences based on tone, pace, and vocabulary Relate listenings to personal experiences and values Organize and synthesize information from the listenings

SPEAKING	VOCABULARY	GRAMMAR	PRONUNCIATION
Express and solicit opinions Relate personal experiences Role-play a scripted conversation Express wishes Add information and opinions to others' ideas Participate in and summarize a discussion	Use context clues to infer meaning Identify and use word forms Identify synonyms and idiomatic expressions	Wish statements—expressing unreality	Stressing important words
Express and solicit opinions and values Relate personal experiences Express agreement and disagreement Role-play a scripted conversation Introduce, defend, and express the different sides of an issue	Use context clues to determine sequence Identify and use word forms	Modals—degrees of certainty	Reduction of the auxiliary *have*
Describe personality Express opinions Express and defend preferences Begin and maintain conversations Role-play discussion in a personality consulting company	Use context clues to infer meaning Use colloquial language Identify and use synonyms and idiomatic expressions Categorize descriptive language	Adjective clauses—identifying and nonidentifying	Grouping words together

SCOPE AND SEQUENCE

UNIT	CRITICAL THINKING	LISTENING
4 The Tipping Point **Theme:** Trends **Listening One:** *The Tipping Point* A radio interview **Listening Two:** *Tipping Points in Fighting Crime* A radio interview	Interpret graphs Analyze book reviews Infer word meaning from context Analyze different opinions Investigate reasons for trends and changes Understand metaphorical language	Predict content Listen for main ideas Listen for details Make inferences based on tone, pace, and vocabulary Relate information to others' viewpoints Organize and synthesize information from the listenings
5 Feng Shui: Ancient Wisdom Travels West **Theme:** Cross-cultural insights **Listening One:** *Interview with a Feng Shui Expert* A radio interview **Listening Two:** *Feng Shui in the Newsroom* A radio interview	Consider the impact of a philosophy on daily life Infer word meaning from context Infer information not explicit in the interviews Compare and contrast differing viewpoints Support opinions with information from the interviews Choose information in a passage to mark and highlight	Make predictions Listen for main ideas Listen for details Make inferences based on vocabulary choices and tone of voice Relate listenings to personal experiences Organize and synthesize information from the listenings
6 Spiritual Renewal **Theme:** Religion **Listening One:** *The Religious Traditions of Fasting* A radio interview **Listening Two:** *Describing Monastic Life* A radio interview	Separate fact from myth Infer word meaning from context Analyze and discuss different opinions Recognize similarities and differences among various religions Understand the importance and value of religious rituals	Make predictions Listen for main ideas Listen for details Make inferences about a speaker's intention Organize and synthesize information from the listenings
7 Workplace Privacy **Theme:** Business **Listening One:** *Interview on Workplace Surveillance* A radio interview **Listening Two:** *Managers and Employees Speak Out* A radio broadcast	Interpret a cartoon Analyze editorial blogs and individual responses Infer word meaning from context Analyze and discuss different opinions Frame arguments Debate ideas and cases	Make predictions Listen for main ideas Listen for details Make inferences based on tone and word choice Organize and synthesize information from the listenings Relate information in the listenings to one's viewpoints

SPEAKING	VOCABULARY	GRAMMAR	PRONUNCIATION
Identify and use different forms of the same root word Understand and use metaphorical expressions Role-play a scripted conversation Discuss trends and viral marketing Add to others' ideas Create and present a public service announcement	Use context clues to infer meaning Identify and use word forms Identify and use synonyms and metaphorical expressions	Adverb clauses of result	Stress changing suffixes
Express and solicit opinions Relate personal experiences and knowledge Role-play a scripted conversation Use target vocabulary in free responses Emphasize a point Present an argument based on a written article	Use context clues to infer meaning Identify and use word forms Identify and use idiomatic expressions	Spoken discourse connectors	Intonation on sentence introducers
Discuss background knowledge and personal beliefs Role-play scripted and semi-scripted conversations Tell and encourage others to tell an anecdote Role-play a group discussion	Use context clues to infer meaning Identify and use word forms Identify and use idiomatic expressions	Count and non-count nouns and their quantifiers	Vowel alternation
Use and check understanding of new words and expressions Agree and disagree with opinions Role-play scripted and semi-scripted conversations Frame oral arguments Conduct a debate on a case related to workplace privacy	Use context clues to infer meaning Identify and use synonyms Identify and use idiomatic expressions	Verb + gerund or infinitive—two forms, two meanings	Stress on two-syllable words

SCOPE AND SEQUENCE

UNIT	CRITICAL THINKING	LISTENING
8 Warriors without Weapons **Theme:** The Military **Listening One:** *Warriors without Weapons* A radio interview **Listening Two:** *Michael Ignatieff's Views on War* A continuation of the radio interview	Respond to pictures and symbols Share experiences Gather background information Infer word meaning from context Analyze and discuss different opinions Distinguish between direct and indirect speech	Make predictions Listen for main ideas Listen for details Make inferences based on tone and word choice Organize and synthesize information from the listenings
9 Boosting Brain Power through the Arts **Theme:** The Arts **Listening One:** *Does Music Enhance Math Skills?* A radio interview **Listening Two:** *Music, Art, and the Brain* A radio interview	Interpret a cartoon Analyze scientific experiments and studies Infer word meaning from context Analyze and discuss different opinions Analyze figurative language Compare and contrast results from experiments and studies	Make predictions Listen for main ideas Listen for details Make inferences based on implied information Organize and synthesize information from the listenings Relate information in the listenings to others' viewpoints
10 Microfinance: Changing Lives $50 at a Time **Theme:** Poverty **Listening One:** *Microfinance* A radio interview **Listening Two:** *Interview with a Microfinance Director* A radio interview	Interpret photographs Share background knowledge and impressions Analyze and evaluate aid programs Identify and use supporting information Infer word meaning from context Analyze and discuss different opinions	Listen for main ideas Listen for details Make inferences based on vocabulary choices and tone of voice Paraphrase and relate information in the listenings to others' viewpoints Organize and synthesize information from the listenings

SPEAKING	VOCABULARY	GRAMMAR	PRONUNCIATION
Role-play a scripted conversation Use direct and indirect speech when re-telling a story Respond appropriately to complex and controversial questions Create a public service announcement	Use context clues to infer meaning Identify and use synonyms and commonly confused words Identify and use idiomatic expressions	Direct and indirect speech	Vowels
Recognize and use figurative language Role-play a scripted and a semi-scripted conversation Discuss experiments and studies Use linking expressions to discuss similarities and differences Role-play a public meeting	Use context clues to infer meaning Distinguish between literal and figurative meanings Identify and use synonyms Identify and use idiomatic expressions	The passive voice and the passive causative	Joining final consonants
Share predictions and opinions Discuss proposals Paraphrase and react to quotes Role-play conversations Add details and examples to support main ideas Simulate a policy meeting	Use context clues to infer meaning Identify and use word forms Identify and use paraphrases and synonyms Identify and use idiomatic expressions	Unreal conditionals—present, past, and mixed	Stress in two-word units used as nouns

ACKNOWLEDGMENTS

The Third Edition of this book could not have been written without the support and assistance of my colleagues, friends, and family.

I would like to thank Frances Boyd and Carol Numrich, the architects of the *NorthStar* series, for their extraordinary vision of combining innovative language learning with topics of high interest to students. Once again, I am grateful to Frances Boyd, my series editor, for her imaginative insights, her sense of humor, and her passionate dedication to the task. For the third time, Frances' exceptional creativity and intelligence motivated and inspired my writing.

I also owe an enormous debt of gratitude to the following people at Pearson Longman: Paula Van Ells, Development Director, deserves credit for her clever, patient, and respectful editing. I appreciate her unflagging support, suggestions, hard work, and particularly her sense of humor. At Pearson Longman, I was also fortunate to have had an outstanding production team committed to editorial excellence and the highest standards of production quality: Shelley Gazes, Production Editor, and Robert Ruvo, Associate Managing Editor. For making significant direct contributions throughout every step of the project, I owe an enormous debt of gratitude to Debbie Sistino, Editorial Manager. I would also like to thank Aerin Csigay for his tremendous help with the art program.

I am particularly grateful to people who contributed generously of their time and materials to the book: David Alpern of *Newsweek on Air;* Dorothy Ferebee of *Fresh Air with Terry Gross;* Eric Molinsky, independent radio producer; Will Bullard, contributor to the unit on Microfinance; Yasha Jampolsky, feng shui consultant; and Linda Lane of Columbia University, author and editor of pronunciation materials.

Between the first and third editions, I had the fortunate experience of traveling worldwide and working with teachers and students who were using the *NorthStar* series. My observations and their feedback provided much of the impetus for this revision. I appreciate their willingness to engage students in material that challenges their assumptions and allows them to think critically about themselves and the world.

Finally, I owe heartfelt thanks to my mom, Bernice, my mother-in-law, Rita, my husband, Rich, and my children, Elyse and Alex, for providing me with constant love, support, and understanding.

Sherry Preiss

For a complete list of reviewers and affiliations, see page 288.

UNIT 1

The Internet and Other Addictions

"Hi. My name is Barry, and I check my E-mail two to three hundred times a day."

1 FOCUS ON THE TOPIC

A PREDICT

Look at the cartoon, and read the caption. Barry introduces himself with his first name and a fact about himself. What kind of problem could he have? What kind of group is this? Discuss your thoughts with a partner.

B SHARE INFORMATION

*Read the opinions and write **A** (agree), **D** (disagree), or **?** (can't decide) in the blank. Work with a partner and compare answers.*

_____ **1.** I think anyone who spends 40 hours a week on non-essential computer use could be called an Internet addict.

_____ **2.** In my view, it's as easy to get addicted to the Internet as it is to get addicted to nicotine or other harmful substances.

_____ **3.** To me, communication by e-mail, chat rooms, and instant messaging is cold and impersonal.

_____ **4.** If you asked me, I'd say that Internet addiction is not as serious as other addictions, such as gambling, nicotine, and drugs.

_____ **5.** I'll bet the typical Internet addict is probably a college student.

_____ **6.** In my opinion, television addiction is worse than Internet addiction.

_____ **7.** It's obvious that cell phone addiction is more widespread and harmful than Internet addiction.

C BACKGROUND AND VOCABULARY

1 CD 7 (2) *Read and listen to the magazine article. Discuss your reaction to the idea of Internet addiction.*

Bill, a student at the University of Maryland who doesn't want his last name used, said recently: "I **surf** the Internet probably 8–10 hours a day, most days. So I guess that's over 60 hours a week. Am I an addict? I don't know, but I can't get through the day without being online—downloading music, googling[1] acquaintances, blogging[2], checking Facebook®[3], or 'IM-ing'[4] my friends."

Students like Bill are becoming increasingly common on college campuses all over the world. Can **engaging in** a behavior such as computer use actually be considered an addiction? Should professors and students be **turning each other in** to college mental health professionals? For years, researchers have been trying to make sense of the biology and psychology of addiction, its causes, and its cures. *Addiction* used to mean abuse of substances such as drugs, alcohol, and nicotine. These days, though, the word is also being applied to Internet use, gambling, sex, shopping, cell phone use, and even travel.

---

[1] **googling:** obtaining information on the Internet using the Google® search engine

[2] **blogging:** maintaining or adding content to a "blog," a journal-like website where individuals contribute comments, ideas, and thoughts

[3] **Facebook®:** an online directory that connects people through social networks at colleges and universities, and at some high schools and workplaces

[4] **IM-ing:** instant messaging; using the Internet to send text messages in "real time" between two or more people

Researchers at Stanford University conducted a random telephone survey of 2,513 adults in the U.S. and found that 70% of the respondents were regular Internet users.

Here are additional statistics from the study:

- 14% found it difficult to stay away from the Net for more than several days at a time.
- 12% stayed online longer than they had intended.
- 12% had tried to cut back on Internet use.
- 9% attempted to hide non-essential Internet use from family, friends, employers.
- 8% used the Internet as a way to escape problems or relieve negative moods.
- 6% of respondents felt their relationships suffered as a result of excessive Internet use.

If some young people are **devoting** this much time and energy to online activities, does it mean they have an addiction? Without defining it precisely, psychologists who have noticed the **compulsiveness** of Internet users suggest that some kind of **therapy** may be needed. In fact, some campus health professionals have responded by **putting together** weekly **support groups** for students who **present with** a variety of addiction-like symptoms, including repetitive stress syndrome (severe wrist pain), excessive fatigue or tiredness, and back and eye strain.

Medical experts, journalists, and sociologists are observing carefully the kinds of issues **coming out** as a result of increasing Internet use in our society. They notice that heavy Internet users are not doing much of anything else: not much socializing, going to movies, eating out, or taking care of their children. Volunteering is decreasing; loneliness is increasing. **Fulfillment** becomes limited to interaction on a screen. The medical community, in particular, is alert to the dangers, both physical and psychological. They are seriously considering recognizing "Internet addiction" as an official psychological condition.

The Internet has revealed unprecedented opportunities for learning, communication, and business. However, as it plays an increasing role in our society, further studies should be conducted to explore the complex effects this technology has on the individual's daily life.

2 *Match the expressions on the left with the definitions or synonyms on the right. If necessary, read the article again for clues about the meaning. Write the appropriate letter in the blank.*

_____ **1.** surf
_____ **2.** engaging in
_____ **3.** turning each other in
_____ **4.** devoting
_____ **5.** compulsiveness
_____ **6.** therapy
_____ **7.** putting together
_____ **8.** support groups
_____ **9.** present with
_____ **10.** coming out
_____ **11.** fulfillment

a. treatment of problems by talking about them
b. inability to control certain behavior
c. becoming publicly known
d. personal satisfaction
e. people who meet to help each other with a problem they all share
f. show signs of an illness by having a particular type of behavior or condition
g. giving or using something (time, effort) for an activity or purpose
h. look for information (on the Internet)
i. organizing
j. taking part in or becoming involved in
k. identifying each other to the police or an authority

2 FOCUS ON LISTENING

A LISTENING ONE: Interview with an Internet Addiction Counselor

Because so many students overuse the Internet, some university health services offer help with the problem. Dr. Jonathan Kandell, a psychologist from the University of Maryland in the United States, was interviewed by Ira Flatow, host of *Science Friday* from NPR® (National Public Radio). Dr. Kandell discusses his approach to students with symptoms of Internet addiction.

CD 1, 3 *Work with a partner. Listen to the first 35 seconds of the interview. Write down three questions that you think Ira Flatow might ask Dr. Kandell, the counselor.*

1. ______________________________
2. ______________________________
3. ______________________________

LISTEN FOR MAIN IDEAS

CD 1, 4 *Look at the chart. Listen to the interview and take notes on the main ideas. Use a separate piece of paper if necessary. (You will note details later.) Work with a partner to compare and revise your notes.*

MAIN IDEAS	DETAILS
Focus of interview unusual or "other" addictions	Examples of addictions gambling, . . .
Kandell's view of Internet addiction	Evidence for this view
Chief symptoms/warning signs of Internet addiction	Other symptoms/warning signs
Possible treatment	Reasons this treatment is helpful

LISTEN FOR DETAILS

CD 1, 5 *Read the chart again. Fill in as many details as possible to support the main ideas. Then listen to the interview again to check your work. Work with a partner to compare and revise your notes.*

MAKE INFERENCES

When you are listening, making inferences means understanding something that is not literally stated, but which you believe is true based on the intention, attitude, voice, pausing, and choice of words of the speakers.

Read the questions. Then listen to each excerpt from the interview. Write your answers and then discuss them with a partner. Give reasons for your choices. Each question has more than one possible answer.

CD 7 6

Excerpt One

A *groupie* usually refers to someone, especially a young woman, who likes a musician, movie star, or sports star and follows this person around hoping to meet the star. Why does Ira Flatow, the host, use the word *groupie* when he advises the radio audience to listen carefully? What does the word *groupie* imply in this context?

____

____

CD 7 7

Excerpt Two

Dr. Kandell doesn't answer Flatow's question directly. What expressions show his hesitation? Why doesn't he answer Flatow directly?

____

____

CD 7 8

Excerpt Three

How does Flatow feel about this topic at this point in the interview? How do you know? What words and tone of voice does he use to indicate his attitude?

____

____

EXPRESS OPINIONS

Discuss the questions with the class. Give your opinions and give reasons for them.

1. Do you know people who overuse the Internet? Do you overuse it? What are the warning signs? What treatment would you recommend for Internet addicts?
2. Dr. Kandell runs a support group for Internet addicts at his university. Do you think that universities should have this service? How helpful can such a support group be? Explain. What other support groups do you know of? Would you ever join one? Why or why not?
3. Anne Lamott, author of a book of essays called *Bird by Bird*, writes, "Getting all of one's addictions under control is a little like putting an octopus to bed." What does she mean? How do you feel about her analogy? Explain.

B LISTENING TWO: Time to Do Everything Except Think

David Brooks, a well-known journalist and commentator, speaks about our growing fascination with and dependence on wired and wireless gadgets to communicate, including laptops, wireless handheld devices, and cell phones. He is interviewed by David Alpern and Warren Levinson on *Newsweek on Air,* a popular radio broadcast.

CD 1 9 *Listen to the excerpt from the interview. Take notes in the chart. Using the topic headings, fill in the main ideas on the left side of the chart, and support those ideas with as many details as possible on the right. Discuss your notes with a partner, and revise if necessary.*

MAIN IDEAS	DETAILS
Brooks's view of communication and information Creates problems	• bombarded with so much information
Advantages of so much information	• increase in IQ • •
Disadvantages of so much information	• creativity threatened •
Effects on Brooks	• always hooked to cell phone •

C INTEGRATE LISTENINGS ONE AND TWO

STEP 1: Organize

Dr. Jonathan Kandell, the psychologist, and David Brooks, the journalist, each discussed some problems and solutions of addiction to certain kinds of technology. Review your notes on pages 4 and 6. Look at the list of problems and mark which speaker identified that problem. Then do the same for solutions.

PROBLEMS	KANDELL	BROOKS
1. Loss of creativity and productivity		X
2. Sense of being overwhelmed by information		
3. Depression when you are not online		
4. Loss of social skills		
5. Poor grades or job performance		
6. Relationship problems		

SOLUTIONS	KANDELL	BROOKS
1. Join a support group		
2. Take time to think and make connections		
3. Find causes of addiction		
4. Read books		
5. Change behaviors to break the online habit		
6. Try to balance online activities with other activities		

◖ STEP 2: Synthesize

Work with a partner. Discuss the questions. Use the information from Step 1.

1. Imagine that you are David Brooks, the journalist, and you are asked to describe the character in the cartoon above. Do you relate to his problems?
2. Imagine you are Dr. Jonathan Kandell and you are asked to give advice to the character above. What would you tell him?
3. Do you think the character and the cartoon are funny? Why or why not?
4. Does the idea behind the cartoon apply to other addictions? Give examples.

3 FOCUS ON SPEAKING

A VOCABULARY

REVIEW

1 *Work with a partner. Fill in the other forms of the words in the chart. A dash (–) indicates that there is no related form or that the form is not commonly used.*

NOUN	VERB	ADJECTIVE
1. addict **2.** addiction		**1.** addicted **2.**
	—	anxious
1. compulsiveness **2.** compulsion	—	
		1. depressed **2.** depressive
enhancement		
fulfillment		**1.** **2.**
	isolate	
—		**1.** overwhelmed **2.** overwhelming
	—	problematic
	strategize	
support		**1.** **2.**
symptom	—	
therapy	—	

2 *Work in groups of three to fill in the blanks in the conversation. Use the correct form of the words from the chart on page 9. Not all words will be used. Then, in your groups, role-play the conversation with drama and enthusiasm. Add to or change the lines if you like.*

Psychiatrists have been studying another unusual addiction: shopaholism, or "compulsive shopping disorder." According to recent research, 8 percent of all Americans may be shopaholics, and 90 percent of them are women. Like other people trying to overcome addictions, shopaholics attend support group meetings. Here is a transcript of a support group session for shopaholics.

A: Hi. I'm Teresa. I became a **(1)** _________________ shopper almost overnight. My job had become just too stressful. So, to unwind after work, I'd head off to the mall. I started buying small things I really didn't need, but then I started spending more and more, and coming home later and later. It was "shop 'til you drop." My spending spun out of control until I was **(2)** _________________ with debt.

B: Sounds familiar, Teresa. Hi, everyone. I'm Olivia. For me, work was not the **(3)** _________________ at all. Rather, my personal life was a mess. The guy I had been dating for 12 years suddenly left me for another woman. So I ended up feeling nervous and unsettled; I started having sudden **(4)** _________________ attacks.

C: You mean headaches, rapid heartbeat, and sweaty palms?

B: Yeah, those were the **(5)** _________________. But as soon as I pulled out my credit card, my "best friend," I felt better, kind of energized. I felt strangely satisfied and **(6)** _________________.

C: I feel the same way when I hold that little piece of plastic. Oh . . . sorry . . . I forgot to introduce myself. I'm Maria. Whenever I feel sad or **(7)** _________________, charging a few hundred bucks on my card just cheers me up. I've tried a bunch of different **(8)** _________________ to try to kick the habit, but so far I haven't found a way to do it. So, now here I am . . . hoping you all will help.

A: Sure, we will. Ummm . . . have any of you gotten **(9)** _________________ to online shopping, catalogue shopping, home TV shopping, or something like that?

C: Nope, not me. Shopping at home is way too lonely and **(10)** _________________. I'd much rather be in a crowded shopping mall.

B: Yeah, me too, Maria. You know, this group is so helpful. We can really be **(11)** _________________ of each other by sharing our feelings openly like this.

A: Yes. I think so, too. It's more **(12)** _________________ than taking that new medicine for shopaholism or seeing a private shrink. And the best part is that we are here and not at the mall . . . at least for now.

EXPAND

Match each boldfaced word or phrase with a similar expression from the list on page 12. Write the corresponding letter in the blank. Then work with a partner and compare answers.

_____ **1.** She was so thrilled at winning $2,000 playing "pachinko," a Japanese pinball-slot matching game, that she **turned into** a real pachinkoholic.

_____ **2.** One of the students in Kandell's support group reported he **felt empty**, confused, and lonely after he went cold turkey and suddenly gave up talking to his friends in chat rooms every night.

_____ **3.** When Dr. Kimberly Young's research on Internet addiction first came out, she was **bombarded with** requests for interviews. Reporters were shocked by her conclusions that Internet addiction was a serious illness.

_____ **4.** Some psychologists believe that electronic forms of communication (e-mail, voice mail, mobile/cell phone, pagers, chat rooms) are seriously **shaping** our social interactions.

_____ **5.** In some parts of the United States, using a cell phone in the car is now illegal. Too many drivers are **multitasking**—eating, talking, working—while driving, which causes accidents.

_____ **6.** Upon returning from a week or two of vacation, many employees are simply **overwhelmed** by the huge amount of e-mail that builds up. Some may receive nearly 400 messages a week.

_____ **7.** After he gave up cigarettes, he **went through** withdrawal: hunger, discomfort, and other uncomfortable symptoms.

_____ **8.** Many business people see technology as a positive way to **enhance** customer service through more immediate and consistent communication.

_____ **9.** Although he's completed most of the treatment for gambling addiction, he is not totally **out of the woods** yet, and still has to take medication.

_____ **10.** Some parents should be blamed for **feeding** their children's addiction to television or computer games because they have no rules to limit use.

_____ **11.** **Driven** to win the "top sales manager of the year" award, he turned into a total workaholic, putting in 18-hour days for months.

_____ **12.** College administrators really don't know what's **going on** in many computer labs. They think students are doing research and studying, but in many cases the students are playing computer games and chatting with their friends online.

_____ **13.** Right before the holidays, she **went on a** shopping **binge** buying gifts for dozens of friends and relatives, and ending up flat broke.

_____ **14.** Wanting to start his marriage with a **clean slate**, he gave up cigarettes, alcohol, and even his cell phone.

_____ **15.** In order to finally break the **vicious cycle** of her technology addictions, her therapist recommended she give away her three computers, cell phone, TVs, and a Blackberry®.

a. improve, enrich

b. doing different things at the same time

c. attacked by a lot of information, data, or questions

d. influencing in a particular way

e. upset, strongly affected

f. became (something different)

g. happening

h. experienced

i. free from a dangerous situation

j. increasing

k. was unhappy (because nothing seemed important or interesting)

l. trying extremely hard

m. began to overdo something

n. fresh beginning

o. serious situation that is very difficult to stop

CREATE

1 *Work with a partner.*

Student A: Ask Student B questions 1 through 3.

Student B: Cover the left column. Answer Student A's questions using the key words in your column in any order. Answer in several sentences and give an example if possible. Then switch roles after question 3.

Example

STUDENT A: Have you ever been addicted to a particular TV program?

STUDENT B: (problematic, turn in, compulsive) Oh, sure! A couple years ago, I felt totally **compulsive** about watching a TV show called *Lost*. It was quite **problematic** because I used to arrange my social life and my homework around the time of the show, so I could be sure to watch it. For several hours each night, I watched old episodes on the Internet and did Internet searches to read about the show and its stars. My roommate threatened to **turn** me **in** to a counselor because she thought I had become addicted.

Student A

1. Can you describe a time in your life when you were really hooked on a hobby?
2. If your friend was a dataholic, what kind of advice would you give him or her?
3. Why do you think students get hooked on their cell phones?

Now switch roles.

4. Why do some highly successful journalists get addicted to dangerous travel?
5. If a close friend of yours insisted on bringing her laptop with her on her vacation, how would you convince her not to?
6. Can you describe a time when you were overly enthusiastic about a new product coming out on the market?

Student B

1. shape, fulfill, driven
2. enhance, bombarded, clean slate
3. multitask, what's going on, vicious cycle
4. driven, on a binge, out of the woods
5. feel empty, overwhelmed, feed
6. come out (on the market), turn into, go through

2 *On a separate piece of paper, write a paragraph describing a person you know who has an addiction. Use at least 8 to 10 words from page 9 and pages 11–12. Use as many different forms of the words as possible.*

B GRAMMAR: Wish Statements—Expressing Unreality

1 *Work with a partner. Study the short conversations, and discuss the questions that follow.*

Q: Is your son going to quit [sky diving]?
A: No, but **I wish he would**.

Q: Are your kids addicted to online video games?
A: Yes, unfortunately, but **I really wish they weren't** [addicted to video games]. They're not doing their homework.

Q: Do you know how I can stop drinking so much coffee?
A: No, but **I wish I did** [know how to stop]. I spend too much money at cafés.

Q: Did you start gambling when you were a teenager?
A: Yes, and **I wish I hadn't** [started gambling].

1. How are the first three boldfaced phrases similar?
2. How is the last boldfaced phrase different from the first three?

WISH STATEMENTS—EXPRESSING UNREALITY

Use the verb ***wish*** when you want to express unreality—a desire for reality to be different or a regret that it was not different. The verb tenses and structures used in the clause after *wish* to express future, present, or past situations are outlined below.

Wish Situation	Examples
Present and Future Wish Use ***wish*** + ***would*** or ***could***.	• I know. **I wish they'd turn their phones off**. They drive me crazy. • **A friend of mine wishes she could get rid of her phone**, but she can't because she is totally hooked on it.
Present Wish Use ***wish*** + past form of the verb.	• The problem is out of control. **I just wish people didn't feel compelled** to answer their phones all the time.
Present Wish (verb *to be*) Use past form: ***wish*** + ***were***.	• In a way, **I wish they weren't so cheap** because then people wouldn't use them so much. • You've got it. **If they were more expensive**, teenagers wouldn't turn into cell phone junkies.
Past Wishes Use ***wish*** + ***had*** + past participle.	• It's like a new culture. The phones have their pluses, but **I wish they hadn't** become so popular. They can be really annoying. • Don't be ridiculous! I'll bet **you just wish you'd predicted** the trend and started a cell phone company. • Yeah, I guess so. But more than that, **I just wish I hadn't been so careless** and forgot to use my hands-free yesterday. I got a ticket for using my phone while driving!
Past Wishes: *Could* Use ***wish*** + ***could have*** + past participle.	• Sorry to hear that. Did you get out of it? • No. **I wish I could have**, but the cop wouldn't listen.

GRAMMAR TIP: The tense of the verb *wish* does not affect the tense of the verb in the clause following *wish*.

In spoken informal English, we often use short answer phrases with *wish* statements. (See the phrases in Exercise 1.)

2 *Work with a partner.*

Student A: Ask Student B questions 1 through 6. Check Student B's answers with the correct answer in parentheses.

Student B: Cover the left column. Answer Student A's question using a short-answer wish *statement. Then switch roles after question 6.*

Student A	**Student B**
1. Will your friend install the new computer program for you tonight? (No, but I wish he would or could.)	**1.** No, but I wish he ________.
2. Does your husband play poker every Friday night? (Yes, and I wish he didn't or wouldn't.)	**2.** Yes, and I wish he ________.
3. Are you still buying lottery tickets every week? (Yes, but I wish I weren't.)	**3.** Yes, but I wish I ________.
4. I heard you couldn't get any cell service in the conference room this morning. (No, but I wish I could have.)	**4.** No, but I wish I ________.
5. Did they know that television watching could be addictive? (No, but they wish they had known.)	**5.** No, but they wish they ________.
6. Is it really true that your younger brother was addicted to computer games by the time he was six years old? (Uh-huh, and he wishes he hadn't been.)	**6.** Uh-huh, and he wishes he ________.

Now switch roles.

7. Will she overeat at the holiday parties?
   (Yes, but she wishes she wouldn't.)
8. I noticed that your husband is compulsive about cleanliness.
   (Yes, and I wish he weren't.)
9. Does she know how to use all the features of her new cell phone?
   (No, but she wishes she did.)
10. Did he go through withdrawal when he stopped smoking?
    (Yes, and he wishes he hadn't.)
11. It's too bad you couldn't figure out how she got so addicted to online gambling.
    (Uh-huh, but I wish I could have.)
12. Were you able to find a program to help end your compulsive shopping?
    (No, but I wish I had or could have.)

7. Yes, but she wishes she ________.
8. Yes, and I wish he ________.
9. No, but she wishes she ________. She only knows how to make calls.
10. Yes, and he wishes he ________.
11. Uh-huh, but I wish I ________.
12. No, but I wish I ________.

C SPEAKING

PRONUNCIATION: Stressing Important Words

In a sentence, one or two words usually express the most important information. These are words that the speaker wants the listener to notice.

CD 1 10 Listen to how the capitalized words are stressed in these sentences:

I've GOT to get some coffee.

I REALLY need to check my e-mail again.

We stress the most important words by saying them

- on a high pitch, or
- with strong stress: the stressed vowel is long and loud.

When you speak, make sure your voice is high enough when you stress an important word.

In English, we emphasize

- new information (in English, new information is usually the last important word of the sentence)

  Today we're going to talk about MULTI-tasking.
- information that contrasts or corrects

  The kids are doing E-mail instead of HOMEwork.

1 CD 7 Track 11 *Listen to the sentences. Underline the words that are stressed. Some sentences may have more than one stressed word. Then practice saying the sentences with a partner.*

Patty

1. Patty was running up huge sums of money on her credit cards.
2. She spent thousands of dollars.
3. Nothing could stop her.
4. She was totally out of control.

Jim

5. Drinking fifteen cups of coffee a day was the only thing that kept Jim going.
6. Totally overwhelmed by work, he drank from 5 in the morning to 11 at night.
7. Now, he was addicted to both coffee and the Internet, and his life was a complete disaster.
8. He couldn't get to a therapist's office fast enough.

2 CD 7 Track 12 *Read the conversation. Work with a partner, and underline the stressed words. Then listen to the conversation to check your answers. Correct any errors. Practice reading the conversation with your partner, emphasizing the stressed words.*

A: Workaholism isn't really an addiction. Some people have to work long hours.

B: But others are workaholics because they love their work.

A: Agreed, but success at any cost may not be such a good thing.

B: Yeah, that makes me think of my father. He was so hooked on work. When he drove, he was on his cell phone; at a red light, he checked his e-mail.

A: You must be joking. That's multitasking at its best!

B: Well, not exactly. He lost his driver's license after his third accident, which was also his fifth ticket.

FUNCTION: Expressions for Building on Others' Ideas

The following is a list of useful expressions that can be used in conversation to build and expand on each others' ideas.

- **To add to your idea,** I think students socialize differently online than they do when they are face to face.
- **Not only that, but I would also say that** people interact more creatively when they interact face to face.
- **Your point makes me think of** another issue, which is the trend toward using cell phone texting more than e-mail.
- **Another thing I'd like to bring up is** the fact that some addictions are more destructive than others.
- **You speak of** needing to stay connected; **then, can I also assume that** you carry your cell phone with you at all times?

Work with a partner.

Student A: Read each of the first four opinions aloud.

Student B: Cover the left column. Build upon, add to, and expand on what your partner has said. Use the expressions listed above. Support your opinion with a few other statements. Then switch roles after item 4.

Example

STUDENT A: We live in a world overwhelmed with information. It will become even more so in the future.

STUDENT B: Not only that, but I would also say that this world will create a generation of dataholics, people who love data and think it's the most important thing in the world.

Student A	Student B
1. Workaholism cannot really be an addiction. Working hard is good for you.	**1.**
2. "Power drinks"—soft drinks with extra caffeine—are just as addictive as coffee.	**2.**
3. Our "plugged in" lives destroy opportunities for creativity and innovation.	**3.**
4. Employers are responsible for employees who have become addicted to technology.	**4.**

Now switch roles.

5. Companies need to come up with strategies to help employees cope with information overload.	**5.**
6. We have time to do everything these days, except think.	**6.**
7. Because students need the Internet to do research, preventing Internet addiction is virtually impossible.	**7.**
8. Technology is dividing us as much as uniting us.	**8.**

PRODUCTION: A Group Discussion

In this activity, you will ***plan a professional discussion about addiction***. Try to use the vocabulary, grammar, pronunciation, and the expressions for building on others' ideas that you learned in the unit.*

Divide into three groups. Read about the situation and the roles for this simulation activity.

Situation and Roles

Every year, the National Psychological Association holds a conference to discuss professional issues. This year's theme is "Addiction." You are psychologists attending the conference. The afternoon sessions, or meetings, are made up of interactive discussions about addiction. During these special sessions, participants share and build on each other's ideas. Then they must summarize their discussions for the participants in the other sessions.

SESSION ONE: ADDICTIVE PERSONALITIES

Discussion Topic: Are some people more likely to develop an addiction than other people?

- Discuss if there is such a thing as an "addictive personality."
- Identify different addictive personality types, and give examples from your own life or people you know.

*(Use **wish** to express regret.)*

---

*For Alternative Speaking Topics, see page 21.

Session Two: Recovery Methods

Discussion Topic: What are some of the different methods used around the world to help people recover from addiction?

- Identify different recovery strategies.
- Discuss the pros and cons of each method.

*(Use **wish** to express regret about failure.)*

Session Three: Psychology of Online Communication

Discussion Topic: How is the Internet affecting our personal relationships?

- Identify the ways the Internet, e-mail, and other forms of electronic communication may be affecting people's relationships.
- List the pros and cons of online communication.
- Make recommendations for the future use of online communication.

*(Use **wish** to express some recommendations.)*

1. Break up into three groups, decide which session each group will role-play, and choose a leader and a note taker.
2. Conduct an interactive discussion session. Make sure the note taker writes down the main points. Use expressions like the following:
   - Not only that, but I would also say that ________________.
   - Your point makes me think of ________________.
   - Another thing I'd like to bring up is ________________.
   - OK, and to add to that idea, I'd say ________________.
3. Summarize your discussion for the whole class.

ALTERNATIVE SPEAKING TOPICS

Choose a topic. Use ideas, vocabulary, grammar, pronunciation, and expressions for building on others' ideas.

Topic 1

Some people say that the Internet has opened up unprecedented resources for research, but like all technology, it comes with dangers. Do you agree or disagree? Explain.

Topic 2

Some 15 percent of Chinese adolescents are said to suffer from "Internet addiction disorder," according to the China Internet Information Center. For this reason, the Chinese government now provides two services: 1) lectures on the dangers of broadband burnout to all elementary school students; 2) mandatory attendance at a spring camp for kids seriously affected. Do you think these strategies will be effective? Why or why not? What advice would you give to the Chinese government to slow down this trend among young students?

Topic 3

"The Internet, cell phones, MP3 players, and online games are distractions that keep people from dealing with real problems and concerns." Do you agree or disagree with this statement? Do you think we are becoming a society compulsively absorbed by technology? Would it be possible or even desirable to stop this trend?

RESEARCH TOPICS, see page 259.

UNIT 2

Honesty Is the Best Policy

"Thank you, sir. I am proud of my resume. And I think you'll find that most of it is true."

1 FOCUS ON THE TOPIC

A PREDICT

1. Look at the cartoon, and read the caption. The man is proud of his résumé yet admits that some of the information on it might not be true. Why does he admit that fact in an interview? Do you think the cartoon is funny? Why or why not? How common do you think lying on a résumé is? Have you or do you know anyone who has lied on a résumé?
2. A "white lie" is a small lie, or a "half-truth" that someone tells because he or she thinks it won't hurt someone else. Is lying on a résumé a white lie? Why or why not? When was the last time you told a white lie?
3. Look at the title of the unit. Is honesty always the best policy? Why do people tell lies or try to deceive others by making them believe something that is not true? Work with a partner. Brainstorm the reasons for lies or deceptions.

B SHARE INFORMATION

"Lying has long been a part of everyday life. We couldn't get through the day without being deceptive," says Professor Leonard Saxe of Brandeis University in the United States. Most lies can be categorized according to a broad spectrum—from seemingly harmless little white lies, or fibs, to more serious lies that could change someone's life. Which lies might be acceptable, and when?

Read the following lies, fibs, or deceptions. Then indicate when, or if, each one is acceptable by putting a check (✓) in the appropriate column. Work with a partner and discuss the reasons for your choices.

LIE	NEVER	SOMETIMES	OFTEN	ALWAYS
1. Parents misrepresent the ages of their children in order to qualify for discounts on travel, theater tickets, or restaurant meals.				
2. Parents tell their young children that their beloved grandfather, who recently died, just "went away for a while."				
3. At a wedding, a guest presents a new, unopened gift to the couple. The guest had actually received the gift at her own wedding a few months ago but had never used it.				
4. A doctor withholds information from a dying patient to keep her from worrying.				
5. A student is required to read a long novel but instead reads a condensed version or watches a movie based on the novel.				

6. A professor exaggerates a student's abilities in a recommendation letter in order to help the student to get into graduate school or to get a job.				
7. A job candidate falsifies his résumé by claiming to have a degree from a prestigious university. He thinks it will get him an interview.				
8. A lawyer knows her client has committed a crime but claims in court that the client is completely innocent.				
9. A company exaggerates the effectiveness of its weight-loss product in advertisements.				
10. In order to get elected, a political candidate makes promises that he or she does not intend to keep.				

C BACKGROUND AND VOCABULARY

Plagiarism, or presenting another's work or ideas as your own, affects many people, especially because other people's work and ideas are now so available on the Internet. This is a common topic of discussion at educational institutions. What can or should be done about it?

The administration at a large university has decided to purchase access to anti-plagiarism software. A dean, a professor, and a student express their thoughts in the online editorials on pages 26 and 27.

1 CD 1, 13 *Read and listen to the letters. Then read the list of definitions that follows. Work with a partner. Write the number of the boldfaced word or phrase next to its definition.*

www.universityonlinenews.com/Editorial

Home
News
Around Campus
Employment
Publications
Media Relations
Contact Us

LETTERS TO THE EDITOR

Plagiarism: An Important Message from the Administration

To the Editor:

As many know, the university has decided to subscribe to a service which provides software designed to detect plagiarism. The service checks a student's work against over a million other sources to reveal the amount of matching text. More than 8,000 academic institutions in 90 countries use this service.

With the rise of the Internet, plagiarism has become more **(1) pervasive** and problematic on campuses worldwide, including our own. A recent survey found that 54 percent of U.S. students admitted to plagiarizing from the Internet. In many cases, students do not intend to deceive. Rather, they are unclear about the concept of intellectual property[1] and about the seriousness with which such issues are taken in academia. Plagiarism is not a **(2) trivial** matter. It is a serious and illegal form of stealing. We cannot depend on students **(3) tattling on each other** to expose cheaters; nor can we rely only on professors' intuition and experience to identify plagiarized work. Therefore, this administration feels we have no choice but to use a tool specifically targeted to detect and battle plagiarism.

–Janet Miller, Dean of Academic Studies, Midlake University

Plagiarism: A Professor Speaks Out

To the Editor:

I would like to take this opportunity to respond to Dean Miller's editorial regarding the administration's decision to invest in anti-plagiarism software.

First, I feel it is important to acknowledge that plagiarism is a problem not limited to the college or university campus. Even governments sometimes **(4) mislead** the public by plagiarizing others' work, as when the British government plagiarized a student's doctoral dissertation in a document it submitted to the United Nations. Or we can recall the embarrassing case of Jayson Blair, the *New York Times* reporter found guilty of copying his work directly from other newspapers. Blair maintained his **(5) veneer** as a respected journalist for years before his crime was uncovered. So, as you see, this problem affects many parts of society!

When it comes to plagiarism in academia, why are administrators engaged in such a **(6) relentless** pursuit of cheaters? Is that really their job? I suggest that the administration give professors the main responsibility for dealing with this problem. First, professors can give "plagiarism-proof" assignments which require original research, first drafts, and creative problem solving. They should also avoid using the

---

[1] **intellectual property:** creation of the mind, such as literary and artistic works and also inventions and designs

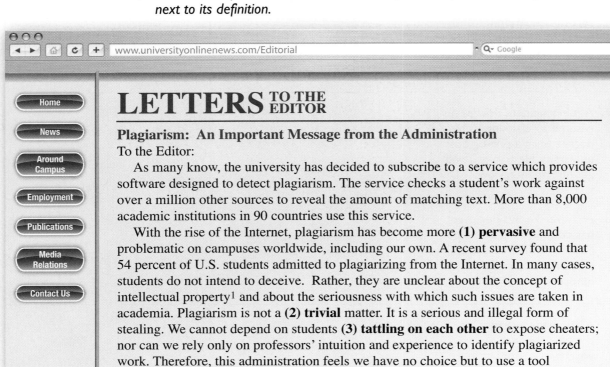

same essay or exam questions year after year. When we suspect dishonesty, we can use free tools on the Internet that have already been proven effective in detecting plagiarism. Most professors who take the time to know students and to give them regular writing assignments have a **(7) finely honed** sense of each student's writing style or ability, making it difficult for the student to **(8) conceal** unoriginal material.

It is our job to help students stay honest. The administration's total **(9) preoccupation** with plagiarism and with this software is a costly waste of time and resources.

–Jerome Anderson, Chair, Department of Political Science, Midlake University

Plagiarism: A Student Speaks Out

To the Editor,

Now we know the truth: The administration doesn't trust us. Clearly, they don't realize that most students don't approve of cheating, and most students don't cheat. Administrators may try to sugarcoat the issue, but the fact remains that this is an unreliable and overly **(10) intrusive** method which leads to the **(11) erosion** of trust between students and teachers at our university. The promoters of this software have an **(12) inflated** opinion of its value. This software won't catch all plagiarists, but it *will* succeed in fueling mistrust between students and professors.

Most students are not interested in getting through college by deception, by lying. Only the most overconfident narcissists[2] think they can really get away with cheating. The rest of us know that cheaters lose in the long run. At the end of the day, it is up to us as students to be honest with ourselves and follow our own moral compass.

–Margarita Hernandez, Junior, Biochemistry

---

[2] **narcissists:** people who admire themselves

_____ **a.** tell something bad that another person has done

_____ **b.** exaggerated; overly important

_____ **c.** a cover that hides the way someone or something really is

_____ **d.** affecting someone's private life in an annoying way

_____ **e.** sharpened; perfected

_____ **f.** hide something carefully

_____ **g.** the condition of thinking about only one thing

_____ **h.** existing or spreading everywhere

_____ **i.** unimportant; of little value

_____ **j.** make someone believe something that is not true

_____ **k.** continuing without stopping or losing strength

_____ **l.** the gradual reduction or wearing down of something

2 *Work with a partner. Discuss your opinions of anti-plagiarism software.*

2 FOCUS ON LISTENING

A LISTENING ONE: Interview with a Psychiatrist

Lying is a topic of public discussion in the media. In the interview, you'll hear Dr. Paul Ekman, a psychiatrist, explain why people lie. What do you think Dr. Ekman will say?

CD 7 14 *Write down your predictions. Then listen to the excerpt and check your predictions.*

____

____

____

LISTEN FOR MAIN IDEAS

CD 7 15 *Now, listen to the entire interview. Stop after each part and write the one main idea about the topic. Work with a partner. Compare your main idea statements. Revise them and write them in the Listen for Details chart on page 29.*

Part One

Main idea: Liars are narcissistic.

Part Two

Main idea: ______________________________

Part Three

Main idea: ______________________________

Part Four

Main idea: ______________________________

Part Five

Main idea: ______________________________

LISTEN FOR DETAILS

Listen to the interview again. Add details that support the main idea. Some have been done for you.

MAIN IDEA	DETAILS
Liars are narcissistic.	• Exaggerated sense of themselves • • • Focus on the moment and not the future. Lack sense of self.
	• • Most avoid lying because of consequences—loss of trust •
	Two criteria: • • No advance notice of lying Ways to lie: • Conceal information • •
	1. 2. 3. 4. 5. 6. 7. 8. 9.
	• • Difficult to repair trust

MAKE INFERENCES

The interviewer, Dr. Fred Goodwin and his guest, Dr. Paul Ekman are very engaged in the interview. Remember that making inferences means understanding something that is not literally stated but that you believe is true based on the intention, attitude, voice, pausing, and choice of words of the speakers. Discuss your answers with a partner and then with the class.

Excerpt One

1. How does the interviewer feel about the narcissist who lies?
   a. Angry and disgusted
   b. Sympathetic
   c. Neutral; he has no feelings
2. To support your answer, note the interviewer's tone, pace, and choice of words.
   a. Tone: ______________________
   b. Pace: ______________________
   c. Choice of words: ______________________

Excerpt Two

3. The interviewer thinks that Eckman's definitions are _____.
   a. complicated
   b. surprising
   c. too simple
4. Explain your answer to question 3.

Excerpt Three

5. Dr. Ekman believes that this kind of lie is _____.
   a. normal
   b. childish
   c. foolish
6. To support your answer, note Dr. Ekman's tone, pace, and choice of words.
   a. Tone: ______________________
   b. Pace: ______________________
   c. Choice of words: ______________________

EXPRESS OPINIONS

Working in small groups, discuss your answers to these questions.

1. People are generally honest. Do you agree or disagree? Explain.
2. The best way to deter plagiarism is by using anti-plagiarism software. Do you agree or disagree? Explain.
3. What kinds of lies have you told? Use the chart on page 29 to help describe them.

B LISTENING TWO: Family Secrets

Concealing the truth is a kind of lying. In this excerpt, you will hear a filmmaker, Pola Rapaport, discuss a time when she uncovered a family secret. She made a documentary film about this important part of her life.

1 CD 7 20 *Rapaport's story is divided into three parts. Before listening to each part, brainstorm predictions with a partner. Jot them down on a piece of paper. Then listen and check to see if your predictions were correct.*

1. In Part One, Rapaport discovers a small photograph of a young boy from Romania in her father's desk drawer, 10 years after her father's death. Predict what relationship this boy could have to her. Give two or three possibilities.
2. In Part Two, in an excerpt from the film, Rapaport discusses the reason for her father's secret. Predict why her father might have hidden the boy's identity. Give two or three possibilities.
3. In Part Three, Rapaport shares her feelings about discovering the family secret. Predict how she might feel. Give two or three possibilities.

2 CD 7 21 *Work with a partner. Number the events below in the order in which they occurred in Rapaport's life. Then listen again to check your answers.*

_____ Rapaport finds the photograph signed *Pierre* in her father's desk.

_____ Rapaport's mother receives a letter from a stranger named Pierre.

_____ Rapaport goes to Romania to meet Pierre.

_____ Rapaport wonders if Pierre is a relative.

__1__ Rapaport's father dies.

_____ Pierre confesses that he is Rapaport's half-brother.

_____ Rapaport realizes that Pierre could be looking for a long-lost family.

_____ Rapaport and Pierre exchange letters.

3 *Share your opinions about the story. Discuss the questions in a small group.*

a. Do you think Rapaport's father did the right thing by concealing the truth about the family? Why or why not?

b. How do you think Rapaport felt about her father when she found out that Pierre was her half-brother? How would you feel in that situation?

c. Do you think Rapaport was trespassing—going somewhere she shouldn't go—in her search for the truth? Why or why not?

d. Many families have "skeletons in the closet," or secrets. Do you think family secrets erode trust? Why or why not? Do you discuss family secrets with other people? Why or why not? If you are comfortable, share a family secret.

C INTEGRATE LISTENINGS ONE AND TWO

STEP 1: Organize

Review Listenings One and Two. In the chart, write down the truths that were concealed in Pola Rapaport's family. (Refer to the list of events from Exercise 2 on page 31 to help you.) Then review your notes from Listening One and write which of Ekman's nine reasons (on page 29) might apply in each case. You may find more than one reason.

CONCEALMENTS AND LIES FROM RAPAPORT'S STORY	POSSIBLE REASONS FOR THE CONCEALMENT OR LIE
Pierre didn't tell his father's family who or where he was.	

STEP 2: Synthesize

Use the information and language in the chart to role-play a conversation between Pola and Dr. Eckman.

Pola: Explain how you uncovered the family secret and why you want to know what motivated your father to keep the secret.

Dr. Eckman: Explain to Pola what may have motivated her father to conceal the family secret.

3 FOCUS ON SPEAKING

A VOCABULARY

REVIEW

English is rich in the vocabulary of honesty, dishonesty, and half-truths. Review the list of words and phrases on page 33 from Listenings One and Two as a class. Then complete the short paragraphs on the next page using the words or phrases.

conceal	mislead	preoccupation	relentless
finely honed	mull over	put one over	tattling
inflated	pervasive	put the pieces together	

Take Notes!
The Art of Liar Spotting

Most people care deeply about the truth and do not like it when authors **(1)** ________________ on them with false information. Therefore, editors and publishers must be **(2)** ________________ in determining whether a nonfiction work is true. They need to check many sources and verify all their facts. Recently, an editor with a **(3)** ____________________ sense of telling fact from fiction came across some suspicious details in a memoir manuscript. After closely examining the author's story, she **(4)** _________________________ and realized he had lied about certain facts from his life. The publisher canceled publication immediately, and the editor remarked that "saving readers from this writer's con was an elating experience."

Are liars easy to spot? Many people think it's a snap. They actually have an **(5)** ________________ sense of their ability to catch a liar by noticing physical signs of deception: covering the mouth, looking around, fidgeting nervously with hands, and so on. However, studies show that catching a liar is tough for two reasons. First, lying is **(6)** ________________. Everyone lies. And second, there are so many ways to hide or **(7)** ________________ the truth. In fact, recent research has revealed that probably less than 5 percent of the population has the ability to detect a liar. Scientists continue to study precise visible signs of deception—the body's own way of **(8)** ________________ on a person who is lying.

(continued on next page)

An international study of lying shows that while children from nearly all cultures deceive each other, most cultures have different attitudes about lying and their ability to trick or **(9)** ___________________ others. One group of researchers found that honesty was not a huge **(10)** ___________________ for some people in the United States. They felt confident that they could get away with lying 56 percent of the time. Another group of researchers found that Chileans and Argentineans think they will be caught about 60 percent of the time while those living in Moldova and Botswana believe they will only be detected fibbing less than 25 percent of the time. Scientists must now **(11)** ___________________ the results, since some of the data are inconclusive.

EXPAND

Part One: A Scientist Blows the Whistle on a Colleague

Beatriz, a young food science researcher, suspects that her friend and colleague, Martin, has lied about the results of his experiment using a new artificial sweetener on laboratory animals. She decides to tattle on Martin to the lab director, Dr. Sanborn.

1 *Read each line of the conversation between Beatriz and Dr. Sanborn. Work with a partner. Write the letter of each of Dr. Sanborn's responses next to Beatriz's lines. The boldfaced word provides a clue. Then listen to the conversation and check your answers. Read the conversation aloud with your partner.*

Beatriz

_____ **1.** Dr. Sanborn, I hate to have to tell you this, but I am concerned that Martin has **fudged** the results of his study.

_____ **2.** Yes, I am pretty sure that he is **bluffing** about the safety of his sweetener.

_____ **3.** Well, apparently his ambition is blinding him. I'm telling you, he's going down a **slippery slope** with this project.

_____ **4.** I know, but he's too afraid to **fess up** to the fact that his sweetener might pose a health risk.

_____ **5.** Trust me, Dr. Sanborn, Martin's project is definitely a **recipe for disaster**. His results will not be duplicated, I'm sure.

Dr. Sanborn

a. Come on, Beatriz. It's really hard to believe that Martin would **lie** about his work. He has always been an accurate, honest researcher.

b. I can't bear to hear that such a bright, intelligent researcher would be **headed toward disaster**.

c. Thanks, Beatriz. I understand. If his project is a **failure**, our lab will lose funding. I'll speak to Martin tomorrow.

d. You mean he has **manipulated** the data in order to get the result he wanted?

e. Beatriz, I've known Martin for years. I can't believe he wouldn't **tell** me if his experiments were failing.

Part Two: The Colleague Defends Himself

The next day, Martin confronts Beatriz about her conversation with Dr. Sanborn.

2 CD 1 23 *Read each line of the conversation between Martin and Beatriz. Working with a new partner, write the letter of each of Beatriz's responses next to Martin's lines. The boldfaced word provides a clue. Then listen to the conversation and check your answers. Read the conversation aloud with your partner.*

Martin

_____ **1.** Wow, Beatriz. I absolutely cannot believe the **whopper** you told Dr. Sanborn about my experiment. You're just jealous that I'm finally getting the results that will make me famous.

_____ **2.** I thought I did, Bea, but you are **two-faced**. I can't trust you now.

_____ **3.** That's not true. The chubby mice have lost weight, and my sweetener is safe. I am being totally **up front** with you and everyone else about my results.

_____ **4.** My reputation does depend on this project, but I would never risk my career to **pull the wool over everyone's eyes**.

Beatriz

a. Martin, I'm not being **deceptive**. Whatever I told Dr. Sanborn, I would tell you directly. Look, I don't trust the results of your study. You are falsifying the data.

b. You can't really believe that! You're so preoccupied with success, you're not being **honest**.

c. I'm sorry, Martin, but the facts show you *are* trying to **trick** us, despite our lab policy to "relentlessly pursue knowledge and truth."

d. Are you kidding? I didn't tell him a **lie**, and I am not envious of you. You should know me better than that.

CREATE

Work with a partner.

Student A: Read statements 1 through 4 on page 36 to Student B. Complete each one according to your own opinions or experiences.

Student B: Respond to Student A using the word listed. You may agree, disagree, ask a question, or share information of your own. Then switch roles after item 4.

Example

STUDENT A: In a family relationship, it is important to be up front about things that happened in your past.

STUDENT B: Maybe, but I think all people have some experience that they would rather conceal forever, even from a family member.

Student A	**Student B**
1. In a family relationship, it is important to be up front about . . .	**1.** conceal
2. My culture/family/best friend has a preoccupation with . . .	**2.** pervasive
3. The best/biggest whopper I ever told was . . .	**3.** fess up
4. I remember putting one over on my parents when I . . .	**4.** tattle
Now switch roles.	
5. Governments should relentlessly punish people who . . .	**5.** mull over
6. In my opinion, bluffing about _________ is never OK.	**6.** recipe for disaster
7. One time, I fudged the truth by . . .	**7.** deceive
8. The news media misleads the public when . . .	**8.** inflated

B GRAMMAR: Modals—Degrees of Certainty

1 *Working with a partner, examine the statements, and discuss the questions that follow.*

- Some studies have concluded that most people lie, fib, or sugarcoat the truth once or twice a day. In order to identify a liar, you **could** pay attention to a change in voice or you **could** watch for unusual body language.
- You **should** be able to spot a liar by noticing a contradiction between his or her words and facial expressions.

1. Which statement is more certain?
2. Which modal verbs could you substitute for the boldfaced words and keep the same meaning?

MODALS—DEGREES OF CERTAINTY

Use **modal verbs** to express different **degrees of certainty** about the present, the past, and the future. The modal you use shows how strongly you believe something is true or not true.

Almost Certain

Present	***must***	The students' papers are identical, although they insist they didn't cheat. Clearly, one of them **must** be lying.
Past	***Must*** + ***have*** + past participle ***(must've)****	He claimed to have received a music award in high school, but there is no official record of it. He **must have (must've)** lied on his application.

Almost Certain, Negative (Impossible)

Present / Future	***Can't / couldn't***	His excuse for missing the exam due to illness **can't** possibly be true. I just know he is telling a big, fat whopper!
Past	***Can't / couldn't*** + ***have*** + past participle ***(couldn't've)****	I'm shocked. The university's president **couldn't have (couldn't've)** committed plagiarism in his speech. He is known for his impeccable integrity.

Quite Sure

Future	***Should / ought to***	Due to improvements in technology, brain scans **should** soon be able to help us detect liars and cheaters more accurately.
Past	***Should*** + ***have*** + past participle ***(should've)****	He **should've** read the university's Honor Code by now. All first-year students do.

Less Certain

Present / Future	***Could / may / might***	The final grades in the professor's class look a bit inflated. He **might** be fudging them to make himself look like a better teacher.
Past	***Could / may / might*** + ***have*** + past participle ***(might've)****	Walt has always been so honest, but he **might have (might've)** cheated on the exam because of the intense competition and the pressure from his parents.

* In speaking, the auxiliary *have* [modal + *have* + past participle] is pronounced /əv/ and is joined to the preceding word. This form is used only in speech.

2 *Work with a partner.*

Student A: Cover the right column. Ask a question or make a comment.

*Student B: Cover the left column. Respond using the cues and a present, past, or future modal verb of certainty. Refer to the chart on page 37. Be sure to pronounce the reduced modal forms (**must've, couldn't've, should've, might've**) correctly. Then switch roles after question 4. Use expressive intonation.*

Example

STUDENT A: Will Tomás be punished for lying to his boss about his work hours?
STUDENT B: (less certain) Maybe. There's a chance he might even lose his job.

Student A	**Student B**
1. Do you think I'll be able to tell if she is lying by just looking at her?	**1.** (quite sure) Probably. You (able / tell) by watching for small changes in her facial expressions.
2. Will she be able to conceal the fact she copied her paper from the Internet?	**2.** (impossible) No way. She (get away with) plagiarizing. Her professor uses anti-plagiarizing software.
3. Do you know why some doctors lie to their dying patients?	**3.** (almost certain) I think so. They (want) to protect the patients and their family from hearing bad news.
4. Why does Stella send exam answers to her friends over her cell phone?	**4.** (less certain) I'm not really sure. Her friends (pay) her for the answers.
Now switch roles.	
5. Is Mohammed feeling better now that he finally fessed up to fudging the results of the experiment?	**5.** (quite sure) He (be / relieve). It usually feels better to be up front about things.
6. The baseball player's drug tests came back positive. He has to leave the team.	**6.** (impossible) Unbelievable! He just (deceived) his fans like that. They adored and trusted him.
7. Bad news. The results of Gordon's experiment cannot be duplicated.	**7.** (almost certain) Hmmm . . . he (cut corners) on the research.
8. Why didn't Marco ever tell anyone about his name change?	**8.** (less certain) Well, I'm not sure, but he (conceal) his identity to protect himself.

3 *Work with a partner.*

Student A: Cover the right column. Ask the question. Check Student B's answer against the words in parentheses.

Student B: Cover the left column. Answer the question using an appropriate past modal of certainty. Use short-answer forms. (See example.) Be sure to pronounce the modal perfect forms correctly. Then switch roles after question 4.

Example

STUDENT A: Did Maria know that her boyfriend lied to her about his "whereabouts" last Saturday night? (must've)

STUDENT B: (almost certain) Well, she _must've_. She told me she was pretty sure she saw his car in front of Sarah's apartment.

Student A

1. Did she tattle on her brother when she found out he had been driving without a license? (must've)
2. Did that young Harvard student really write that book that just won a major award? (couldn't've)
3. She refused to look in my eyes when she answered my question. Do you think she was lying? (could've been / might've been / may've been)
4. Did he really have to spend a year in jail for cheating on his taxes? (must've had to)

Now switch roles.

5. Do you think she lied about her plans so she wouldn't have to go to the party? (could've / might've / may've)
6. Have all the airports installed the special tracking device to spot people lying about their identities? (should've)
7. Were the lab directors pleased with the doctoral students' results? (couldn't have been)
8. Do you think Ms. Rapaport could tell immediately that Pierre was her half-brother? (must've known)

Student B

1. (almost certain) Yes, she _____. She looked happy. He looked miserable and their parents looked furious.
2. (impossible) No, she _____. The book was too good. In fact, they think she plagiarized 50 percent of the novel.
3. (less certain) Hmmm . . . she _____. Not making eye contact is one sign of lying.
4. (almost certain) Yes, he _____. I heard he hadn't paid any taxes for six years!
5. (less certain) I'm not sure, but she _____. She is sort of two-faced, so it's hard to know her real feelings.
6. (quite sure) Yes, they _____. The government has required these since 9/11.
7. (impossible) Unfortunately, they _____. The results were misleading.
8. (almost certain) Of course, she _____. He looked exactly like her father.

C SPEAKING

PRONUNCIATION: Reduction of the Auxiliary *Have*

CD 7 24 Listen to the statements. Then read the explanation.

- I know I **should have told** the truth, but I was afraid I'd get in trouble.
- If you had made an excuse for missing the appointment, your client **wouldn't have fired** you. It's not acceptable to say you just didn't feel like working that day.

In spoken English, the auxiliary ***have*** is reduced when used with ***could***, ***might***, ***must***, ***should***, and ***would*** in the unreal conditional tense as well as in modal perfect forms. It is pronounced /əv/, and joins to the preceding word. The main verb is stressed.

1 CD 7 25 *Listen to these modal perfects and repeat them.*

1. could have done
2. would have done
3. should have done
4. might have done
5. must have done
6. couldn't have done
7. wouldn't have done
8. shouldn't have done
9. might not have done*
10. must not have done*

2 CD 7 26 *In this conversation, Anton has just heard Molly compliment their friend, José, on his new haircut. Listen to the conversation and fill in the blanks with modal perfects. Draw a line through the **h** of **have** and use an underline to link the modal and **have**. Then practice the conversation with a partner.*

Anton: I think José's hair looks awful. I could have given him a better haircut with my eyes closed. Do you really think he looks good?

Molly: No, I agree, he looks terrible. He ________________ his hair long. But I couldn't tell him that.

Anton: No, but he didn't ask you what you thought. You volunteered the compliment. You ________________ anything at all.

Molly: But he saw me staring at him. If I hadn't said anything, he ________________ I didn't like his haircut. He knew I'd noticed, so I told a white lie. What's the harm?

Anton: Well, first, you told a lie when you ________________ nothing. But what's worse, now José thinks he looks good when he really doesn't.

Molly: But if I hadn't said anything, it ________________ awkward. Anyway, when his hair grows, I'll tell him he looks even better.

---

*After *might* and *must*, the full negative *not* is more common than the contraction *n't*.

3 *Work with a partner.*

Student A: Cover the right column. Read your statements to Student B.

*Student B: Cover the left column. Respond to your partner using **would've**, **should've**, **could've**, **might've**, or **must've**, or their negative forms. Then switch roles after item 5.*

Student A

1. Midlake University expelled a student when a professor caught him plagiarizing.

2. But he was caught. He was cheating.

3. How do you know it was his first time? Maybe it was just the first time he got caught.

4. I think the policy is right, but it has caused a lot of distrust between the students and the administration.

5. I wonder if the students really understand plagiarism.

Now switch roles.

6. Yesterday, I decided to do a little experiment. I decided to go for a whole day without telling a lie, not even the smallest deception.

7. Well, I was late for my first appointment with a new client. When I told her I'd forgotten about the appointment, she fired me.

8. Yes, but remember the experiment. Then Joe asked me to go to lunch, and I said no. When he asked me why, I said I didn't feel like listening to his problems.

9. Well, then I decided I'd better go home and not talk to anyone else. But I passed the test— I didn't tell a single lie for the whole day.

Student B

1. Uh-huh. I heard about that. The university should / not / expel him.
 Uh-huh. The university shouldn't've expelled him.

2. Yeah, but it was his first time. They should / give / him another chance.

3. That's true. He might / plagiarize before.

4. I know. I think the university could / handle it better.

5. Well, they must / hear about it in the news.

6. Well, that should / not / be hard for you. You're one of the most honest people I know. What happened?

7. This sounds like an expensive experiment. Could / not / you / say that you were in another meeting and unable to leave?

8. He must / be furious. I know how I'd feel if someone said that to me. So, you lost a client and a friend. What happened next?

9. Maybe you should / start the experiment with a different definition of a lie, one that doesn't lead to lost clients and friends.

◖ **FUNCTION: Seeing Multiple Sides to an Issue**

Lying, cheating, and secrecy, as well as honesty, truth-telling, and openness, require people to reflect on their ethics and values. Ethical dilemmas are rarely clear-cut. Generally, when we make ethical or moral decisions, we need to consider all angles to an issue.

The following is a list of expressions to use when reflecting on an ethical dilemma.

INTRODUCTORY EXPRESSION	ADDITIONAL CONSIDERATION OR RESPONSE
One way to look at _____ is . . .	And another way could be . . .
Of course, it depends on . . .	It could also depend on . . .
On the one hand, you could say . . .	On the other hand, . . .
One thing to take into consideration could be . . .	Another thing might be . . .
There are several things to consider. One . . .	Two . . . Three . . . etc.
One way to think about _____ is . . .	But the flip side would be . . .
If you look at it from the angle of . . .	But seen from another angle . . .

With a partner, discuss the ethics of the common actions listed below.

Student A: Flip a coin. If it lands on "heads," you must defend the action listed, using an introductory expression above.

Student B: Respond using the expression for additional information or opposing response from the right column above. It should correspond to the expression used by Student A.

Switch roles after each item.

Daily Ethical Dilemmas

Is it honest or ethical to:

- Take office supplies from your company for personal use?

Example

STUDENT A: On the one hand, you could say that it's ethical because sometimes I bring things from home to the office.

STUDENT B: On the other hand, the things you bring from home, such as decorations, are not really "supplies" that you need to do your job, so it's not ethical.

- Download music from the Internet without paying?
- Buy a new sweater and then return it after wearing it?
- Turn in a paper you had actually written for another class two years ago?

- Not tell your professor when he or she inadvertently marks an answer "correct" when in fact you find out it is incorrect?
- Claim that computer problems caused you to turn in a project late, when really you just didn't have time to finish it?

PRODUCTION: A Group Discussion

In this activity, you will ***plan a group discussion about dilemmas and lying***. Try to use the vocabulary, grammar, pronunciation, and the language to discuss multiple sides of an issue that you learned in the unit.*

Work in groups of four. Each student will read key information on page 255 about one actual ethical dilemma and then summarize it for the group. As each dilemma is presented, the other group members will take notes on a separate piece of paper. Then, as a group, brainstorm possible solutions or answers to the questions. Take brief notes below each question. Use the modals of certainty on page 37 and the expressions for seeing alternate sides to an issue on page 42. Choose one dilemma to present to the class.

DILEMMA A: TRADING A LEMON	DILEMMA B: VIDEO PIRACY	DILEMMA C: A DOCTOR'S DEBATE	DILEMMA D: TURTLE TROUBLE
• What should he do?	• What should the woman tell her child?	• Should the doctor tell him his diagnosis?	• Was the woman's lie justified?
• What should he tell a potential buyer?	• Should she discuss the issue with the neighbors?	• Should the doctor respect the family's wishes not to tell the patient how serious his illness is?	• What other options did she have?

*For Alternative Speaking Topics, see page 44.

ALTERNATIVE SPEAKING TOPICS

Choose a topic. Use ideas, vocabulary, grammar, pronunciation, and the language to discuss multiple sides of an issue.

Topic 1

Look at the following statistics. Working with a partner, discuss why you think the statistics are true. What accounts for the numbers? What is surprising or not surprising to you?

a. According to an online résumé writing business, of 1,000 résumés vetted over six months, 43 percent contained one or more "significant inaccuracies."

b. One study found that most people lie once or twice a day. Both men and women lie in 20 percent of their social exchanges lasting more than 10 minutes. In one week they deceive 30 percent of those they come in contact with one to one.

c. When students communicate, they often tell lies. In fact fibs occur in 15 percent of e-mail messages, 33 percent of phone calls, 25 percent of face-to-face conversations, and about 20 percent of instant message chats.

Topic 2

Work in a small group. Read the following quotations about truth and lying. Paraphrase them. Discuss whether you agree or disagree with them and why.

- "Lying is done with words and also with silence." (Adrienne Rich, twentieth-century American poet)
- "A little inaccuracy sometimes saves a lot of explanations." (Saki, twentieth-century British writer)
- "Why would anyone lie? The truth is always more colorful." (James Hall, twentieth-century American musician)
- "Lying is an art. For parents, however, it may be an absolute necessity." (Bernice Kanner, twentieth-century American author)
- "He who is not sure of his memory should not undertake the trade of lying." (Michel de Montaigne, sixteenth-century French author)
- "A lie has short legs." (Estonian proverb)
- "Man was given a tongue with which to speak and words to hide his thoughts." (Hungarian proverb)
- "We need lies in order to live." (Friedrich Nietzsche, nineteenth-century German philosopher)
- "Speech was given to man to disguise his thoughts." (Maurice de Talleyrand, nineteenth-century French diplomat)
- "A lie can get halfway around the world before the truth can get its boots on." (Mark Twain, nineteenth-century American author)

RESEARCH TOPICS, see page 260.

UNIT 3 The Bold and the Bashful

1 FOCUS ON THE TOPIC

A PREDICT

Look at the cartoon above and the title of the unit. Bookstores sometimes sponsor events at which authors can meet people and autograph books for them. What is the message of the cartoon? Do you think it's funny? Why or why not? What kinds of self-help tips might be offered in this book? How do you think it feels to be bashful or shy?

B SHARE INFORMATION

1 *Who's shy and who isn't? Take the quiz and calculate your score.*

HOW SHY ARE YOU?

For each statement, rate yourself on this scale. Circle your answer.

	Never	Almost Never	Sometimes	Often	Always
1. I'm tense and nervous when I'm with people I don't know well.	1	2	3	4	5
2. It's difficult for me to ask other people for information.	1	2	3	4	5
3. I'm often uncomfortable at parties and other social gatherings.	1	2	3	4	5
4. When I'm in a group of people, I have trouble thinking of the right things to say.	1	2	3	4	5
5. It takes me a long time to overcome my shyness in new situations.	1	2	3	4	5
6. It's hard for me to act in a natural way when I'm meeting new people.	1	2	3	4	5
7. I'm nervous when I'm speaking to someone in authority.	1	2	3	4	5
8. I find it hard to talk to strangers.	1	2	3	4	5

WHAT YOUR SCORE MEANS:

30–40 = very shy
21–29 = somewhat shy
below 21 = probably not shy, although you may feel shy in some situations

TOTAL SCORE:______

2 *Discuss the results of the shyness quiz in a small group.*

1. Who had the highest score in your group? Who had the lowest score? Did your own results seem right to you?
2. When you speak English, do you feel shy or bold? In what situations do you feel shy? Describe those situations.
3. In your opinion, is shyness a positive or negative quality? Explain. In cultures you know, how is shyness perceived or regarded?

C BACKGROUND AND VOCABULARY

1 CD 1 27 *Shyness has personal, situational, as well as cultural dimensions. First, read and listen to the sentences. Then try to determine the meaning of the boldfaced words from the context of the sentences. Write a definition or similar expression under the sentence.*

1. In English class, some students tend to speak out a lot. Others are somewhat **reticent**.

   ____

2. A public-speaking **phobia**, called glossophobia, prevented the businessman from delivering formal presentations at work.

   ____

3. If people cannot explain their ideas well when they speak, others may assume those ideas have no **merit**.

   ____

4. Dr. Zimbardo, a university professor who studies shyness, found that Israelis were not shy and introverted. On the contrary, they were outgoing and **extroverted.**

   ____

5. In China, being shy may not have **adverse** consequences as it does in some countries. In fact, some studies have indicated that Chinese children who are shy are well accepted by their peers and often end up in leadership roles.

   ____

6. Researchers have found that Scandinavians have higher rates of shyness, often defined as a social anxiety **syndrome**, with both physical and emotional symptoms. They say it could be because of the cold weather.

   ____

7. **Chronic** shyness—shyness that persists from childhood to adulthood—can have negative consequences, such as low self-esteem and loneliness.

   ____

(continued on next page)

8. My friend and I regard each other as **kindred souls**. We are both painfully shy.

____

9. The public often make **misattributions** about top business executives. People assume they are outgoing, aggressive, and bold. But data shows that 40 percent of chief executive officers (CEOs) worldwide describe themselves as shy.

____

10. Of the students from India surveyed, 82 percent reported that shyness was a problem or **handicap** that made them unhappy and unfulfilled.

____

11. Off-screen, film actor Brad Pitt is said to be **aloof** and unfriendly. But in truth, he is just very shy and protective of his personal life.

____

12. It was not her intention to be rude or **condescending** toward her staff. She behaved this way in order to cover up her extreme shyness.

____

2 *Now match the words on the left with the correct definition or similar expression on the right. Write the appropriate letter in the blank. Then work with a partner and compare answers.*

_____ **1.** reticent	**a.** condition
_____ **2.** phobia	**b.** distant
_____ **3.** merit	**c.** very strong fear
_____ **4.** extroverted	**d.** negative
_____ **5.** adverse	**e.** disadvantage
_____ **6.** syndrome	**f.** unwilling to talk
_____ **7.** chronic	**g.** false assumptions
_____ **8.** kindred souls	**h.** very sociable
_____ **9.** misattributions	**i.** people having similar traits
_____ **10.** handicap	**j.** value
_____ **11.** aloof	**k.** treating others as inferior
_____ **12.** condescending	**l.** continual (in a medical sense)

2 FOCUS ON LISTENING

A LISTENING ONE: Americans Are Getting Shyer

What is the reputation of people from your country: bold or bashful? Is this a stereotype? How do they see themselves? Internationally, Americans are seen as bold. However, one professor's research has shown that they consider themselves quite bashful. Americans believe that being bashful is a problem: "Shyness is undesirable, [it] has adverse consequences," explains Professor Philip Zimbardo in an interview aired on NPR®.

CD 1 28 *Work with a partner. Predict some of the problems that you think shy people may have as a result of their shyness (for example, staying in a dead-end job, avoiding social situations). Discuss your ideas with your partner. Then listen to this excerpt of the interview to check your predictions.*

LISTEN FOR MAIN IDEAS

CD 1 29 *Read the topics. Then listen to Part One of the interview, and write a main idea statement related to each topic. Do the same for Part Two. Work with a partner and compare notes.*

TOPIC	MAIN IDEA
PART ONE	
1. *Results of Dr. Zimbardo's new study*	1.
2. *Reasons Americans are becoming shyer*	2.
PART TWO	
3. *Descriptions of shyness*	3.
4. *Dr. Zimbardo's advice to shy people*	4.
5. *Problem that shyness presents to attractive people*	5.

LISTEN FOR DETAILS

CD 7 30 *Read the sentences and circle the letter of the answer that completes each sentence correctly. Answer as many items as you can. Then listen to the interview again. As you listen, complete any remaining items. Work with a partner and compare answers.*

Part One

1. According to the interviewer, Alex Chadwick, these days Americans are having difficulty _____.
   a. meeting people
   b. dressing appropriately
   c. asking questions

2. Dr. Zimbardo _____.
   a. teaches in a shyness clinic
   b. runs in Palo Alto
   c. manages a shyness clinic

3. Dr. Zimbardo's latest research focused on shy _____.
   a. adults
   b. children
   c. children and adults

4. The researchers discovered that over the past 10 years, the number of Americans who label themselves as shy has increased to _____.
   a. 48 percent
   b. 18 percent
   c. 20 percent

5. One thing that Dr. Zimbardo does not say about shy people is that they are _____.
   a. competitive
   b. reticent
   c. self-conscious

6. The electronic revolution means that many people's jobs are being replaced by computers. Dr. Zimbardo doesn't mention _____ as being replaced by computers.
   a. gas station owners
   b. bank tellers
   c. telephone operators

Part Two

7. In Dr. Zimbardo's survey, _____ of people said shyness was undesirable.
   a. 70 percent
   b. 79 percent
   c. 75 percent

8. One example of situational, or momentary, shyness not mentioned by Dr. Zimbardo is _____.
   a. going on a blind date
   b. playing the piano in public
   c. speaking in public

9. Quasimodo is the hunchback in Victor Hugo's novel *The Hunchback of Notre Dame.* Dr. Zimbardo compares shyness to Quasimodo's hump because _____.
   a. everyone notices it
   b. you always carry it with you
   c. it's not chronic

10. Dr. Zimbardo feels that shy people should be aware that nearly _____ of the population is shy.
   a. 15 percent
   b. 50 percent
   c. 40 percent

11. According to Dr. Zimbardo, when you are too shy, people may assume you are also _____.
   a. unintelligent
   b. motivated
   c. unattractive

12. Dr. Zimbardo tells Alex Chadwick that he is not shy because he is the oldest child in a _____.
   a. small Italian family
   b. large Sicilian family
   c. large Greek family

MAKE INFERENCES

Read the questions. Then listen to each excerpt from the interview. Remember that making inferences means understanding something that is not literally stated, but that you believe is true based on the intention, attitude, voice, pausing, and choice of words of the speakers. Discuss your answers with a partner, then with the class.

CD 7 31

Excerpt One

1. What do you think the interviewer, Alex Chadwick, means by the phrase "Friends, take heart"? Why does he use the word *friends* to address the anonymous radio audience?
2. What is Chadwick's attitude toward the topic of shyness? How does he use his tone of voice to express this attitude?

Excerpt Two

3. Dr. Zimbardo clearly believes that his research is important and interesting. How does he show this attitude in the excerpt? How does he use his tone of voice? What words does he use to express this attitude?

Excerpt Three

4. How does Dr. Zimbardo feel when Chadwick asks him whether he is shy? What can you hear in his voice and choice of words?

EXPRESS OPINIONS

1 *Work with a partner. If you were a parent of a shy child or if you had a good friend who was shy, what five strategies would you use to help your child or friend "come out of his / her shell"? In other words, what tips would you give a "shrinking violet" to blossom? Or, alternatively, how would you convince a "shrinking violet" to simply accept and be comfortable with his or her reserved temperament? Discuss your opinions.*

2 *Are we born shy, or do we become shy? Work with a partner. Read the factors that psychologists believe make people shy. Decide how important you think these factors may be in causing shyness. Write them in one of the columns. Then discuss the reasons for your choices.*

genetics
cultural values
birth order (oldest, middle, or youngest)
gender
competition
parents' behavior
lack of social skills
physical attractiveness
use of computer and video games
use of electronic communication (e-mail, voice mail, chat rooms)
life experiences (moving, changing schools, divorce in family)

VERY IMPORTANT	SOMEWHAT IMPORTANT	NOT VERY IMPORTANT

3 *Work with a partner. Look at the cartoon, and discuss the answers to the questions that follow.*

Drawing by M. Twohy, © 1996 The New Yorker Magazine, Inc.

1. What does "low self-esteem" mean? Do you think all shy people have low self-esteem? What could cause low self-esteem?
2. Is writing in a diary a useful way to express your feelings and cope with problems? What advice would you give to the man to boost his self-esteem?

B LISTENING TWO: The Pollyanna Syndrome

Are you an optimist or a pessimist? Have you ever run into an overly optimistic person? In this on-air essay from Public Radio International, Julie Danis gives her opinion about Pollyannas—people who refuse to accept that anything bad can happen. The name comes from the heroine of a 1913 novel, Pollyanna, who had a consistently optimistic outlook on life, which many people today see as unrealistic.

In the commentary, Danis gives examples of ways that one coworker was able to "make lemonade out of lemons." What might this phrase mean? Have you ever known any Pollyannas? If so, describe them.

CD 7 34 *Read the items on the left. Then listen to Julie Danis's commentary. Listen again, and match Danis's unlucky event with Pollyanna's "bright side" view on the right.*

Danis

_____ **1.** went to the eye doctor but did not get a diagnosis for the problem of blurred vision

_____ **2.** stop-and-go commute

_____ **3.** computer crashes and 1-800-HELP line is very busy

_____ **4.** snowed in with no hope of flying

_____ **5.** toothache and no dental insurance for the root canal

Pollyanna

a. time to purge, or clean out, the computer files

b. time to catch up on movies

c. a chance to skip the mascara and rest eyes every two hours

d. no solution

e. a chance to listen to language tapes while doing relaxation exercises

C INTEGRATE LISTENINGS ONE AND TWO

STEP I: Organize

Using the information in Listening One and Listening Two, complete the chart. Use information that is directly stated and information that is implied.

PERSONALITY TYPES	POSITIVE ATTRIBUTIONS	NEGATIVE ATTRIBUTIONS	WAYS TO COPE
Dispositionally shy	X	• unpopular •	• find others who are shy
Situationally shy	X	• •	
Optimist	• outgoing • •	•	X
Pessimist	•	• •	• •

STEP 2: Synthesize

Work with a partner. Read the situations and use the words and phrases from Step 1 to improvise a short conversation between a Pollyanna and a shy person. Then present the conversations to your class.

Situation 1

Student A: You are a situationally shy employee who has just been told by your manager that you have to give a presentation to 75 salespeople about a new product your company has just launched. Following the presentation, you will have to host the reception, making sure everyone feels comfortable. You are petrified. Explain all of your feelings and symptoms.

Student B: You are the Pollyanna coworker. Give advice to Ms. Situationally Shy to help her succeed in her task. Help her make lemons out of lemonade.

Situation 2

Student B: You have just been chosen as the president of the campus environmental club because of your intelligence, knowledge of the subject matter, and ability to get things done. However, you are very dispositionally shy. In this role, you have to be a leader, organize events, give speeches, and convince your members to follow your agenda. You are not sure you can manage. Discuss all of your feelings and symptoms.

Student A: You are a Pollyanna and you are Mr. Dispositionally Shy's club adviser. Convince him that he should be "comfortable in his own skin" and that he can do the job. Give him tips for doing it. Help him find the silver lining.

3 FOCUS ON SPEAKING

A VOCABULARY

REVIEW

How does birth order affect personality? Some researchers believe that being the firstborn, the only child, or the "baby" in a family has a significant impact.

(continued on next page)

Read the letters to a newspaper, and fill in the blanks with the correct form of the appropriate expression from the list. Use the hints below the blanks to help you. Work with a partner and compare answers.

break the ice	fill the void	outlook	virtually
carried away	grouchy	take things as	widespread
draw out	mark (v.)	think of	wind up

STAR DAILY.com Each week the *Star Daily* posts our favorite responses to questions posed to our readers. Here are our favorites:

BIRTH ORDER: DOES IT MATTER?

Dear *Star Daily*:

I'm the youngest of five children. I know that ________________ all later-born
1. (almost)
children are reserved, but not necessarily aloof. Rarely ________________ , I have a
2. (in a bad mood)
positive ________________ on life and
3. (point of view)
________________ they come.
4. (accept experiences as)

NANCY KAKOWSKI
Springfield, Missouri

Dear *Star Daily*:

I realize that acceptance of this birth order theory is becoming more ________________ ,
5. (common)
but I just can't buy it. I mean, it's ridiculous! Everyone is just getting so ________________
6. (overly excited)
with these ideas and attributing every kind of behavior to birth order! First of all, I think personality traits are determined by genetics. Second, theories like birth order are actually harmful in that they may ________________
7. (label)
people unfairly, leading to misattributions about people's personalities.

MARTHA JOHNSON
New York City, New York

Dear *Star Daily*:

I'm the firstborn in my family. My siblings complain that I'm arrogant, but I don't ________________ myself that way. At social
8. (consider)
gatherings, I ________________ being the
9. (end up)
life of the party. I see my role as ________________ my more introverted
10. (encouraging)
friends.

MARK BALDINO
Portland, Oregon

Dear *Star Daily*:

I'm an independent, only child. So I spent a great deal of time alone. To ______________________ , I had to learn many

11. (overcome loneliness)

new skills. For example, I learned how to lose my awkwardness and self-consciousness. Now, I'm usually the one at social occasions to

____.

12. (get people socializing and enjoying themselves)

PATTY LAFOND
Austin, Texas

EXPAND

1 *English has a wealth of vocabulary to talk about personality and temperament. Work with a partner. Write each word in the most appropriate category on the chart. Some words may fit in more than one category. For help, use information from the unit and a dictionary.*

assertive	life of the party	positive	standoffish
bashful	methodical	reserved	talk a blue streak
bold	negative	reticent	timid
gloomy	open	self-conscious	upbeat
gregarious	outgoing	shrinking violet	wallflower
inhibited	petrified	sociable	whiny
killjoy	Pollyanna	social butterfly	

BEHAVIOR		ATTITUDE	
Introvert	**Extrovert**	**Pessimist**	**Optimist**

2 *Work with a partner. Describe yourself to your partner using the words from the chart you completed in Exercise 1. Overall, what kind of person are you—an introvert, extrovert, pessimist, or optimist?*

CREATE

Work in small groups. Read the questions. Discuss the answers, and defend your opinions. Use words from the box on page 57 to help you express yourself. Play devil's advocate if possible. (If you "play devil's advocate," you support a less popular opinion in order to encourage debate.) Add your own examples.

Who Would You Rather Have?

1. Who would you rather have for your doctor?

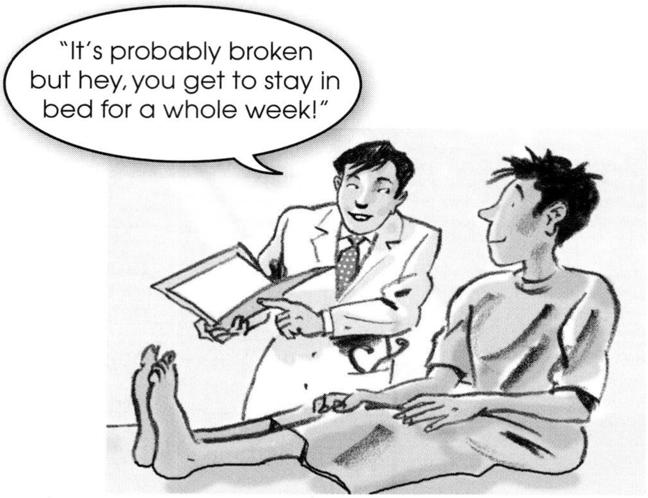

Someone who is _____.

a. highly experienced, but also reticent and a bit aloof

OR

b. a recent medical school graduate, but also outgoing . . . always makes lemons out of lemonade.

2. Who would you rather have for your teacher?

Someone who is _____.

a. gregarious, can talk a blue streak, but also at times gloomy

OR

b. reserved, confident, but also at times a bit self-conscious

3. Who would you rather have as your spouse?

Someone who is _____.

a. sensitive, kind, but also reticent and introverted

OR

b. the life of the party, gregarious, but also at times a bit standoffish and sometimes grouchy

4. Who would you rather have as your tour guide on vacation?

Someone who is _____.

a. extremely knowledgeable, detail-oriented, but a killjoy

OR

b. sociable, assertive, but inexperienced and a bit scattered and disorganized

B GRAMMAR: Adjective Clauses—Identifying and Nonidentifying

1 *Work with a partner. Study the sentences and discuss the questions that follow.*

- Our research, which we've been conducting since 1972, focuses on adults who are shy.
- We are losing the social lubrication that's essential for people to feel comfortable in the presence of others.
- I am more like a Zorba the Greek-type person whose job in the world it is to make people feel comfortable.
- Negative personality traits, most of which are totally false, are often applied to shy, attractive people.

1. What is the purpose of the underlined clauses?
2. Compare the five underlined clauses. How are they similar? How are they different?

ADJECTIVE CLAUSES

Adjective clauses are used to add variety, sophistication, and interest to sentences. They are useful in combining sentences to provide more detail and information. There are two kinds of adjective clauses: identifying and nonidentifying.

Identifying Adjective Clauses

An **identifying adjective clause**:

- has a subject and a verb
- modifies specific nouns and pronouns
- can be introduced by ***who***, ***whom***, ***which***, ***that***, ***whose***, ***where***, and ***when***
- is not set off by commas
- is essential to the meaning of the sentence

Examples

- We are losing the social lubrication **that's essential for people to feel comfortable in the presence of others**.
- Consider the division between those **who always see the bright side** and those **who'd rather wallow in their misery**.

Nonidentifying Adjective Clauses

A **nonidentifying adjective clause**:

- has a subject and a verb
- is used with the relative pronouns ***who***, ***whom***, ***which***, and ***whose***. It is also used with ***where*** and ***when*** and cannot be used with ***that***
- must describe a specific person or thing
- is set off by commas
- is not essential to the meaning of the sentence and may be omitted

Examples

- Our research, **which we've been conducting since 1972**, focuses on adults.
- Dr. Lynn Henderson, **who is co-director of the Shyness Clinic**, says nearly everyone experiences shyness.

Quantifying Expressions

Nonidentifying adjective clauses often contain **expressions of quantity** such as ***many of***, ***most of***, ***some of***, ***none of***, ***two of***, ***several of***, ***half of***, ***all of***, ***each of***, ***both of***, and ***a number of***.

Use the structure: quantifier + preposition + relative pronoun (only ***who***, ***whom***, ***where***, ***when***, or ***which***).

Examples

- Negative personality traits, **most of which are totally false**, are often applied to shy, attractive people.
- The participants, **all of whom were adults**, met with the therapist twice a week to talk about their problems with shyness.

2 *Read the paragraph. Underline all the adjective clauses. Circle the pronouns. Draw an arrow from each clause to the noun it modifies. Label the clause **I** (identifying) or **N** (nonidentifying).*

The Palo Alto Shyness Clinic was founded by Dr. Philip Zimbardo, who is a professor at Stanford University, in Palo Alto, California. The clinic provides group and individual therapy for people who are trying to overcome loneliness and shyness. The clinic, which is currently directed by psychologist Dr. Lynn Henderson, uses a specialized treatment model called the Social Fitness Model that trains people in social skills in much the same way that people get trained in physical fitness. Dr. Henderson, who invented the Social Fitness Model, believes that problems of shyness, most of which can be overcome, must be explored in a supportive, positive environment.

N

3 *Work with a partner.*

Student A: Ask Student B questions 1 through 4.

Student B: Cover the left column. Answer the questions. Use a variety of adjective clauses in your answers. Then switch roles after question 4.

Student A	**Student B**
1. Who is Dr. Philip Zimbardo?	**1.** *Oh. He's the one who runs the Shyness Clinic.*
2. What is Stanford University?	**2.** Hmm. I think (that) . . .
3. What's an extrovert?	**3.** As far as I can remember . . .
4. What's situational shyness?	**4.** I'm not sure I remember, but I think . . .
Now switch roles.	
5. What's an introvert?	**5.** Well . . .
6. What's a Pollyanna?	**6.** Oh . . .
7. What's a shrinking violet?	**7.** I guess it's . . .

C SPEAKING

PRONUNCIATION: Grouping Words Together

When you speak, group your words into shorter phrases or thought groups. Thought groups help the listener understand speech in the same way that punctuation marks help readers understand writing. Pronounce the words in a thought group together.

- I'm the firstborn from a large family.

Join thought groups together smoothly. Hold (or lengthen) the end of one thought group briefly before you start the next group. There is often a small change in the pitch of your voice between thought groups.

- I'm the firstborn from a large family.

There are no fixed rules for the length of thought groups. Many thought groups are also grammatical groupings, like nonidentifying clauses.

- Dr. Lynn Henderson, who is co-director of the Shyness Clinic, says nearly everyone experiences shyness.

As you become more fluent, you will be able to use longer thought groups.

1 CD 1 35 *Listen to the sentences. Underline the thought groups. Then work with a partner to compare your groupings, and practice reading the sentences. If you and your partner have different groupings, discuss these differences.*

1. We discovered that about 40 percent of all Americans label themselves as currently shy.
2. Over the past 10 years, that figure has increased to about 48 percent.
3. Do you find these days that it's more difficult meeting people?
4. Two out of every five people you meet think of themselves as shy.
5. There are just many things in a culture, our culture, which lead lots of people to be shy.
6. Children don't see . . . don't have the opportunity to see their parents and relatives relating in a natural, easy, friendly way.
7. When you're at a party, or just in a conversation with someone anywhere and you recognize that they're shy, what do you do to draw them out or try to make them more comfortable?
8. Admitting your shyness is really an important first step because if you don't, people make misattributions.

2 CD 7, 36 *Listen to the sentences, and circle the letter of the one you hear. Then, working in pairs, choose sentence **a** or **b** to read to your partner. Your partner will tell you which one you have chosen. Then switch roles.*

1. **a.** "Philip," said the doctor, "doesn't suffer from shyness."
   b. Philip said, "The doctor doesn't suffer from shyness."
2. **a.** My sister, who lives in California, is a Pollyanna.
   b. My sister who lives in California is a Pollyanna.
3. **a.** Suzanne's manager told me she's gotten over her shyness.
   b. Suzanne's manager told me, "She's gotten over her shyness."
4. **a.** Zimbardo interviewed the students, who had admitted they were shy.
   b. Zimbardo interviewed the students who had admitted they were shy.
5. **a.** Everything he said was based on research.
   b. "Everything," he said, "was based on research."
6. **a.** The therapy, which the clinic provides, gets people to be more outgoing.
   b. The therapy which the clinic provides gets people to be more outgoing.

FUNCTION: Breaking the Ice and Maintaining a Conversation

At the end of the interview with Alex Chadwick, Dr. Zimbardo says, "I'm a firstborn from a big Sicilian family, so my job was making all the other kids feel comfortable, and so I . . . I am more like a Zorba the Greek-type person whose job in the world it is to make people feel comfortable, you know, at life's party."

Dr. Zimbardo admits that "making people comfortable at life's party" is a social skill that comes naturally to him. However, for many people, feeling comfortable and relaxed in social situations is a challenge. There are social skills that anyone can learn in order to help cope with feelings of shyness or awkwardness in social situations.

An important first step is learning how to break the ice and maintain a conversation.

BREAKING THE ICE	EXAMPLES
Introduce yourself.	"Hi, how are you?" "Hello, I'm Philip Zimbardo."
Comment on something shared: • weather • shared situation • uncontroversial news	"Nice weather, don't you think?" "How do you know the host?" "What a game last night, huh?"

MAINTAINING A CONVERSATION	EXAMPLES
Ask open-ended and follow-up questions.	"What brings you to Palo Alto?" "What kind of work do you do?"
Volunteer information.	"I run a shyness clinic here in the city."
Listen actively and look interested.	"Really?" "You're kidding!" (Use eye contact.) (Smile or nod your head occasionally.)
Change the topic if the conversation is dying, or excuse yourself.	"On another topic, did you see . . . ?" "Excuse me. I'd like to get a drink."

Work with a partner. Role-play a situation from the list. Student A starts the conversation. Both students keep it going for at least three minutes, throwing it back and forth like a ball. Use the chart above as a guide. Then change roles and role-play a second situation.

Situations

a. You are in a long checkout line at the supermarket. Start a conversation with the person behind you.

b. You are stranded at an airport gate waiting for a delayed flight. Start a conversation with the person next to you.

c. You are on a bus. Start a conversation with the person in the next seat.

d. You are at a party and feeling very self-conscious. Start a conversation with a person who also looks shy or awkward. Admit your uneasiness. As Dr. Zimbardo advises, look for a kindred soul.

PRODUCTION: A Case Study

In this activity, you will ***play the role of consultants who advise companies on how to build effective teams*** to achieve better results. Try to use the vocabulary, grammar, pronunciation, and the language for breaking the ice and maintaining a conversation that you learned in the unit.*

Work in groups of three or four.

What's the perfect personality mix to accomplish a given task? The choice can make the difference between success and frustration or failure. Try your hand at team building.

You are consultants working in a company called Personality Profiles, Inc. Personality Profiles is a highly specialized company which provides expert consultation to other companies on "team selection" for special projects. In other words, if a company needs to make sure a specific project team is composed of people with the appropriate personalities, they ask Personality Profiles to define the specific personalities and the best mix of personalities for that project. In addition, Personality Profiles is responsible for interviewing final candidates. The successful execution of the job depends on choosing the right people and the right combination of people. Sometimes the team members are as different as night and day!

This month, you have three clients who have asked you to define the personality mix and character attributes for three important projects. For each project:

1. Read the client's case.
2. Discuss what kinds of individuals would be best suited to perform the task. Use adjective clauses to characterize people: *We need people who are . . . Demanding people, who are. . . People who would not be suitable are . . .*
   Use expressions for maintaining the conversation when it begins to die.
3. Complete a chart with descriptions of the type of team members needed and interview questions to evaluate potential candidates. See the chart on page 67.

Imagine the class is your client. Choose one of the cases to present. Explain the reasons for your recommendations.

*For Alternative Speaking Topics, see page 67.

Client One: Global Space Project International (GSPI)

GSPI, an international consortium of space travel professionals, has asked Personality Profiles, Inc. to assist in the process of selecting a three-person crew for a mission to Mars. The mission will last approximately 2.5 years.

Some of the specific challenges of this mission include:

- Long periods of confinement and isolation
- Possibility of emergencies
- Low physical activity
- Intense, rigorous scientific experiments
- Repetitive and monotonous tasks

Client Two: *Canadian Post* Newspaper

Canadian Post newspaper has asked Personality Profiles, Inc. to assist in the process of selecting a three-person team of young university students to accompany a well-respected, famous investigative reporter on a 10-city tour of Africa. The trip will last approximately three months. The reporter and his three-student team of reporters will report on health, economic, and educational conditions in the 10 poorest areas of the African continent.

Some of the specific challenges of this mission include:

- Rough, unsophisticated living conditions
- Unpredictable and risky travel
- Lack of cell phone or electronic communication at times
- Exposure to illness, disease, and death
- Daily reporting and writing deadlines

Client Three: Cactus Production Studio

Cactus Production is the leading Mexican movie studio and has asked Personality Profiles, Inc. to assist in the process of selecting a three-person team to develop, create, and execute a creative and competitive marketing campaign for a new, highly anticipated movie by a prominent Mexican director and starring a popular Mexican movie star. The team will have only three weeks to develop the campaign, which will include television advertising, billboards, movie previews, newspaper and magazine advertising, a website, actor tours, and interviews.

Some of the specific challenges of this task include:

- Tight, unreasonable deadlines
- Conflicting needs, interests, and demands from actors, producers, directors
- Insufficient advertising budget
- Very high expectations for the movie to make a lot of money
- Complex campaign which includes several media (television, web, billboards, print, etc.)

Example

Client: Canadian Post

TEAM MEMBERS	PERSONALITY	DETAILED PERSONALITY REQUIREMENTS	PROBING QUESTIONS FOR INTERVIEW
1.	Dispositionally shy	*Good listener, excellent observer, doesn't have to be the center of attention*	1. How will you feel meeting new people every day? 2.
2.			
3.			

ALTERNATIVE SPEAKING TOPICS

Choose a topic. Use ideas, vocabulary, grammar, pronunciation, and expressions for breaking the ice and maintaining a conversation.

Topic 1

Gail Vennittie, a principal with PricewaterhouseCoopers, said, "I grew up as the middle child of seven kids. Depending on the situation, I had to try and figure out how to interact. Every scenario is slightly different." Being the middle child, Gail has had to be sensitive to other points of views as well as learn to be an independent thinker. Do you agree with Gail? Think about your own birth order. How has this birth order affected your personality or your skills?

Topic 2

Bill Gates, co-founder of Microsoft, is often described as shy and antisocial. In fact, research has shown that 40 percent of top CEOs tend to be introverts. Why do you think this is so? What makes them successful? Do you think there is a difference between shyness and introversion? If so, what is the difference?

Topic 3

Surprisingly enough, despite great success and public attention, many celebrities consider themselves shy. One well-known singer-songwriter, Suzanne Vega, speaks openly about her shyness. The following song, which appeared in the movie *Pretty in Pink*, expresses Vega's feelings and perspective on her shy temperament.

1 *Listen to the song. Then listen again, and fill in the missing words. Compare your answers with those of a partner.*

Left of Center

If you want me
You can find me
Left of center
Off of the ________________
In the ________________
In the fringes*
In the corner
Out of the ________________

(Repeat)

When they ask me
"What are you looking at?"
I always ________________
"Nothing much" (not much)
I think they know that
I'm looking at them
I think they think
I must be ________________

But I'm only
In the outskirts
And in the ________________
On the edge
And off the ________________
And if you want me
You can find me
Left of center
Wondering about you

---

* more common: on the fringes

I think that somehow
Somewhere inside of us
We must be ________________
If not the same
So I continue
To be wanting you
Left of center
Against the ________________

If you want me
You can find me
Left of center
Off of the strip
In the outskirts
In the fringes
In the corner
Out of the grip

When they ask me
"What are you looking at?"
I always answer
"Nothing much" (not much)
I think they know that
I'm looking at them
I think they think
I must be out of touch

But I'm only
In the outskirts
And in the fringes
On the edge
And off the avenue
And if you want me
You can find me
Left of center
Wondering about you
Wondering about you

2 *Read the lines from the song. Then circle the letter of the expression that best explains the line(s).*

1. "If you want me / You can find me / Left of center / Off of the strip"

In this line and in the title of the song, "left of center" refers to a _____.

a. physical location
b. psychological state of mind
c. temporary physical sensation

2. "In the outskirts / In the fringes / In the corner / Out of the grip"

The singer implies that she is _____.

a. withdrawn and shy
b. lost and lonely
c. excluded and angry

3. "When they ask me / 'What are you looking at?' / I always answer / 'Nothing much' (not much) / I think they know that / I'm looking at them. / I think they think / I must be out of touch"

These lines imply that the singer feels other people regard her as _____.

a. emotionally unstable
b. unaware
c. unconnected to the group

4. "I think that somehow / Somewhere inside of us / We must be similar / If not the same"

These lines suggest that the singer feels _____.

a. other people are shy like herself, but hide it well
b. all shy people are the same
c. like she wants to meet someone who is not shy

5. "So I continue / To be wanting you / Left of center / Against the grain"

"Against the grain" implies that the singer's love is _____.

a. a secret
b. forever and endless
c. different and unusual

3 *Discuss the questions with a partner.*

1. What are Vega's feelings about her shyness? What is the main point of the song?
2. Do you think the song illustrates shyness well? Why or why not?
3. Have you ever felt like the character in the song? Explain.

RESEARCH TOPICS, see page 260.

UNIT 4

The Tipping Point

MURDERS IN NEW YORK CITY

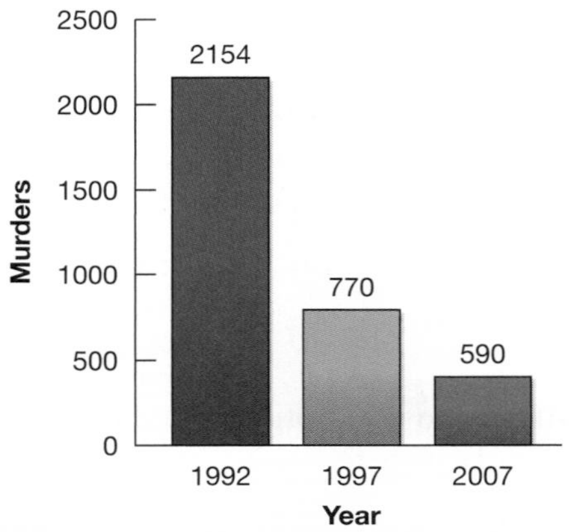

GROWTH AND FORECASTED GROWTH OF CELL PHONE SUBSCRIBERS

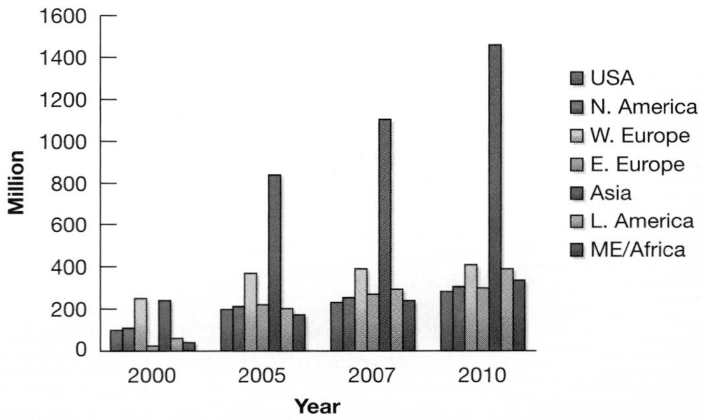

Source: http://www.etforecasts.com/products/ES_cellular.htm

1 FOCUS ON THE TOPIC

A PREDICT

Look at the graphs above. Working in a small group, analyze the data, and answer the questions.

1. What do the two graphs have in common? Look for patterns in the data.
2. For each graph, discuss several factors that may have contributed to the sudden changes illustrated.
3. Look at the title. What do you think this unit will be about?

B SHARE INFORMATION

1 *Work with a partner. Interview your partner to find out what factors influence his or her behavior or ideas. There can be more than one factor. Record the letter(s) of your partner's answers on the blank lines. Then have your partner interview you.*

What influenced you to . . .

_____ **1.** see the last movie or TV show you saw

_____ **2.** read the last book you read

_____ **3.** go to your last vacation spot

_____ **4.** check out the last website you visited

_____ **5.** choose the last restaurant you ate at

_____ **6.** perform some charitable act (volunteer, donate money, etc.)

_____ **7.** buy the last piece of clothing or shoes you bought

_____ **8.** (do something else you did)

Factors

a. word of mouth (everyone is talking about it!)

b. someone you respect told you

c. saw it on the Internet

d. saw it on television

e. read about it in a newspaper or magazine

f. other (specify)

2 *Work with your partner. Discuss the questions.*

1. Review your answers to Exercise 1. What patterns do you notice? What people or things influence your behavior and thinking the most?
2. The graphs on the preceding page show a dramatic decrease in the murder rate in New York City and a dramatic increase in cell phone usage in Asia. Why do you think certain trends develop so suddenly?

C BACKGROUND AND VOCABULARY

1 CD 7 38 *Read and listen to the examples of online customer reviews of Malcolm Gladwell's book* The Tipping Point.[1] *Then discuss why the book is so popular and whether it interests you.*

[1] *The Tipping Point: How Little Things Can Make a Big Difference* is a best-selling book. As a result of its popularity, the expression "tipping point" has entered the language.

http://www.onlinereviewer.com

Home

Shopping Cart

New Search

412 of 717 people found this review helpful:

Wonderful book

Reviewer: **A future thinker**

Malcolm Gladwell, a staff writer for *New Yorker* magazine, in *The Tipping Point*, writes an engaging book exploring why and how things happen. He asks questions such as: How do advertisers get us to buy products or go see movies? Why do people suddenly stop doing something the way they have always done it? According to Gladwell, the **(1) transmission** of ideas often occurs in the same way as the passing of germs from one person to another. Every day, people spread messages. One of Gladwell's examples deals with the sudden popularity of Hush Puppies[1], a kind of shoe which had been unfashionable for many years. But suddenly, a bunch of cool kids started wearing Hush Puppies in New York City and telling all their friends about them. Fashion **(2) mavens**, expert designers who set fashion standards, adored the "cool" shoes and got the fashion industry to fall in love with the new styles. Before long, everyone on the street was wearing Hush Puppies. Simple **(3) word-of-mouth** advertising sparked the Hush Puppy fashion **(4) epidemic**.

Comment | Was the review helpful? Yes No

---

4 of 10 people found this review helpful:

Pretty good for an easy read

Reviewer: **Martin**

I found Gladwell's simple yet informative book full of great examples. One of my favorites was his look at *Sesame Street*, a popular children's television show. In the late 1960s, educational television producers wanted to **(5) generate** interest and enthusiasm for reading and writing among preschool children. To figure out how to make preschool TV shows "sticky," or memorable, among preschoolers, the producers **(6) got a hold of** the top psychologists in the country, who began conducting experiments on children's television viewing habits. **(7) Consumed by** trying to find the "stickiness factor," psychologists and TV executives carefully recorded specific moments when kids paid attention to shows and when they stopped watching. Relentless in their search, the researchers finally figured it out. From their many studies, they found that kids always paid attention when real adults and children were shown on the TV screen at the same time as the puppets. The children's show producers also discovered that they could **(8) win** kids **over** to certain programs by making scenes not only flashy and exciting with puppets, but comprehensible with real people. To me, this was one of the best parts of the book.

Comment | Was the review helpful? Yes No

---

1 **Hush Puppies:** 

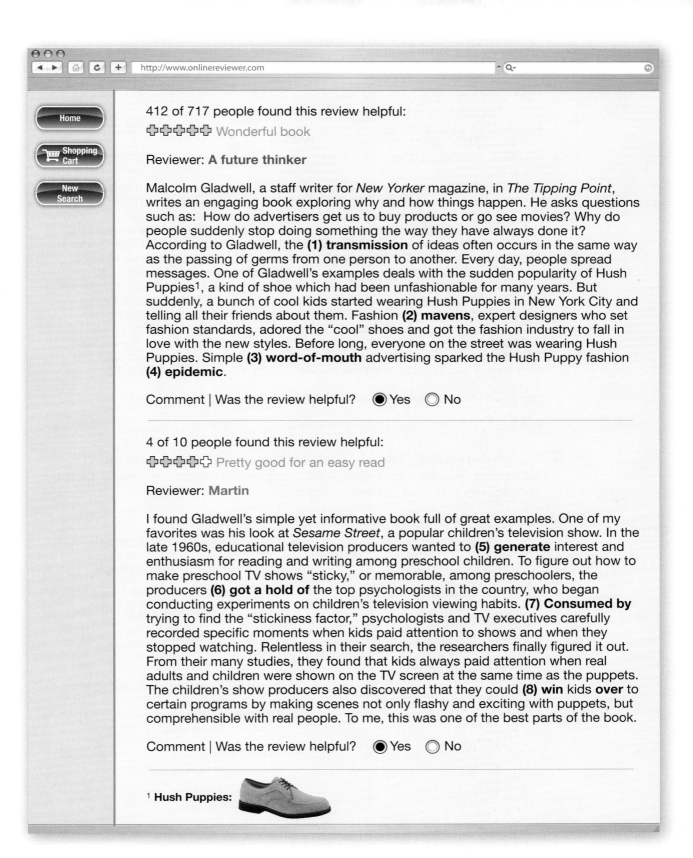

http://www.onlinereviewer.com

320 out of 660 people found this review helpful:

Fascinating read

Reviewer: **Sarah, a Gladwell addict**

OK, I will admit it. I am a total Malcolm Gladwell groupie. I have been to three of his book readings, seen him on TV talk shows, and heard him interviewed on the radio. I just can't get enough of his ideas! So, when this book came out, I just devoured it! As a management consultant, I found his ideas on employee effectiveness the most intriguing. Gladwell **(9) profiled** the high-tech firm Gore Associates. Gore Associates adheres to the "rule of 150"—a belief that a group made up of fewer than 150 people operates more effectively than a larger group. According to Wilbert "Bill" Gore, the CEO of Gore Associates, the **(10) root** of many companies' problems is that employees work in groups with more than 150 people. Gore's "sticky and infectious" philosophy **(11) goes a long way toward** ensuring the company's profitable performance. Some people believe that the "rule of 150" **(12) holds** for religious groups, schools, and communities, not only companies. They think that it is more efficient to manage a group with fewer than 150 members. If you want to see more examples, run out now and buy this book!

Comment | Was the review helpful? ◉ Yes ○ No

2 *Work with a partner. Match the words and phrases on the left with the correct definition or synonym on the right. Write the appropriate letter in the blank. Compare your answers with those of other students.*

_____ **1.** transmission
_____ **2.** mavens
_____ **3.** word-of-mouth
_____ **4.** epidemic
_____ **5.** generate
_____ **6.** got a hold of
_____ **7.** consumed by
_____ **8.** win [someone] over
_____ **9.** profiled
_____ **10.** root
_____ **11.** goes a long way toward
_____ **12.** holds

a. is true
b. contacted; communicated with
c. related to people telling people
d. large number of cases of an infectious disease occurring at the same time
e. totally involved in
f. cause; source
g. persuade someone to do something
h. passing of something from one person, place, or thing to another
i. people who know a lot and talk a lot about a particular subject
j. produce or create
k. succeeds in
l. described

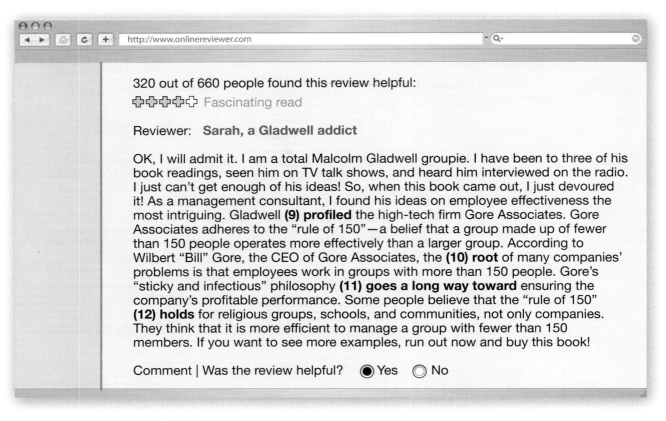

2 FOCUS ON LISTENING

A LISTENING ONE: *The Tipping Point*

In his book *The Tipping Point: How Little Things Can Make a Big Difference,* Malcolm Gladwell explores why changes in behavior or ideas happen unexpectedly and suddenly. Why did the New York City crime rate drop so dramatically? Why did cell phones become popular so quickly in Asia?

CD 1 39 *In the interview, Gladwell describes a type of person called a* **connector**. *He says that connectors play a huge role in spreading ideas. What kind of person is a connector? Work with a partner and complete the sentence with as many descriptions as possible. Then listen to the excerpt to check your predictions.*

Connectors are people who . . .

- make a lot of phone calls.
- ______________________________
- ______________________________
- ______________________________

LISTEN FOR MAIN IDEAS

CD 1 40 *Gladwell identifies three kinds of people who spread ideas: mavens, connectors, and salesmen. Listen to the interview. Then complete the sentences. Work with a partner and compare answers.*

1. Connectors are people who ______________________________
____
2. Mavens are people who ______________________________
____
3. Salesmen* are people who ______________________________
____

LISTEN FOR DETAILS

CD 1 41 *Listen to the interview again. Read the sentences, and mark them* ***T*** *(true) or* ***F*** *(false). Correct the false statements. Then discuss your answers with a partner.*

_____ 1. Word-of-mouth epidemics are transmitted by a huge number of exceptional people.

_____ 2. Gladwell gives a "names test" to people to find out how many people they know with the same last name.

* The more commonly accepted term is "salespeople."

_____ 3. By using his "names test," Gladwell concluded that out of 350 people, most people know more than 130 people.

_____ 4. People who score well on Gladwell's names test are called "connectors" because they know a lot of people and can spread ideas quickly.

_____ 5. Gladwell can't start a word-of-mouth epidemic because his circle of friends is too small.

_____ 6. Connectors can spread ideas and news quickly to a lot of people in a very short time.

_____ 7. Ariel, a friend of Gladwell, is a professional restaurant critic.

_____ 8. Most restaurants in lower Manhattan are filled with customers who are friends of Gladwell and Ariel.

_____ 9. There are only about two dozen restaurant mavens in Manhattan.

_____ 10. Gladwell describes mavens as the "Ariels of the world."

_____ 11. A word-of-mouth epidemic is most successful if a maven works with a connector to spread the epidemic.

_____ 12. According to Gladwell, Tom Gau is a very successful salesman because he can easily persuade you to do or believe in something.

MAKE INFERENCES

Work in a small group. Listen to the excerpts, and answer the questions. Pay special attention to tone, pace, pausing, intonation, and word choice. Then discuss your answers with the group.

Excerpt One

1. How would you describe the interviewer's style:
   a. rude and impatient
   b. interested and attentive
   c. distracted and bored
   d. serious and academic

Excerpt Two

2. Lydon says, "I'm afraid I'm one of them" because he is _____.
   a. saying that he is afraid
   b. showing his embarrassment
   c. pretending to be sorry
   d. trying to be funny

CD 7 44
Excerpt Three

3. Gladwell asks "right?" because he _____.
   - **a.** thinks Lydon is a restaurant expert
   - **b.** is not sure about what he is saying
   - **c.** is implying that the interviewer would agree with them
   - **d.** expects the interviewer to interrupt him

CD 7 45
Excerpt Four

4. By repeating the interviewer's, "You can't sell," Gladwell intended to _____.
   - **a.** demonstrate sympathy for Lydon's inability to sell
   - **b.** confirm he had heard what Lydon had said, and move the conversation forward[1]
   - **c.** confirm that he knows that the interviewer really can't sell
   - **d.** emphasize the importance of what Lydon had said about himself

EXPRESS OPINIONS

Many readers have reacted strongly to the ideas put forth in *The Tipping Point.* Below are some opinions posted to blogs and other websites.

*Read the opinions and write **A** (agree) or **D** (disagree) next to each statement. Then work in small groups and explain your opinion.*

VOICE OF THE PEOPLE

_____ 1.

Martin from Ashland, Oregon, U.S.:

I think that Gladwell's categories of mavens, connectors, and salesmen are really useful to describe just about everyone I know. I, for one, am a maven.

_____ 2.

Rosa from Buenos Aires, Argentina:

I am an independent thinker, resistant to trends and trendsetters. And there are many people like me—people who are never influenced by "social messengers" such as mavens, connectors, or salesmen.

_____ 3.

Choi Soon Young from Seoul, South Korea:

The former U.S. vice president, Al Gore, won an Oscar and a Nobel Peace Prize because of his movie *An Inconvenient Truth,* and this started a big movement against global warming. I am completely convinced that Gore hit "the tipping point" that Gladwell describes.

[1] move the conversation along faster in order to make his own point

_____4. 

Pedro Sanchez from Chihuahua, Mexico:

Gladwell oversimplifies the idea of social change. Change is gradual, and I don't buy the notion that a few people can jumpstart a larger trend. Where I live, it would take more than that.

_____5. 

Melek Orbay from Istanbul, Turkey:

I guess that the rise of teenage smoking has something to do with Gladwell's ideas of social epidemics spread by messengers. I think that the spread of teenage smoking could also be stopped by getting a "social messenger" to create a tipping point in the other direction.

_____6. 

(name withheld):

Gladwell should write more about this: Antisocial and even violent behavior is glorified on some websites and spread to isolated or sick individuals. Through the Internet, evil people can try to create support for their hateful ideas. The tipping point can spread a social disease, not just create a social trend.

B LISTENING TWO: Tipping Points in Fighting Crime

In this second interview, Malcolm Gladwell discusses the dramatic decline in crime in New York City.

1 CD 7 46 *Read the incomplete sentences on page 79. Then listen to the excerpt. Circle the letter of the correct phrase to complete the sentence. Then compare your answers with those of another student.*

1. Todd Mundt, the host and interviewer, believes that the reason crime fell so dramatically in New York is _____.
   a. well known and documented
   b. unknown
   c. being researched now

2. Gladwell believes that crime fell because of _____.
   a. community action
   b. behavior of certain influential people
   c. sudden small changes

3. According to George Kelling's "broken windows" theory, _____.
   a. criminals are definitely affected by the environment
   b. criminals may be affected by the environment
   c. criminals are not affected by the environment

4. According to Kelling, a broken window in a car probably means that the car is parked in an area which is _____.
   a. poor
   b. dangerous
   c. unsupervised

5. Traditional conservative thinking blames high crime rates on _____.
   a. an ineffective police force
   b. the criminals themselves
   c. the environment

6. Kelling believes crime can be reduced by _____.
   a. encouraging criminals to be more sensitive to the environment
   b. teaching moral and socially responsible behavior to all citizens
   c. making small environmental changes

7. In the early 1980s, the subway system in New York City was _____.
   a. disorganized and messy
   b. confusing and chaotic
   c. dirty and dangerous

8. Former New York City Police Chief William Bratton tried many ways to improve the subways. He tried everything except removing _____.
   a. graffiti
   b. turnstiles
   c. garbage

9. The police helped reduce subway crime by _____.
   a. encouraging people not to litter or throw garbage on the ground
   b. washing off the graffiti
   c. arresting anyone who entered the subway without paying

2 *Work in small groups. Explain the broken window theory in your own words. Do you think it is an effective or ineffective approach to reducing crime? Why or why not? Can you think of any other societal problems that might be solved by this approach?*

C INTEGRATE LISTENINGS ONE AND TWO

STEP 1: Organize

In Listening One, Gladwell described the way in which "social epidemics" are spread by a few people—mavens, connectors, and salespeople. In his book *The Tipping Point,* he calls this phenomenon **"The Law of the Few."**

In Listening Two, he discusses the way in which small but significant environmental changes can create a large change. In the mid-1990s murder rates in New York City fell by two-thirds in five years. Gladwell credits the removal of litter, graffiti, and garbage as an environmental "tipping point" that caused a dramatic decline in crime on the subway and in certain neighborhoods of New York City. He refers to this effect as **"The Power of Context."**

Put the statements into the flowchart on page 81 to show your understanding of ***The Law of the Few*** *and* ***The Power of Context****.*

The Law of the Few

- The connector tells a salesperson and many other people about a restaurant.
- The restaurant quickly becomes very popular.
- A connector calls the maven to ask about a new restaurant.
- ~~The owners of a new restaurant invite a maven to dine at their new restaurant.~~
- The salesperson tells a few people, including another connector, about the new restaurant.

The Power of Context

- The number of serious crimes drops dramatically.
- The city sanitation department cleans up the garbage and graffiti.
- ~~The subway is very dangerous because of serious crime.~~
- Criminals understand that someone is paying attention to the subway.
- The police arrest people for jumping turnstiles and other minor crimes.

The Law of the Few

The owners of a new restaurant invite a maven to dine at their new restaurant.

The Power of Context

The subway is very dangerous because of serious crime.

STEP 2: Synthesize

Work in a small group. Choose a current problem to address. (See the list of suggestions below or create your own.) Discuss how you would use The Law of the Few or The Power of Context to address this problem. Use the flowchart on page 82 to take notes. Be specific. Present your ideas to the class.

- The mall or shopping center near your home has a rising crime rate and people are afraid to shop there, especially in the evening.
- You and your business partner open a coffeehouse near your school. It is successful, but six months later a large and well-known chain of coffeehouses opens a store on the same block.
- Big trucks rumble down your residential street to avoid a new toll road that was put in place nearby.
- The recycling program at your school is not popular with students. They don't recycle.

Problem:

Circle one: The Law of the Few
The Power of Context

3 FOCUS ON SPEAKING

A VOCABULARY

REVIEW

Work with a partner. Fill in missing forms of the words in the chart. In the verb column, you may use phrasal verbs (two-word verbs). A dash (–) indicates that there is no related form or that the form is not commonly used.

NOUN	VERB	ADJECTIVE
transmission		
	generate	
		consumed
	profile	
root		rooted
	—	contagious
trigger		
	vandalize	
mess		
		immune
	infect	

EXPAND

1 *Some words and phrases can have both literal and metaphorical meanings. Look at the example. Then complete the activity that follows.*

Example

The murderer pulled the **trigger** of the gun and killed the security guard. (Here, *trigger* is used literally: The *trigger* is the part of the gun that you press with your finger to fire it.)

"Maybe we can go into those little **triggers**, because I find this really interesting, because we're talking about such a big change that takes place, uh, being **triggered** by very small things, uh, what do you think some of those were?" (Here, *trigger* is used metaphorically: *Triggers* are things that cause or inspire change.)

Work in a small group. Look at the words and phrases with metaphorical meanings, and place them in the appropriate column.

Band-Aid® solution	infected	swim against the tide
be immune to an idea	make a splash	the tide is turning
contagious idea	a ripple effect	viral marketing
float an idea	a social epidemic	wave
a flood of ideas		

Metaphors Related to Illness	Metaphors Related to Water or Weather
______________________	______________________
______________________	______________________
______________________	______________________
______________________	______________________
______________________	______________________
______________________	______________________
______________________	______________________

2 *Look at the boldfaced words. Try to determine their metaphorical meaning from the context. Work with a partner. Complete the sentences to show you understand the meaning of the boldfaced words. Discuss your sentences with those of another pair.*

1. Many companies now rely on viral marketing to get customers to buy or use their products.

   A **viral marketing** strategy they might use is to get trendy people to wear the company name on clothing products.

2. An epidemic occurs when many cases of a disease occur at the same time.

   Although epidemics are usually not desirable, an example of a positive **social epidemic** is ____________________

3. The cold virus is incredibly contagious, easily passed from person to person.

   An example of a highly **contagious idea** is ____________________

4. If you infect people with a disease such as a cold, you give them that illness.

   A "salesman's" enthusiasm for an idea **infects** others simply by ____________________

5. People who are immune to a particular illness cannot be affected by it.

   In the same way, those who are **immune to new ideas** or trends ____________________

6. A wave is a ridge of water that rises and curls in the ocean.

   We may experience a crime **wave** when ____________________

7. When the 250-pound Olympic wrestler jumped into the swimming pool, he made an enormous splash and got everyone nearby totally wet.

   The first Polaroid customers who brought their instant picture-taking cameras to parties also **made a splash**. In a few short months, Polaroid ____________________

8. After three days of rain, the river flowed over its banks and flooded the town.

   After Sony game developers asked customers for ideas for new video games, the Sony website was **flooded** with ____________________

9. Ocean beach lifeguards face the difficult challenge of swimming against the tide when they dive in to help someone.

   When it comes to fashions, some people like to **swim against the tide** by ____________________

10. The tide must be turning because the waves were reaching the top of the beach, but now they are only reaching the rocks.

In the late 1990s stock in Internet companies, "dot-coms," was considered very valuable. Suddenly, however, the **tide turned** and ________________________

____

11. In order to find out if a boat will float, it must be tested in the water.

Most people will mention a new idea to a select group of people at first to watch their reaction. The New York City mayor **floated** his crime-fighting **ideas** with his advisors because ________________________________

12. If you drop a stone into calm water, you will notice a ripple effect—low waves on the surface that spread out in circles.

In business, a **ripple effect** occurs when ________________________________

____

13. A Band-Aid is a piece of thin material that you use to cover cuts and other small wounds. Using a Band-Aid is an inexpensive, fast, and convenient treatment.

International terrorism is a big problem that cannot be solved by a **Band-Aid solution** such as ____

____

CREATE

Read this imaginary interview between David McIntosh, senior manager at the Center for Business Innovation, and author Seth Godin, who, like Malcolm Gladwell, researches the spread of ideas. First, complete each sentence with the best form of the word or phrase from the box. Then, with a partner, role-play the interview. Read aloud with drama, interest, and expression.

come around	"ideavirus"	"sneezers"	viral marketing
contagious	immune	~~spread~~	went a long way
epidemic	infected	transmit	went through the roof
get a hold of	ripple effect	trigger	

Ideaviruses: A Conversation with Seth Godin

A (McIntosh): Seth, in your book, *Unleashing the Ideavirus,* you argue that an idea (1) ____spreads____ like a bad cold. Is that right?

B (Godin): Yes, exactly. Ideas can spread rapidly or become (**2**) ______________ just like a virus.

A: So, if a company wants to spread, or (**3**) ______________, an idea, it should imitate a virus?

B: That's right.

A: And in your book, you introduced a special term, (**4**) ______________, now often used in business circles. The term refers to a very powerful form of person-to-person communication. If this type of marketing succeeds, it's possible we can witness a very big change in attitude, preference, or habits.

B: Exactly! To persuade people, or to get them to (**5**) ______________ to a new idea, you have to make a big impact. You need a "virusworthy" idea, something everyone wants to talk about. And if the right people (**6**) ______________ the idea, it will spread incredibly fast.

A: Oh, I see. And in that case, we'll witness a word-of-mouth (**7**) ______________. Interesting. Now Seth, can you give me an example of this thing you call, ummm, a virusworthy idea?

B: Sure, think about Google. Every time you do a web search using the Google search engine, you see the Google logo. (Google) You can't miss it. Nobody is (**8**) ______________ to the Google ideavirus.

A: And in your book, you give a special name to people who spread ideaviruses: (**9**) ______________. Is that correct?

B: Yes. For example, Oprah Winfrey, the well-known talk show host and actress, is one. Ms. Winfrey used to recommend books on her show, and those books would suddenly become hot bestsellers. Each viewer told his or her friend or neighbor. The friend or neighbor told another friend and then another. The group of readers just got bigger and bigger, like a stone thrown in a pond; the recommendations created a (**10**) ______________.

A: I see. Basically, her recommendation is a **(11)** ________________ for millions of Americans to run out and buy her recommended book. Hmmm. Another question: In your talk, you also mention Post-it®[1] notes, those sticky little pieces of notepaper that everyone seems to use. How did people become **(12)** ________________ with the Post-it Note virus?

B: It's a great story. The secretary at the 3M Company liked the Post-it Notes. So she sent them to the secretaries in other big companies. In about two months, sales exploded. They **(13)** ________________!

A: So the Post-it Note trend is an example of the classic **(14)** ________________. The secretary "sneezed" by sending those very first packages to other secretaries.

B: Yeah, those packages **(15)** ________________ toward making Post-it Notes one of the best-selling office products of the twentieth century.

A: Thanks, Seth, for talking with me.

B: My pleasure.

B GRAMMAR: Adverb Clauses of Result

1 *Examine the pairs of sentences. Then, with a partner, discuss the questions that follow.*

1. **a.** Tom Gau is an extraordinary salesman.
   b. Tom Gau is **such an extraordinary salesman that** people from all over the world want to learn his secrets of persuasion.
2. **a.** George Kelling's "broken windows" theory led to effective solutions.
   b. The solutions were **so effective that** the crime rate in New York City dropped dramatically in the early 1990s.
3. **a.** Criminals are sensitive to subtle environmental changes.
   b. New York City criminals were **so sensitive to subtle environmental changes that** they stopped committing subway crimes when the graffiti was removed.

- What is the difference between **a** and **b** in each pair?
- Why is *such* used in **1b** and *so* used in **2b** and **3b**?

[1]Post-it® notes, the original "sticky notes" with an adhesive backing, is a brand owned by the 3M Company.

ADVERB CLAUSES OF RESULT

Adverb clauses of result with ***such . . . that*** and ***so . . . that*** present the result of a situation that is stated in the first clause.

Adverb clauses of result are introduced by:

such + noun or noun phrase + ***that*** + clause of result	• The subways were **such a mess that people hated to ride them**.
so + adjective + ***that*** + clause of result	• The shoe brand became **so popular that sales went through the roof in only a few short months**.
so + adverb + ***that*** + clause of result	• The flu spread **so quickly that 50 percent of Manhattanites were sick on New Year's Day**.

So is also used before ***many***, ***few***, ***much***, and ***little***.

so + ***much / little*** + uncountable noun + ***that***	• Rachel Carson's book *Silent Spring* brought **so much attention to the dangers of pollution that the modern environmental protection movement was born**.
so + ***many / few*** + count noun + ***that***	• Carson exposed **so many environmental dangers that the government began to scrutinize the chemical industry**.

NOTES:

1. In spoken English, ***that*** is often omitted.
2. Placing ***such*** or ***so*** at the beginning of the sentence results in an inverted word order. This structure is emphatic.
   - **So** sensitive **were** New York City criminals to the subway environment that they stopped committing crimes after the graffiti was removed.
   - **Such** enormous impact **did** Carson's book **have** that President John F. Kennedy ordered a special advisory committee to examine the issues the book raised.

2 *Read the story of two historical figures who, on horseback, tried to spread the news of the start of the American Revolution in the eighteenth century. One man succeeded; the other did not. Fill in the blanks with* ***so, such,*** *or* ***that****. Work with a partner and compare your answers.*

Midnight Riders: Spreading the Message

In April 1775, a young boy working at a livery stable[1] in Boston, Massachusetts, overheard a British army officer say, "Tomorrow is the day. Tomorrow we will attack the colonists." The boy was **(1)** ________________ frightened and excited upon hearing about the imminent battle **(2)** ________________ he immediately ran to report the news to a silversmith[2] named Paul Revere.

Revere was **(3)** ________________ a popular and well-known citizen **(4)** ________________ he had already heard from several others the very same news. Revere became **(5)** ________________ convinced of the truth of these rumors **(6)** ________________ he immediately jumped on his horse and under the cover of darkness began his legendary "midnight ride" to Lexington. In just two hours, he covered 13 miles, shouting "The British are coming!" The sensational news spread **(7)** ________________ quickly **(8)** ________________ the colonial American army had enough time to organize and meet the British enemy with fierce resistance.

That same night, another colonial American revolutionary named William Dawes had heard the same forecast that "the British were coming." Like Revere, Dawes jumped on his horse and carried the message in another area near Boston. Unfortunately, though, Dawes's ride was ineffective.

(9) ________________ few men from his area showed up the next day to fight **(10)** ________________ most people thought Dawes had ridden through a pro-British community. But he hadn't.

Why was Revere's ride successful and Dawes's a failure? Revere was a "connector" and Dawes wasn't. In fact, Revere was **(11)** ________________ an intensely social

[1]**livery stable:** a place where people paid to have their horses cared for, or a place where horses could be rented
[2]**silversmith:** someone who makes things out of silver

"connector" **(12)** ________________ when he died, thousands of Bostonians attended his funeral. Knowing everyone, belonging to every club around, enormously popular, Revere had built **(13)** ________________ a wide circle of friends **(14)** ________________ he knew exactly how to spread that piece of critical news as far as possible. Revere's ride and the word-of-mouth epidemic he started are mentioned in every history textbook about early America. And William Dawes? He was **(15)** ________________ anonymous **(16)** ________________ almost no one remembers his ride from that night.

3 *Work with a partner.*

Student A: Ask Student B questions 1 through 4.

Student B: Answer the question using the cue and the information provided in parentheses. Use ***so that*** *or* ***such that*** *in your answer. You may rephrase the information in your own words. Then switch roles after question 4.*

Student A	**Student B**
1. How popular were Hush Puppies in the fall of 1995?	**1.** (popular shoes) They were ________________ ________________ the famous designers Calvin Klein and Donna Karan asked their models to wear them in their fashion shows.
2. Did Rachel Carson's book *Silent Spring,* really educate people about the dangerous chemical called DDT?	**2.** (few) Clearly it did. Before her book came out, ________________________ Americans understood DDT ________________ no one worried about it.
3. Is the Internet a powerful tool to make ideas tip?	**3.** (powerful tool) Absolutely. The Internet is ______________________________ connectors can use it to spread infectious ideas with a single e-mail.
4. How anonymous was William Dawes in Boston right before the start of the Revolutionary War?	**4.** (anonymous) William Dawes was ______________________________ no one listened to his warnings of the British invasion.

Now switch roles.

5. How influential was Kelling's "broken windows" theory?

5. (influential theory) Well, it was ________________ ________________ the mayor based his crime strategy completely on Kelling's ideas.

6. Is yawning contagious?

6. (contagious) Believe it or not, it is ________________ ________________ if you start to yawn, it is likely that the person next to you will yawn, and soon everyone in the room will be yawning.

7. Was the first Yale University tetanus shot campaign a success?

7. (a failure) Unfortunately, the first one wasn't. It was ________________________ only 20 out of 2,000 students got inoculated.

8. How strongly does the CEO of Gore Associates feel about the "Rule of 150"?

8. (strongly) Obviously he feels ________________ about it ________________ each Gore-tex factory has only 150 parking spaces. When cars begin to park on the grass, the company builds a new factory. Gore has 15 factories all within a 12-mile area.

C SPEAKING

PRONUNCIATION: Stress Changing Suffixes

One syllable in a word has primary stress. The vowel in that syllable is long and loud. When you add certain suffixes to base words, a different syllable may be stressed:

defíne	+ tion	→	definítion
próverb	+ ial	→	provérbial

Stress usually falls on the part of the word just before these suffixes:

-tion / -sion	connéction
-ial / -cial / -tial	fináncial
-ity	publícity
-ic / -ical	realístic

1 CD 1 (47) *Listen to the words, and repeat them. Make the stressed vowel long and loud. Put a stress mark (´) over the stressed syllable.*

1. a. sensitivity	**b.** criminality	**c.** responsibility	**d.** popularity
2. a. energetic	**b.** fantastic	**c.** realistic	**d.** apologetic
3. a. transmission	**b.** organization	**c.** decision	**d.** documentation
4. a. financial	**b.** artificial	**c.** commercial	**d.** influential
5. a. logical	**b.** musical	**c.** critical	**d.** theoretical

2 CD 1 (48) *Listen to the words, and repeat them. Make the stressed vowel long and loud. Put a stress mark (´) over the stressed syllable. Check your stress marks with a partner.*

1. a. able	**b.** possible	**c.** public
2. a. invite	**b.** inoculate	**c.** complicate
3. a. president	**b.** benefit	**c.** office
4. a. category	**b.** chaos	**c.** symbol

3 *Work with a partner. Add the suffix to the words, and put a stress mark over the stressed syllable in the new words. Take turns reading the new words. Listen to each other to make sure you stress the correct syllable and pronounce it with a long, loud vowel.*

	-ity		**-ial / -cial / -tial**
1. a. able	abílity	**3. a.** president	____________
b. possible	____________	**b.** benefit	____________
c. public	____________	**c.** office	____________
	-tion / -sion		**-ic / -ical**
2. a. invite	____________	**4. a.** category	____________
b. inoculate	____________	**b.** chaos	____________
c. complicate	____________	**c.** symbol	____________

FUNCTION: Making a Point with Metaphors

Malcolm Gladwell values metaphors for their ability to demonstrate comparisons in a powerful and imaginative way. He uses many metaphors to communicate his concept of the "tipping point." Politicians, journalists, public speakers, advertisers, and poets use metaphors frequently because they can be such an effective communication tool.

1 *Underline the metaphors, or expressions that imply a comparison between two things.*

- "There is a small number of exceptional people who play a huge role in the transmission of epidemic ideas."
- "Crime is such a fundamentally contagious thing."

2 *Work in pairs.*

Student A: Read items 1 and 2 on the next page silently. Then put the statements in your own words, using words or expressions that can be used metaphorically from the left column in the chart below.

Student B: Listen to Student A's statements. After each item, restate the information that Student A gave you, using the introductory expressions from the right column in the box below. You may also add any words and expressions that can be used metaphorically. Switch roles after item 2.

Example

Student A reads silently: Yale University students were asked to get tetanus shots but rarely did so. University officials asked for and received *many* ideas for getting students to come to the Health Center for shots. In the end, the university distributed a map and appointment times, which *finally brought crowds of* students in for shots.

Student A says: Yale University students were asked to get tetanus shots but rarely did so. University officials asked people how to get students to come to the Health Center for shots, and then they were *flooded* with ideas. In the end, the university distributed a map and appointment times, which *turned the tide* on this problem.

Student B responds: *In other words,* just a little bit of the right information triggered a great response!

WORDS AND EXPRESSIONS THAT CAN BE USED METAPHORICALLY	CLARIFYING INTRODUCTORY EXPRESSIONS
contagious	In other words . . .
epidemic	So, . . .
float an idea	What you're saying, then, is . . .
flood	To put it another way . . .
go through the roof	
immune	
infected	
make a splash	
open the floodgates	
ripple effect	
trigger	
turn the tide	
wave	

1. Cleaning up litter and graffiti were small things that caused a big change in New York City's crime rate.

2. At a fashion show in 1994, two famous designers drew a lot of attention when they wore Hush Puppies shoes. Immediately, sales of the shoes increased. Kids everywhere were suddenly wearing Hush Puppies.

Now switch roles.

3. Before *Sesame Street* appeared on television, the creators tested the idea out on a lot of kids. Educational experts strongly opposed the show because they mistrusted television's ability to be educational. In the end, *Sesame Street*'s proven success created a lot of interest in children's educational television.

4. Rachel Carson's interest in the environment was sparked when she began investigating chemical pesticides. Prior to the 1962 publication of her book *Silent Spring*, most people felt protected from any harmful environmental dangers. The book was criticized by the chemical industry, which didn't believe Carson's accusations against it.

PRODUCTION: A Public Service Announcement

In this activity, you will ***create your own public service announcement (PSA)***. Try to use the vocabulary, grammar, pronunciation, and the language to make a point that you learned in the unit.*

In order for an epidemic to "tip," there are two critical factors:

- the messenger
- the message

The messengers—"mavens, connectors, and salesmen"—help spread ideas. But the content of the message is important, too. The message can only be successful if it has the quality of "stickiness"—meaning that it sticks in our minds, or that we can remember it. If the message is sticky, it can create change.

Public Service Announcements (PSAs) are short messages broadcast on television and radio. Their purpose is to inform the public of important health and safety issues. Generally, in the United States, nonprofit organizations produce PSAs, and television and radio stations are required to broadcast them.

*For Alternative Speaking Topics, see page 97.

1 CD 7 (49) *Listen to the PSA about improving your community. Work with a partner, and answer the questions.*

- What is the message of the PSA? Is it memorable? Why?
- Could it help change attitudes and behaviors? Why?
- How would you improve the PSA to make it a "stickier" message?

2 CD 7 (50) *Listen again. Fill in the outline that gives the general structure of the PSA.*

PSA campaign: ____________________

Number of speakers: ____________________

Speakers: ____________________

Sound effects: ____________________

Opening line (used to get the listener's attention): ____________________

Problem: ____________________

Suggestions to solve the problem: ____________________

3 *Work in small groups. Write and present a PSA.*

1. Decide on an issue of public concern such as water quality or water use, air quality, teenage smoking, Internet addiction, safe driving, saving endangered species, clean environment, and so on.
2. Use the outline above as your guide in writing a PSA about your chosen issue.
3. Make sure your PSA is "sticky," so it can tip an important issue. Choose sound effects, and record it.
4. Present your PSA to the class. Play the recording. Have the other students in the class answer these questions: What is the message? Is it sticky? Why or why not?

ALTERNATIVE SPEAKING TOPICS

Choose a topic. Use ideas, vocabulary, grammar, pronunciation, and the language to make a point.

Topic 1

There are many trends currently having an impact on people's lives worldwide in this decade. What will be the impact of some of these trends? Working with a partner, look at the chart and discuss the potential impact of the following. Ask each other the following: "What would be the impact on (category) _____ if (trend) _____ . . . etc.?" Fill in the chart with your group's decisions.

CATEGORY	TREND	IMPACT
Entertainment industry	80 percent of consumers download games, videos, information, and music from the Internet.	
Health care industry	90 percent of individuals demand tests to reveal genetic future.	
Business	Over 100 million people desire to live to be at least 100 years old as healthy and active citizens.	
The world	AIDS and other pandemics continue to take the lives of millions.	
The future of society	Global warming and climate change persist for another 50 years with nine billion people living on Earth.	

Source: Adapted from James Canton, *The Extreme Future*, 2006

Topic 2

In his book *Extreme Future,* futurologist James Canton predicts that there will be important innovations that will certainly reach a tipping point by the year 2025 and "rock your world." Look at his list of innovations. Decide if you agree (A) or disagree (D) with his prediction and why. Discuss what might be the impact of these events if and when they reach the tipping point.

_____ **1.** Teleportation of objects around the planet

_____ **2.** Specialized DNA for sale online

_____ **3.** Space tourism to the moon and Mars

_____ **4.** Manipulating matter to make smart products

_____ **5.** Four billion people doing Internet commerce

_____ **6.** Hydrogen engines for transportation

_____ **7.** Cybernetic health enhancement of humans

_____ **8.** Downloading memories and medicine

_____ **9.** Domestic robots

RESEARCH TOPICS, see page 261.

UNIT 5

Feng Shui: Ancient Wisdom Travels West

"A million two does seem a bit heavy for a one-bedroom at first, but this unit has the best feng-shui in the building."

1 FOCUS ON THE TOPIC

A PREDICT

Look at the cartoon above. A New York City real estate agent admits that $1,200,000 is a very high price for a one-bedroom apartment. However, she suggests that good **feng shui** increases the value a great deal. If you have never heard of feng shui (pronounced "fung shway"), can you guess what it might be? How might good feng shui increase the value of an apartment?

B SHARE INFORMATION

1 *Feng shui is the ancient Chinese art or practice of arranging the environment in order to achieve harmony in that space. Work with a partner. Decide if each aspect of the environment listed on the chart creates favorable or unfavorable feng shui. Check (✓) your choice, and discuss the reason for your decision. Then check your answers on pages 256–257.*

ASPECTS OF THE ENVIRONMENT	FAVORABLE FENG SHUI	UNFAVORABLE FENG SHUI	REASON
an aquarium			
plants and flowers			
the colors red and purple			
mirrors			
a desk facing a view			
a room full of windows			
living near a cemetery			
living on a quiet dead-end street			
an odd number of dining room chairs			
pictures of bats on the walls			
a tiger statue outside an office door			

2 *Discuss the environmental aspects with your partner. Which ones seem like good common sense? Which ones seem like superstitions?*

C BACKGROUND AND VOCABULARY

1 CD 2 *Read and listen to the passage, then read the list of definitions on page 102. Work with a partner and write the number of the boldfaced word next to the correct definition.*

Introduction

More and more Western architects, real estate developers, and interior designers are using the principles of the Chinese practice of feng shui in their life and work. Previously, Westerners (1) **frowned upon** feng shui as mere superstition. (2) **Hard-bitten** designers and architects, scientifically trained, refused to acknowledge any possible (3) **transcendent** explanation for successes brought on by the application of feng shui principles. Originally, they dismissed interest in feng shui as a (4) **digression** from established technical and artistic practices. Nowadays, however, feng shui is becoming more accepted in places outside of Asia, such as the United States, Canada, Europe, and Latin America.

The Meaning of Feng Shui

Feng shui, meaning "wind" and "water" in Chinese, is an ancient form of geomancy, or the art of (5) **aligning** things in the environment to create harmony and good luck. An art and a science, feng shui aims to create both physical and psychological comfort. Practitioners believe that the arrangement of the elements in our environment can affect many aspects of our lives such as health, happiness, and fortune. Feng shui experts generally recommend simple changes; for example, they instruct people not to sit with their backs to the door because they can be (6) **caught off-guard** and startled unnecessarily. Or they encourage business owners to put an aquarium in the entrance of their building since an aquarium symbolizes (7) **abundance**, as in the saying, "there are always more fish in the sea."

In classical feng shui water always symbolizes wealth and abundance. Very simply, where there was water, crops could grow. In ancient agrarian society water was the source of wealth. Aquariums represent the water element.

The Theory of Feng Shui

The theory behind feng shui is that there is an invisible life force or energy, called *ch'i* ("chee"), that (8) **circulates** through all things–rooms, buildings, people, hills, rivers, power lines. If ch'i flows smoothly and freely, then things go well for people. If ch'i is blocked, then the people in that space may feel discomfort or unhappiness. Sharp corners, narrow openings, poor lighting, and clutter are some of the many factors that can create blocked or unfavorable ch'i. Relying on tools and knowledge that are centuries-old, trained feng shui experts can (9) **sense** immediately if the ch'i is circulating properly. They consider the shape, size, and location of objects as well as materials, colors, and numbers.

(continued on next page)

The Origin of Feng Shui

Feng shui grew out of the practical experience of farmers in southern China over 3,000 years ago. Those who built their huts facing north were battered by the wind and dust from the Gobi Desert in Mongolia. In contrast, those who built their huts facing south enjoyed the warmth of the sun and protection from the wind. As a result, south became the favored direction. Over the years, south came to be associated with fame, fortune, summer, the number nine, and the color red. In fact, to (**10**) **quote** world-renowned feng shui expert Lillian Too, red, the color of the south, "could well bring you good fortune." Ms. Too encourages red wallpaper, curtains, carpets, and all red in the southern part of a room, office, or building.

The Spread of Feng Shui

Today the work of feng shui masters is in great demand among Chinese populations in China, Taiwan, Singapore, Hong Kong, Malaysia, and the Philippines. It is estimated that nearly 85 percent of Hong Kong residents apply feng shui principles when choosing an apartment or business. Now the ancient art of feng shui has migrated to the West. Well-known architects, designers, and business people no longer view the practice (**11**) **skeptically**. In fact, there are many popular books filled with (**12**) **anecdotes** about people whose lives have been dramatically changed by feng shui.

_____ **a.** properly positioning

_____ **b.** disapproved of

_____ **c.** personal stories

_____ **d.** tough, experienced

_____ **e.** surprised

_____ **f.** beyond the limits of ordinary experience

_____ **g.** moves, flows

_____ **h.** a large quantity of something

_____ **i.** with doubt

_____ **j.** feel and know

_____ **k.** idea that is unrelated to the topic

_____ **l.** repeat what someone else has said or written

2 *Divide into groups of five. Each person should choose one section of the background information. Read your section quickly, taking brief notes on a separate piece of paper. Then close your books, and use your notes to summarize your paragraph to the group. Discuss your reaction to feng shui.*

2 FOCUS ON LISTENING

A LISTENING ONE: Interview with a Feng Shui Expert

Sedge Thomson, the radio host of *West Coast Live* from San Francisco, interviews Kirsten Lagatree, author of the book *Feng Shui: Arranging Your Home to Change Your Life*. At the end of the interview, Thomson asks Lagatree about the impact of favorable feng shui on how one feels.

CD 2, 3 *Work with a partner. Predict how favorable feng shui might make a person feel. Write your predictions on the lines. Then listen to an excerpt from the interview to check your answers.*

1. ____
2. ____
3. ____
4. ____
5. ____

LISTEN FOR MAIN IDEAS

CD 2, 4 *Listen to the interview, and then complete the chart by writing the main idea of the topic discussed. Share your answers with a partner.*

TOPIC	MAIN IDEA
Part One 1. definition of feng shui	a system of arranging things around you to create harmony and balance, and to make you feel better
2. popularity of feng shui in other countries	
3. Donald Trump's attitude toward feng shui	
4. basic design of Lagatree's home office	

(continued on next page)

TOPIC	MAIN IDEA
Part Two **5.** role of mirrors	
6. Lagatree's overall attitude toward feng shui	
7. who can sense good feng shui	

LISTEN FOR DETAILS

CD 2 5 *Read the questions. Then listen to the interview again, and write short answers. Compare your answers with those of a partner. Complete the questions with as much detail as possible.*

Part One

1. Lagatree doesn't think feng shui is a way to keep out evil spirits. Why not?

____

2. Thomson says that feng shui is very important in Asia. What three examples does he give to support this statement?

____

3. What two countries make up part of Lagatree's background? What influence have they had?

____

4. Why do some Chinese people living in San Francisco ask to have one-way street signs removed?

____

5. Why didn't Lagatree place her desk facing the window?

____

6. How does she feel about the impact of feng shui on the design of her home office?

____

Part Two

7. What two reasons does Lagatree give for not putting mirrors in the bedroom?

____

8. What three reasons does she give for putting mirrors in other rooms?

____

9. As a journalist, how did Lagatree feel about feng shui at first?

____

10. When Lagatree's skeptical friends asked her if she believed in feng shui, how did she respond?

____

11. You don't have to be a feng shui expert to know if a place has good feng shui. Why not?

____

MAKE INFERENCES

In the interview, Kirsten Lagatree's and Sedge Thomson's opinions and attitudes about feng shui are not made clear just from their words; their attitudes can be inferred by their tone of voice. Listen to the excerpts, paying attention to the speakers' tones and choices of words. Then work in pairs, and discuss the answers.

CD 2 6

Excerpt One

1. Thomson probably feels that feng shui is ________________.
2. Lagatree may feel that Thomson's question is ________________.

CD 2 7

Excerpt Two

3. Lagatree mentions Donald Trump to emphasize that ________________.
4. Thomson's quick response, "a famous feng shui expert, as we all know," implies that he thinks Donald Trump is ________________.

CD 2 8

Excerpt Three

5. Lagatree told her friends, "Don't quote me." She probably said this because ________________.

EXPRESS OPINIONS

Work in a small group, and discuss the answers to the questions.

1. What is the most interesting thing you have learned so far about feng shui?
2. Would you be interested in applying feng shui principles to make changes in your home? If so, what changes would you like to make? If not, why are you skeptical?
3. Does feng shui remind you of any practices from other cultures? Which ones?
4. What do you suppose leads Westerners to adopt Eastern practices, such as yoga, feng shui, and so on? In what ways does a traditional Eastern practice tend to change when it becomes Westernized?

B LISTENING TWO: Feng Shui in the Newsroom

First, look at the ***bagua*** chart on page 107. In feng shui, it is an octagonal grid used to determine how parts of the house or a room relate to various areas of one's life. The feng shui master places the bagua over the floorplan of the room or house to see how to arrange the areas to promote the flow of "good ch'i."

The bagua is used like a compass. Unlike Western compasses, in this Chinese compass, south is placed on the top, the most important direction. The components of the bagua include: five basic elements (fire, earth, water, metal, and wood), colors of nature, numbers, animals, and areas of life (health, wealth, relationships, wisdom, business, and so on).

Lagatree visits a radio newsroom to record this interview. She suggests changes in the newsroom based on feng shui principles.

CD 2 9 *Listen to the interview with host Steve Scher. Then listen again, and fill in the missing information on the bagua chart. Also, draw arrows from the desks (both Steve Scher's and the news writers') and the aquarium to where Lagatree suggests placing them.*

Bagua Chart

Area of Life: Fame
- Fire
- Birds
- Summer

Color: Red
Number: 9

Area of Life: ________
- Wood
- Early Summer
- Fish Ponds

Color: ________
Number: ________

Area of Life: Relationships
- ________
- ________
- ________

Color: ________
Number: ________

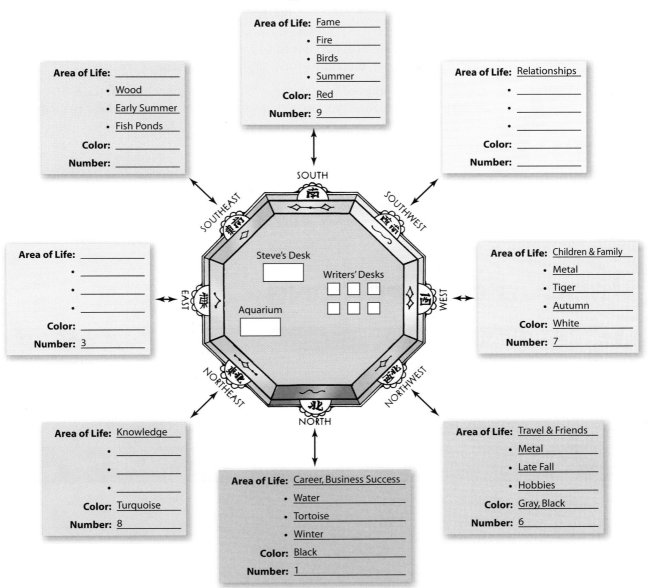

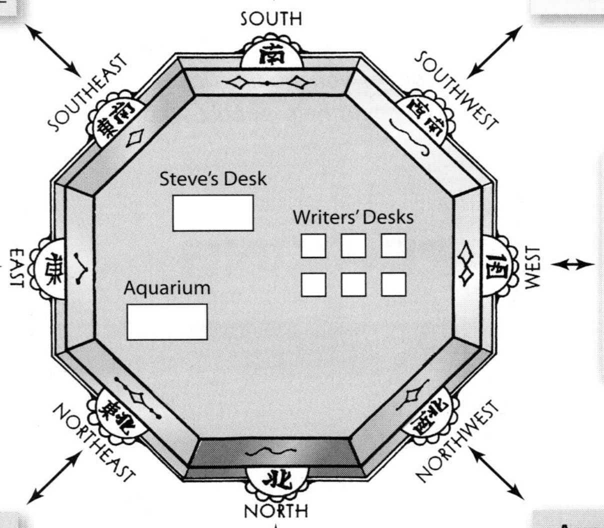

Area of Life: ________
- ________
- ________
- ________

Color: ________
Number: 3

Area of Life: Children & Family
- Metal
- Tiger
- Autumn

Color: White
Number: 7

Area of Life: Knowledge
- ________
- ________
- ________

Color: Turquoise
Number: 8

Area of Life: Travel & Friends
- Metal
- Late Fall
- Hobbies

Color: Gray, Black
Number: 6

Area of Life: Career, Business Success
- Water
- Tortoise
- Winter

Color: Black
Number: 1

C INTEGRATE LISTENINGS ONE AND TWO

STEP 1: Organize

Work in pairs. Follow the directions to apply the feng shui principles you studied in the listenings.

1. Choose a space which is familiar to you and your partner. It could be a place in your school, a store, etc. Brainstorm problems with the space.
2. Review the principles of feng shui as well as the bagua chart on page 107. Brainstorm the changes you would like to make according to these principles.

STEP 2: Synthesize

Draw the space on a separate sheet of paper, including as many details as possible. Present the results to another pair or the whole class. Describe the space before and after. Describe the changes you would make based on the new design. Finally, describe how favorable feng shui could help people who live and/or work in this space.

3 FOCUS ON SPEAKING

A VOCABULARY

REVIEW

Work with a partner. Fill in the other forms of the words in the chart. A dash (–) indicates that there is no related form or that the form is not commonly used.

NOUN	VERB	ADJECTIVE
abundance	abound	
1. acuteness 2. acuity	—	
		aligned
		digressive
—	frown upon	

NOUN	VERB	ADJECTIVE
1. **2.** governance		
1. **2.** quote (informal)		
scholar	—	
1. sense **2.**	**1.** **2.**	
1. **2.**	—	skeptical
	transcend	
		vital
anecdote	tell an _____	

EXPAND

Work with a partner. Take the role of Kirsten Lagatree (the author) or Donald Trump (the famous New York City real estate developer). Complete the imaginary interview with the appropriate forms of the words from the box. Use the phrases under the blanks to help you. Then read the interview aloud with drama, interest, and expression.

at heart	get into	keep out	scare the heck out of
can't hurt	hard-bitten	make a move	sharp
catch off guard	huge	peppy	talk [someone] into
clean	in the midst of	rise or fall	work around

Lagatree: Mr. Trump, ever since I heard you ________________ feng shui, I've
1. (became interested in)

been dying to meet you. Referring to you as not only an astute

(continued on next page)

businessman but also as an artistic designer __________ 2. (essentially), I often quote you when I do interviews or speak on book tours.

TRUMP: Kirsten, the pleasure is mine. I've read your handbook on feng shui and have always thought you were a __________ 3. (quick, smart), intelligent writer.

LAGATREE: Why, thank you, Mr. Trump. Now, I understand that you absolutely do not __________ 4. (take action) in business without consulting your feng shui master, Mr. Tin Sun. Is that true?

TRUMP: Absolutely. I am currently __________ 5. (involved in) complicated negotiations involving some highly valued property on the Hudson River in New York City. However, Master Sun has informed me that the windows and doors are not aligned properly and the views are not that great. I thought about selling the property, but Master Sun __________ me __________ 6. (convinced) keeping it. He said it is very valuable and, by applying feng shui principles, we can easily __________ 7. (compensate for) the problems. Fortunately, the overall design of the building is __________ 8. (simple).

LAGATREE: How did such a __________ 9. (tough, experienced) businessman like yourself get into feng shui?

TRUMP: I've been doing business in Asia for years and am well aware of the fact that feng shui is __________ 10. (very popular) there. In Hong Kong, you know, business deals __________ 11. (succeed or fail) on feng shui.

LAGATREE: Have you used feng shui in your home as well?

TRUMP: Yes, Kirsten, I have. Master Sun started working on my house five years ago. I must admit that when he first came over, he __________ 12. (frightened) me. He connected many of my personal and physical problems to the poor circulation of ch'i in my house. After many adjustments and a great deal of money, I was finally able to ______ (13. prevent from entering) the unfavorable ch'i.

LAGATREE: I'm sure. I know there are many skeptics out there. However, I do believe that if you live in a house with good feng shui, you feel ______ (14. livelier) and more energetic. In addition, you'll be able to live comfortably day in and day out without getting ______ (15. startled) in your own home.

TRUMP: Of course. Anyway, I always tell those hard-bitten businessmen who tease me, "Try feng shui. It ______ (16. can do no harm)."

CREATE

Work with a partner.

Student A: Cover the right column. Ask questions 1 through 5.

Student B: Cover the left column. Answer each question, using the key word or expression in parentheses. Add additional information to clarify and explain. Then switch roles after question 5.

Student A	Student B
1. After learning about feng shui, how would you talk a skeptic into using it?	1. I guess . . . (couldn't hurt) I guess I'd say that it's been around for thousands of years, so it must work. At the very least, **it couldn't hurt. In other words, . . .**
2. Do you really believe that feng shui can affect people's moods and feelings?	2. Hmmm . . . (sharp, peppy) So, what I mean is . . .
3. What other Eastern practices would you be interested in getting into?	3. Perhaps . . . (get into) To put it another way . . .
4. What is your favorite way of keeping out unfavorable ch'i?	4. Let me see . . . I think . . . (keep out) What I mean is . . .
5. Why do you think feng shui has become so popular recently?	5. I imagine it . . . (huge) . . . Actually, what I am trying to say is . . .

(continued on next page)

Now switch roles.

6. Do you prefer simple, clean designs or more complicated, cluttered arrangements?

6. Actually, I think . . . (clean)
So, in other words . . .

7. What kind of ch'i did you sense when you first walked into your current home?

7. I'm not sure I remember, but . . . (sense)
You see, what I mean is . . .

8. Can you describe a place you know with good feng shui?

8. Sure, I felt like I was . . . (in the midst of) good feng shui when I . . .
I think you could also say . . .

9. If your classroom had poor lighting and immovable desks that faced the wall, what would you do to create good feng shui?

9. Wow. That's a tough one. I guess . . . (work around) . . .
To put it another way . . .

B GRAMMAR: Spoken Discourse Connectors

1 *Work with a partner. Examine the excerpt from Listening One, and discuss the questions that follow.*

Before radio host Sedge Thomson invited author Kirsten Lagatree to be interviewed on *West Coast Live,* he asked his researcher, Robin Tennenbaum, about Lagatree's qualifications.

THOMSON: Is Kirsten Lagatree a feng shui master?

TENNENBAUM: Well, Sedge, she doesn't claim to be a feng shui master. I mean, she hasn't studied in China or anything. **But** she has done a great deal of research, especially on the spread of feng shui in the United States. **On top of that**, she's written a well-respected book on the subject, which has led to a number of positive book reviews and successful radio interviews. **As a result**, she's become known as somewhat of an expert on feng shui.

1. What purpose does each of the boldfaced phrases serve? Name all three.

2. What other words could substitute for them?

SPOKEN DISCOURSE CONNECTORS

Discourse connectors are words and expressions that can connect ideas in speaking and writing. They join ideas both within sentences and between sentences. When you express yourself at length or in detail on a topic, then you need to use these words to help the reader or listener understand your ideas. In written English, we use formal connectors—***in contrast***, ***moreover***, ***furthermore***, ***consequently***, ***therefore***—to express the meaning of contrast, addition, and result. In spoken English, we often use more informal connectors to express the same meaning.

Contrast (unexpected result)	Addition	Result
but	plus	so
however	in addition	as a result
on the other hand	on top of that	

2 *Fill in the blanks in the story with the appropriate discourse connectors from the chart above. There may be more than one correct answer. Then read the story aloud with drama, interest, and expression.*

A feng shui master told this story:

One client told me that her business was doing very poorly and she needed to take some action. (1) ________________, she was eager to revive her social life as well. (2) ________________, she hired me and I spent several hours assessing her home. At first glance, I sensed that the ch'i was flowing smoothly throughout the house. (3) ________________, a few minutes later, I did notice an old armchair in her living room blocking the front door. I asked her where she had bought it. She told me it was from the set of a movie about a dangerous killer. (4) ________________ she mentioned that she had only had the chair for about four months and that this was the time when her business and social life began to fail. It was clear to me that the chair had negative energy, which was related to her bad luck. (5) ________________, we moved the chair outside immediately. As soon as we did, the telephone rang. It was a friend asking her on a date. (6) ________________, one month later, her business took off. (7) ________________, she now understands the importance of bringing objects with only positive ch'i into the house.

3 *Work with a partner. Take turns reading the statements aloud. Select a discourse connector for the meaning given, and make additional statements.*

1. Feng shui is an Eastern practice. [contrast]

   But it's becoming very popular in the West. In particular, Western corporations are using feng shui in their business locations.

2. Some people say feng shui is just a superstition. [addition]
3. Placing a plant in a corner can help positive ch'i circulate. [result]
4. Many real estate developers in Western countries are consulting feng shui experts. [result]
5. In Hong Kong, feng shui is taken quite seriously. [contrast]
6. To create positive ch'i, you can put an aquarium in the southeast corner of the room. [addition]

C SPEAKING

PRONUNCIATION: Intonation on Sentence Introducers

Sentence introducers are phrases like ***Well***, ***First***, ***In addition***, and ***On the other hand***. They show how a sentence relates to other sentences in a conversation or longer message. They may also show the speaker's perspective on the information.

In speaking, introducers are often separated from the following sentence, especially when the introducer consists of several words. Short introducers like *Well* or *But* may either be separated from the following sentence or pronounced with it.

CD 2 10 Listen to the boldfaced introducers.

A: **You know**, I don't like this paint color. It's too bright.
B: **Plus** it's too green. What should we do?
A: **Well**, we might get used to it.
B: Maybe. **Anyway**, I don't want to repaint.

Introducers that are separated from the sentence by a pause, or in writing by a comma, have:

- their own intonation pattern
- intonation which often falls at the end of the introducer and then may rise a little

You know, I don't like this paint color.

Introducers that are not separated:

- join closely to the following sentence
- do not have their own intonation pattern

Plus it's too green.

1 CD 2 (11) *Listen to the story about Bruce Lee and fill in the blanks with the introducers you hear. Add a comma after the introducer if it is separated from the following sentence.*

Kung Fu Master Meets Feng Shui Disaster

(1) ______So______ this is the story of a true tragedy that occurred in Hong Kong, involving feng shui. **(2)** ________________ you've heard of Bruce Lee, the famous kung fu actor. **(3)** ________________ he decided to buy a house in a valley that got a lot of wind. **(4)** ________________ wind can destroy ch'i. **(5)** ________________ people couldn't understand why he chose that area. He was wealthy and could have lived anywhere in Hong Kong. **(6)** ________________ he bought the house. **(7)** ________________ to change his feng shui, he put a mirror on a tree in his backyard. **(8)** ________________ a storm destroyed the tree, and he never replaced it or the mirror. **(9)** ________________ doctors concluded that he died of a cerebral edema[1]. **(10)** ________________ a lot of people believe that unfavorable feng shui also played a role.

[1]**cerebral edema:** an accumulation of fluid on the brain

2 *Read the conversation and fill in the blanks with one of the introducers in the box. In some blanks, more than one introducer is possible. Then work with a partner and compare answers. Read the conversation aloud.*

Actually	Plus	So	Well

A: How can you live in this mess?

B: ________________, it doesn't bother me at all.

A: ________________, it looks awful. ________________ it smells like dirty shoes.

B: ________________ I guess you're saying I should do some cleaning.

3 *Work with a partner. Student A, ask your partner questions about his or her surroundings. Student B, use an introducer to begin your answer. Then switch roles after question 4.*

Example

A: How important is it for you to have a view in your living space?

B: Actually, it's really important. I'm living in a dorm room now, and my view is the brick wall of another building. So it really bothers me.

1. How do you feel in a messy room?
2. How well can you concentrate in a noisy room?
3. How do you feel in a windowless room?
4. Can you sleep if it's noisy? Explain.

Now switch roles.

5. Can you concentrate if you're working at a messy desk? Explain.
6. How important is it for you to have an attractive living space? Work space?
7. How important is it for you to have sunlight in your living space?
8. Do paint or furniture colors affect your mood? How?

FUNCTION: Emphasizing a Point

When speaking informally to a skeptical listener, English speakers may use an emphatic speaking style. In Listening One, for example, Kirsten Lagatree knows that Sedge Thomson and many listeners may be skeptical of feng shui. As a result, she emphasizes her point by using certain emphatic expressions such as *boy* and *would no more do [this] than [that]*, and by using emphatic intonation.

1 *Listen to the examples, and read them as you listen. Then look at the explanation and examples on the next page before you do the second exercise.*

- "Well, **I wouldn't say** to keep out evil spirits. **But I would say** it's a system of arranging all the objects around you at home or at work."
- "He **would no more** start working on a building project without a feng shui master **than he would** without, you know, if it was L.A., without a seismologist."
- "The new Regency Hotel in Singapore just opened with two beautiful fountains in the lobby. **Talk about** great feng shui! The hotel is booked solid for the next two months!"
- "Now, based on just simple things I've done, and also lots and lots of people I talked to for the book, **I'd have to say** it works . . . and at the very least it couldn't hurt."
- "We can't see it but, **boy**, is it there doing things!"

EMPHASIZING A POINT		
Expression	**Explanation**	**Example**
Boy . . .	used as an exclamation followed by an inversion, auxiliary then main verb	*Boy,* did Bruce Lee have bad luck!
I wouldn't say . . . , but I would say . . .	used to clarify the meaning	*I wouldn't say* feng shui is huge in the United States, *but I would say* it's becoming popular.
. . . would no more . . . than . . .	followed by something obviously unreasonable	*I would no more* hire a feng shui expert to design my house *than* I would hire a palm reader to predict my future.
Talk about . . .	followed by an explanation	*Talk about* a perfect location! The house was surrounded by lovely streams and beautiful gardens.
I'd have to say . . .	used to emphasize a strong point	Well, since I moved my desk to the northeast corner, *I'd have to say* my writing has improved.

2 *Work with a partner.*

Student A: Ask the question or make the comment.

Student B: Cover the left column. Respond emphatically or skeptically. Use an expression from the chart above and appropriate intonation. Add further comments. Then switch roles after question 5.

Student A

1. You really hired a feng shui expert to boost profits? Did it work?
2. How about hiring a professional "clutter consultant" to clean the clutter out of your house? A trained professional will clear the "stuck energy" in your house and bring you instant luck.

Student B

1. Boy, __did it!__ Profits are up 100 percent.
2. Are you kidding! I would no more hire a professional "clutter consultant" than I would _________ (add something unreasonable).

(continued on next page)

3. Listen to this! You won't believe it! A Chinese American millionaire paid a feng shui expert $50,000 to advise him on the alignment of his building.

3. Talk about _________ (add an explanation)!

4. I think feng shui practitioners are nothing more than superstitious fortune tellers with a compass.

4. Well, I wouldn't say _________, but I would say _________.

5. Don't you think that feng shui is really more than just putting up mirrors or hanging wind chimes?

5. Absolutely! I'd have to say _________.

Now switch roles.

6. My friend Michael had had two robberies in his apartment. Then he used a feng shui expert, who advised him to set up an aquarium. He's had no robberies since.

6. That's amazing! Talk about _________ (add an explanation)! But I don't think feng shui had anything to do with it.

7. Another friend added flowers, wind chimes, crystals, and mirrors in his house. Two days later, he got the biggest promotion of his life.

7. Boy, _________ (use an inversion).

8. Would you buy a house near a cemetery?

8. No, I would no more _________ than _________.

9. What do you think of other Eastern practices like *tai chi,* macrobiotic diets, and so on?

9. Well, I'd have to say _________.

10. Feng shui is trendy in the West now. It'll fade in a few years.

10. I wouldn't say _________, but I would say _________.

PRODUCTION: Present an Argument

In this activity, you will form an opinion and ***present an argument based on an article***. Try to use the vocabulary, grammar, pronunciation, and the language for emphasizing a point that you learned in the unit.*

For years people worldwide have believed that good feng shui fosters positive benefits such as health, happiness, harmony, wealth, creativity, and respect. Individuals and families have redesigned their homes in order to create positive and auspicious energy. Corporations have rebuilt their company buildings and workspaces to create greater prosperity and magnify success.

*For Alternative Speaking Topics, see page 120.

Even educational institutions such as schools and universities have tried to tackle and solve major challenges by implementing feng shui on campus. However, feng shui is a controversial practice and many people are highly skeptical of its potential to create significant change.

Read this case, which combines elements of real cases. Then do the activities that follow.

New University President Plans to Implement Feng Shui on Campus

Government, Faculty Outraged!!

This public university, esteemed for decades for its beautiful campus and strong academic programs, appears to be in shambles: dying trees, brown lawns and withered flower beds, crumbling staircases, cracked walls, water-stained ceilings, windowless classrooms, neglected computer labs, and buildings never repaired properly following several devastating earthquakes in the 1990s. On the inside, one finds demoralized professors fleeing to teach in private universities, and unhappy students with plummeting exam scores, low job placement rates, and few acceptances to graduate programs. Enrollment is still declining, and there have been four campus-wide student strikes so far this year.

Can this picture get any worse?

As one of the oldest public universities in Latin America—once world-renowned and prestigious—this beloved university is desperate for total and complete change.

Can Luis Miguel Sanchez make good on his promise of change?

Hired just three months ago, Luis Miguel Sanchez, grandson of Chinese immigrants, pledged that he would succeed in transforming the university from a devastated educational institution to one the entire country could once again be proud of.

How would he do this?

He will start with 15 million dollars! Yes, it is true. The university suddenly announced that the development office had

received an anonymous 10 million dollar donation from a wealthy donor of Chinese descent to renovate the university. Inspired by his 3-week trip to Hong Kong and wanting to be respectful of the donor's heritage as well as the large number of students of Chinese descent at the university, the president has recommended that planners, architects, designers and builders plan the renovation according to feng shui principles.

What inspired him? After visiting many buildings in Hong Kong, the president became convinced that feng shui could be the key to creating peace and harmony at home and throughout the nation. His idea was to redesign both the public display and private living areas of the university.

President Sanchez is 100 percent confident that implementing feng shui on campus will establish harmony among the students, the

(continued on next page)

government, and faculty; raise academic standards; and return the university to its glory days. The student body is supportive of his innovative plans.

In stark contrast, the faculty and the government are adamantly opposed to his strategy. Skeptical of feng shui, they aim to renovate according to the country's history, tradition, and culture. They advocate rebuilding according to colonial architectural tradition, famous for richness and creativity. Moreover, they see feng shui as superstitious nonsense and doubt that adding ponds and lakes will solve the university's serious problems. Restoring the traditional décor, they believe, will bring pride, honor, and self-esteem to the entire university population and the country as a whole.

1. Divide into two groups:
   - the president and the students
   - the government and the faculty
2. Using the information in the news article, outline the arguments for each side.
3. Conduct the meeting in which both groups present their opinions. Use the discourse connectors presented on page 113 and the expressions for emphasizing a point presented on page 117.
4. As a class, vote on how the president will handle the donation.

ALTERNATIVE SPEAKING TOPICS

Work with a small group. Read the following quotes that discuss the relationship between people and place (our homes, communities, environment). Paraphrase each quote. What does it mean in other words? Comment on each quote. How do you feel about it?

Then discuss this general question: How does the environment in which you live, study, or work affect you? In your discussion, use ideas, vocabulary, grammar, pronunciation, and expressions for emphasizing a point.

"As places around us change—both the communities that shelter us and the larger regions that support them—we all undergo changes inside. This means that whatever we experience in a place is both a serious environmental issue and a deeply personal one."

—Tony Hiss, *The Experience of Place*

"The basic principle that links our places and states is simple: A good or bad environment promotes good or bad memories, which inspire a good or bad mood, which inclines us toward good or bad behavior. The mere presence of sunlight increases our willingness to help strangers and tip waiters, and people working in a room slowly permeated by the odor of burnt dust lose their appetites, even though they don't notice the smell. On some level, states and places are internal and external versions of each other."

—Winifred Gallagher, *The Power of Place*

RESEARCH TOPICS, see page 262.

UNIT 6

Spiritual Renewal

1 FOCUS ON THE TOPIC

A PREDICT

1. Look at the photograph of the monastery. What do you know about monasteries? Why do you think someone would choose to live in a monastery?

2. The number of visitors to monasteries and other spiritual retreat centers has increased dramatically over the past few years. Why do you think this is happening? Why do you think someone would choose to visit a center for spiritual retreat?

B SHARE INFORMATION

In modern life, there are many forms of spiritual renewal. Many people practice small daily rituals, such as intentionally remaining quiet or spending time alone; a growing number of people choose to retreat from society for a few days, often by visiting a spiritual community; and a few people withdraw from mainstream society to live in a monastery.

A *monastery* is a place occupied by a community of persons, called *monks* (males) or *nuns* (females), who follow strict religious vows, or promises. Monasteries transcend cultural, national, and religious boundaries: There are Buddhist, Indian, Christian, hermit, and wandering monks. All monasteries throughout the world share a similar commitment: brotherly or sisterly love, harmony, prayer, and communal work. What else do you know about modern monastic life?

Read the list of statements. Write **F** *(fact) or* **M** *(myth) before each statement. There are three of each. Compare your answers with those of a classmate. Read the explanations on pages 257–258.*

Modern Monastic Life: Fact or Myth?

_____ **1.** Most monks and nuns are quiet, introverted people.

_____ **2.** Monks and nuns never retire and generally work until they die.

_____ **3.** Since they devote themselves to the spiritual world, monks and nuns have made few contributions to the outside world.

_____ **4.** Monks and nuns are chosen from birth to become monks and nuns by the family or the community.

_____ **5.** It is necessary for monks and nuns to be vegetarians, shave their heads, or wear special robes called "habits."

_____ **6.** Although most monks and nuns follow strict daily schedules, most monasteries are open to outside visitors.

C BACKGROUND AND VOCABULARY

Spiritual retreats have become increasingly popular. In these blog entries, a man tells of his journey from Calgary, Canada, to Mt. Athos, Greece. The passages appeared on a travel newsletter website about Athos, the oldest surviving group of monastic communities in the world.

CD 2 13 *Read and listen to the blog entries, and notice the boldfaced words. Then match them to the definitions in the list on page 126. Then discuss whether you would like to visit Mt. Athos.*

http://www.mytravelblog.com/mt.athos.greece

Mt. Athos, Greece

Monday, 27 March early morning – Ouranoupolis

A dream come true: While waiting for the ferry, I look out across the sea toward the sacred thousand-year-old holy mountain, Mt. Athos, which rises more then 6,500 feet (1,981 meters) straight out of the water. Attracted by its beauty, no doubt, **(1) prophets** came here in the first century to practice their ancient **(2) ascetic** traditions of self-denial, such as **(3) fasting**. The mist, the white haze, the feathery silhouette all give the mountain a **(4) divine** presence as it rises high into the clouds. I check my pocket for the zillionth[1] time to make sure I have my four-day permit allowing me to visit the 20 monasteries on the mountain. To preserve the beauty of the monastic mountain, the Greek government **(5) enacted a law** limiting the male-only tourist visits to four days.

Monday, 27 March noon – Daphni

By noon, my ferry has arrived at Daphni, the primary port on the Holy Mountain. I am stunned by the confusion and commotion. It is a **(6) vibrant** and vital port. The noise is pervasive —roaring trucks, police sirens, shouting tourists with cell phones held tight to their ears, barking dogs, blaring radios. I ask myself, "Is this really an escape from my **(7) hectic** life in the city? Will I really be able to **(8) replenish** my soul?"

Monday, 27 March late afternoon – Karyes

Finally, I get to Karyes, a charming, peaceful village at the tip of Mt. Athos. I take a deep breath. A sense of satisfaction and **(9) well-being** fills my heart. I hike the 20 minutes to Monastery Koutloumousiou through thick trees and bushes. A bearded, unsmiling monk wearing black robes greets me. Speaking little, the guest master brings me to a cave-like room for the offering traditionally given to visitors: chewy candies and strong black Greek coffee.

The guest master then explains that all the monks are fasting at this time of the year, meaning they **(10) refrain from** eating and drinking most of the day. Therefore, the evening meal will be later than usual. The monks need a lot of discipline to keep the fast. Besides the fast, they need a strong **(11) will** to endure the many hours of prayer. On top of all that, they have few hours of sleep each night. Wow! This makes me realize that the monk's life is not for me.

Tuesday, 28 March very early morning – Karyes

I wake up at 2:30 A.M. to attend the daily prayer service. Praying and singing together **(12) fosters** a spirit of community and brotherhood in the monastery.

After the service, I take a walk and think about my first 24 hours on Athos. I feel sincere **(13) gratitude** to my hosts for their hospitality. I am in awe of their display of **(14) humility** and generosity to each other and to the hundreds of visitors searching for a few days of silence and solitude. Athos is a mystical place.

---

[1] **zillionth:** fictional number, meaning an incredibly high number

_____ **a.** living without any physical pleasures or comforts, especially for religious reasons

_____ **b.** made a new official rule

_____ **c.** not being too proud

_____ **d.** determination

_____ **e.** eating little or no food for a special reason

_____ **f.** develops

_____ **g.** full of energy and life

_____ **h.** thankfulness

_____ **i.** not do something you want to do

_____ **j.** a feeling of being happy, healthy, or satisfied

_____ **k.** very busy; full of activity

_____ **l.** coming from God or a god

_____ **m.** holy men

_____ **n.** renew and refill

2 FOCUS ON LISTENING

A LISTENING ONE: The Religious Tradition of Fasting

In this radio broadcast, the host, Duncan Moon, talks with four professors about the religious tradition of fasting. Fasting, or denying oneself food for an extended time, is an old and widespread spiritual practice.

CD 2 14 *Work with a partner. Predict the reasons that inspire people of many religions to fast. List your ideas. Then listen to an excerpt from the interview to check your predictions.*

1. ______________________________
2. ______________________________
3. ______________________________
4. ______________________________

LISTEN FOR MAIN IDEAS

CD 2 15 *Read the lists of religions and the reasons for fasting. Then listen to the broadcast. Match each religion on the left with the essential reason for fasting associated with that religion.*

Religion(s)	Reason for Fasting
_____ **1.** Eastern religions	**a.** preservation of an ancient tradition
_____ **2.** all religions	**b.** spiritual renewal
_____ **3.** Judaism	**c.** spiritual discipline
_____ **4.** Episcopalianism	**d.** asceticism
_____ **5.** Mormonism	**e.** anti-competitiveness
_____ **6.** Islam	**f.** anti-materialism

LISTEN FOR DETAILS

CD 2 16 *Read the questions. Then listen to the broadcast, and write short answers. Work with a partner and compare answers.*

1. According to Judaism, Christianity, and Islam, who were the first religious leaders to fast?

____

2. According to Diana Eck, professor of comparative religion at Harvard Divinity School, what does a fast symbolize?

____

3. What does Barbara Patterson, professor of religion at Emory University, think about the stress that might be created by fasting?

____

4. How often do Mormons fast?

____

5. What do Mormons do with the money they save by fasting?

____

6. When do Muslims fast, and for how long?

____

7. According to Ahbar Ahmed, the Islamic studies professor, why is fasting so important now?

____

8. In addition, according to Ahmed, why is fasting so difficult these days?

____

MAKE INFERENCES

In the broadcast, all three speakers use phrases that appear simple on the surface but actually imply deeper and richer meanings. Listen to each excerpt, and choose the correct answer. Explain your responses to a partner.

CD 2 17 **Excerpt One**

1. What is implied about material or earthly things?
   - **a.** They symbolize our desire for food.
   - **b.** They are unnecessary in religious practice.
   - **c.** They can interfere with spirituality.

2. According to Dr. Eck, the value of fasting is _____.
   - **a.** symbolic—it represents a spiritual attitude
   - **b.** practical—it reduces the desire for food
   - **c.** debatable—it reveals what people believe

3. Dr. Eck might feel that people should fast to become _____.
   - **a.** more spiritual
   - **b.** less materialistic
   - **c.** more flexible

CD 2 18 **Excerpt Two**

4. What does Moon imply by the phrase "spiritual gym"?
   - **a.** Fasting strengthens the spirit.
   - **b.** Athletes might be good at fasting.
   - **c.** People go to special gyms to fast.

5. The purpose of the athletic analogy is _____.
   - **a.** to make a humorous comment about fasting
   - **b.** to help listeners understand the effort involved
   - **c.** to portray fasting as something common

CD 2 19 **Excerpt Three**

6. What does Dr. Ahmed imply by the phrase "spiritually exhausted"?
   - **a.** When you don't fast, you feel tired.
   - **b.** When you don't fast, you feel less satisfied.
   - **c.** When you don't fast, you can't think.

7. Dr. Ahmed probably thinks that most people are "spiritually exhausted" because _____.
   - **a.** they are physically tired
   - **b.** they live in a fast-paced world
   - **c.** they don't take time during the day for silent reflection

EXPRESS OPINIONS

Discuss the questions in a small group.

1. Why do you think fasting is a spiritual practice in so many religious traditions?
2. Have you ever fasted? Do you think it had a spiritual effect on you? Describe and analyze your experience.
3. As you heard in the broadcast, many people fast to become more disciplined. How else can this kind of discipline be achieved?

B LISTENING TWO: Describing Monastic Life

Recently, the journalist William Claassen wrote a book describing monastic life in 11 countries. For his research, he visited monastic communities around the world. In Listening Two, he discusses his experiences in Thailand, Greece, and Spain.

CD2 20 *Listen to the interview with William Claassen. As you listen, check (✓) the correct information to complete the sentences. There may be more than one answer for each question.*

1. The main purpose of Claassen's trip was to _____.
   _____ **a.** write a book
   _____ **b.** choose a religion
   _____ **c.** continue a spiritual journey
2. In Thailand, at the Wat Tham Krabok monastery, the monks _____.
   _____ **a.** preserve the forests
   _____ **b.** make wine
   _____ **c.** help AIDS patients
   _____ **d.** help Hmong refugees
   _____ **e.** help drug addicts
   _____ **f.** discourage visitors
3. Wat Tham Krabok is different from other forest monasteries because _____.
   _____ **a.** the monks don't respect the monastic discipline of solitude
   _____ **b.** the monks provide service to the community
   _____ **c.** the monks don't participate in daily chants
   _____ **d.** it is a hectic place
4. On Mt. Athos in Greece, Claassen learned a term, the "two-legged wolf," which refers to people who _____.
   _____ **a.** visit monasteries only for fun and curiosity
   _____ **b.** are not primarily spiritually motivated
   _____ **c.** visit Mt. Athos for seven to 10 days
   _____ **d.** prefer the beaches of Thailand to the monasteries on Mt. Athos

(continued on next page)

5. In Spain, at Monasterio de Santo Domingo, the monks _____.
   _____ **a.** won international acclaim for their music
   _____ **b.** produced an album of their Gregorian chants
   _____ **c.** started recording their music in the early 1990s
   _____ **d.** record music to draw more visitors to their monastery
   _____ **e.** record music to make money
   _____ **f.** use the profits from the albums to support the work of the monastery

C INTEGRATE LISTENINGS ONE AND TWO

STEP 1: Organize

As you heard in the broadcast and the interview, the desire for spiritual renewal is pervasive. However, approaches to achieving this renewal vary widely. Review Listenings One and Two, and complete the chart.

SPIRITUAL GOALS	SPIRITUAL PRACTICES	
	Personal / Solitary	**Communal**
• break attachments to material things	• fasting	• giving to the poor
•	•	•
•	•	•
•	•	•
•		

STEP 2: Synthesize

Use the information in the chart above, and prepare a one minute mini-lecture. Choose two or three spiritual practices from the chart, and explain how they can help people achieve one or two specific spiritual goals. Consider how solitary and communal practices may bring different results. Use details and examples to explain your position. Take turns sharing your mini-lectures in a small group.

3 FOCUS ON SPEAKING

A VOCABULARY

REVIEW

Thomas Merton (1915–1968) was an influential author and philosopher. He was also a monk. Merton was an outgoing teenager who lived in Europe and the United States. Later, as a graduate student in New York City, he experienced a sudden religious awakening. He converted to Catholicism, did charitable work in the city, and became a professor, but gradually Merton withdrew from the "real" world. Ultimately he joined the Trappist order of monks, an order with strict and solitary practices. For 27 years Merton lived at a well-known monastery in Kentucky. During this time, famous writers, professors, and religious leaders visited the monastery to learn more about the life and thoughts of this extraordinary monk.

Read the transcript of an imaginary interview of Merton by Japanese journalist Kenji Masaaki, who traveled to the monastery on a fact-finding journey. The interview took place in 1967, a year before Merton's visit to Thailand, where he died accidentally from electrocution as he stepped out of the bathtub.

Match each boldfaced word in the passage to its synonym or definition on page 133.

MASAAKI: Welcome, Father. I appreciate your taking the time to meet with me. It is a real pleasure to meet you. I have read your works and greatly admire your writing. I was wondering if you could speak briefly about your childhood, which was a bit unconventional, wasn't it?

MERTON: Of course. Well, when I was six years old my mother passed away after a long fight against cancer. My father was a restless artist who just couldn't settle down. So, he periodically shipped me off to stay with relatives and friends in England, France, or America.

MASAAKI: Hmm . . . I see . . . What did that experience teach you?

MERTON: Well, I learned how to enjoy the **(1) hectic**, gypsy sort of life, and I also developed an acute sensitivity to and understanding of people and places around me.

MASAAKI: But didn't you finally settle down in 1938 when you went to graduate school in New York?

MERTON: Yes, I did. While at Columbia I immersed myself in my studies, but in the end, I felt restless and confused, spiritually and philosophically. So, I began a deliberate **(2) quest** to deepen my knowledge of myself and explore the spiritual world.

MASAAKI: Is this what led you to Catholicism? What prompted your sudden change of heart?

MERTON: Well, that's an excellent question. Actually, I can **(3) trace** my conversion **back** to a single day in Manhattan. While sitting in the back of a church, I had an epiphany, a sudden insight: I mysteriously felt so drawn to God that I knew I had to commit myself to the Catholic faith immediately.

(continued on next page)

MASAAKI: I've read that you felt you had to find a practical way to demonstrate your newly found faith, so you **(4) took on** volunteer work in a poverty-stricken neighborhood, right? How did that affect you?

MERTON: That work had a profound effect on me. It **(5) fostered** a sense of calm and **(6) well-being**, because I felt good about helping people. But I also witnessed serious racial and economic injustices, which inspired my active participation in the civil rights movement.

MASAAKI: Oh, I see. So, could you speak briefly about how you finally entered the monastery in 1941?

MERTON: Well, I don't remember all the details, but I do know that in spite of my volunteer work and my newly found Catholicism, I still had a nagging feeling of spiritual emptiness, so I decided to become a monk. Of course, my close friends and family considered the **(7) notion of** entering a monastery a bit odd.

MASAAKI: Yes. I imagine everyone was baffled over why a vibrant, brilliant young man would choose to **(8) pull back** from daily life and commit himself to an ascetic life. What can you tell us about those early days of fasting, silence, and prayer?

MERTON: Sure. Let's see now. I do recall that in the beginning, loneliness and the rigorous monastic life presented the greatest challenges. As you can probably imagine, it took great will for me to **(9) refrain from** smoking, drinking, speaking, and living the life I had previously enjoyed in New York. Worried about my somber mood, the older monks worked hard to **(10) draw** me **out** and help me discover who I truly was.

MASAAKI: Yes, I've heard that **(11) over time** the more experienced monks helped to bring out your true gift: your amazing ability to write about spirituality, contemplation, nature, art, relationships, and God. Can you speak briefly about your writing?

Thomas Merton

MERTON: Of course. My autobiography, *The Seven Storey Mountain*, was published in 1948. Surprisingly, it **(12) caught on** quickly and sold more than one million copies its first year. Since then, I have written more than 100 books, articles, and essays. I donate all my **(13) royalties** from my books to my home here at the monastery.

MASAAKI: Wonderful! And you write about other topics besides religion, don't you?

MERTON: Definitely. In the past five years, I have been writing for the general public on the civil rights movement, non-violence, peace, and the nuclear arms race, subjects dear to my heart. Just last week, I met with legislators from the U.S. Congress who sought my permission to quote from my work as they attempt to **(14) enact** critical civil rights legislation.

MASAAKI: And I understand that you'll be off to Thailand soon to meet with the Dalai Lama in order to discuss ways to deepen understanding between Christians and Buddhists.

MERTON: Hmm . . . I see you've done your homework. Yes, that is the plan.

MASAAKI: Thank you for speaking with me today. I appreciate your time, Father.

_____ **a.** make a rule or law

_____ **b.** became popular

_____ **c.** finds the origins of something

_____ **d.** idea

_____ **e.** started

_____ **f.** search

_____ **g.** feeling of being happy, healthy, or satisfied

_____ **h.** very busy; full of activity

_____ **i.** money paid to a writer

_____ **j.** not do something you want to do

_____ **k.** make someone willing to talk

_____ **l.** developed

_____ **m.** gradually

_____ **n.** withdraw

EXPAND

Nowadays, people everywhere seek calm and clarity as an antidote, or cure, to their busy, frenzied lives. Many decide to spend days, weeks, or even years in a monastery or go on a spiritual retreat in order to reduce stress, practice meditation, contemplate universal questions, or simply "get away from it all."

In earlier times, people recorded details of their lives and thoughts in diaries. Today, bloggers—or web loggers—do the same on the Internet. These popular online journals appear in text form; however, many also include recordings, producing an "audio blog."

Three people express their views on this new trend toward "spiritual vacations." Read about them.

1. Thomas Kruze, a celebrity who vacationed for a week at a well-known Tibetan Buddhist retreat center in Nepal
2. Pam Stone, associate director of Spiritual Adventures International, a nonprofit organization representing more than 1000 non-religious retreat centers
3. Brother Nathaniel, the spiritual leader of the San Franciscan Monastery in Chile, a monastery which has recently opened its doors to outsiders

CD 2 21 *Look at the boldfaced expressions listed in the blog scripts. Then listen to the audio blogs. As you listen, pay attention to the use of these expressions. Circle the word or phrase on page 134 that has the same meaning as the expression.*

Thomas Kruze: In spite of my professional success and wealth, I was drawn to spending a week at St. John's Monastery in Nepal in order to get in touch with my spiritual core. I had been **at odds with** my agent because we just couldn't agree on what would be suitable roles for me. He seemed to think that I was distracted, not focused on my career, and simply **out of touch with** my fans. I knew he spoke the truth, but I couldn't accept it. Spending time at St. John's, enjoying long periods of solitude and reflection, helped me overcome these **stumbling blocks,** and achieve the peace of mind to make clearer decisions.

(continued on next page)

Pam Stone: Our clients come from all **walks of life.** We get corporate executives, religious leaders, housewives, blue-collar workers, teenagers, you name it! Many will be in the midst of some kind of drama in their lives. Some may even be **in dire straits,** struggling with serious **inner turmoil** and looking for **serenity** in order to think clearly about ways to cope with life's challenges. Others are simply **in a rut** and hope that a meditative experience can help them see more clearly to **gain insight** into themselves and their lives.

Brother Nathaniel: In the beginning, most of us were not in favor of the decision to open the gates of our monastery to outsiders because we cherish our contemplative life. Those in favor of the "guest house enterprise" and those opposed to the idea just couldn't **see to eye to eye.** We were afraid of making a business out of spirituality. However, to our great delight, the opposite has happened. The guests are remarkably respectful, and we realized that we are able to help people experience a meaningful way of life.

1. **at odds with**	talking with	disagreeing with	feeling uncomfortable with
2. **out of touch with**	not understanding	unpopular with	disliked by
3. **stumbling block**	physical injury	problem or difficulty	disagreement
4. **walks of life**	geographical areas	ages	positions in society
5. **in dire straits**	in extremely difficult situations	in physical pain	in financial trouble
6. **inner turmoil**	illness	personal distress	family issues
7. **serenity**	peacefulness	counseling	medicine
8. **in a rut**	stuck in the same place	depressed	in conflict with someone
9. **gain insight**	make friends	feel healthy	understand something
10. **see eye to eye**	agree	be friendly	look at each other

CREATE

Work with a partner.

Student A: Cover the right column. Ask Student B questions 1 through 4.

Student B: Cover the left column. Answer the questions, using the key words. Take time to think, using expressions for hesitation. Explain your ideas in detail. Use the information about Thomas Merton from the previous exercise. Then switch roles after question 4.

EXPRESSIONS FOR HESITATION

- Hmm, let's see now . . .
- Hmm, I'm not exactly sure, but maybe . . .
- Well, let me think for a minute . . .
- Well, that's a good question . . .

Student A

1. Can you understand why a young man with an interesting life would choose to go into a monastery?
2. Why do you think Merton was called "The Talkative Trappist"?
3. How do you think Merton's early volunteer work in New York City influenced his writing?
4. What impressed you most about Merton's life?

Now switch roles.

5. Why is Merton's work so popular with the general public?
6. How do you think the other monks at the monastery felt about Merton's writing career?
7. What part of Merton's life would you like to find out more about?
8. What impressed you most about Merton's life?

Student B

1. hectic, quest, well-being

   Hmm, let's see now, he had lived a very **hectic** life, but in his **quest**, he found that he needed solitude to achieve spiritual **well-being**.

2. refrain, draw out, over time, not see eye to eye
3. trace back, take on, foster, in dire straits
4. (Use any of the words from items 1–3 and one of the expressions for hesitation from the box above.)
5. notion, enact, foster, walks of life
6. over time, catch on, royalties
7. pull back, draw out, take on, stumbling block
8. (Use any of the words from items 5–7 and one of the expressions for hesitation from the box above.)

B GRAMMAR: Count and Non-Count Nouns and Their Quantifiers

1 *Work with a partner. Examine the statements, and discuss the questions that follow.*

- Very few spiritual **journeys** can compare to visiting the monasteries on Mt. Athos.
- With 20 monasteries and a limit of four days, it took Claassen quite a bit of **effort** to see more than six monasteries on one trip.
- Some monks are concerned about the growing number of **pilgrimages** to Mt. Athos these days.
- It takes a great deal of **discipline** to fast for a month.

1. Categorize the boldfaced nouns into count and non-count nouns.
2. What do the underlined expressions of quantity tell us?

COUNT AND NON-COUNT NOUNS

All nouns in English can be divided into two groups: count nouns and non-count nouns. **Count nouns** are those that can be counted and made plural (*monasteries, monks*). In contrast, **non-count nouns** can be considered as a mass and cannot be made plural (*spirituality, air*). Non-count nouns may refer to categories made up of different things (*money, furniture*), phenomena that occur in nature (*darkness, weather*), or abstractions (*violence, greed, honesty*).

Certain expressions of quantity, called **quantifiers**, state the amount of the noun. Some quantifiers are used with count nouns, and others are used with non-count nouns.

Quantifiers before Count Nouns	Quantifiers before Non-Count Nouns
a lot of	a lot of
many / a great many	a great deal of
quite a few	quite a bit of
a bunch of	a large amount of
a (large) number of	
certain	
not many	not much
very few (just a few / only a few)	very little (just a little / only a little)
a few / few	a little / little
fewer	less

GRAMMAR TIP: Notice the change in meaning when the indefinite article *a* is placed before *few* and *little*.

Few / Little

- negative meaning
- similar to *not much* and *not many*

A few / A little

- positive meaning
- similar to *some* (when talking about a small quantity)

Compare:

- *Few* people can fast more than three days in a row.
- *A few* people from our group decided to return to the monastery for another visit.

2 *Work with a partner. Decide if the nouns in the box are count or non-count nouns, or both. Write them in the correct column. If a noun is used as either count or non-count, write it in both columns. Seven of them are commonly used as either count or non-count nouns.*

consumption	gratitude	notion	stress
discipline	humility	pilgrimage	will
effort	impact	quest	work
faith	journey	soul	
fast	monastery	spirituality	

Count	**Non-Count**
______________	______________
______________	______________
______________	______________
______________	______________
______________	______________
______________	______________
______________	______________
______________	______________
______________	______________
______________	______________
______________	______________
______________	______________
______________	______________

3 *Read the sentences. Indicate if each boldfaced word is being used as a count (**C**) or a non-count (**NC**) noun. The words or phrases in parentheses give you a hint. Refer to the chart on page 136, and add a quantifier when appropriate. Use a variety of quantifiers. Put an **X** in the blank if a quantifier is not appropriate.*

1. a. __NC__ Obeying the rigorous routine and monastic rules requires __quite a bit of__ **discipline** (controlled behavior) on the part of the monks.

   b. __C__ __Certain__ **disciplines** (areas of knowledge or training) such as yoga, meditation, or fasting develop spirituality.

(continued on next page)

2. a. _____ Addicts being treated at the Wat Tham Krabok monastery must have ______________________ **will** (determination) to endure and succeed.

b. _____ Although the attorney works for the monastery, she doesn't write ______________________ **wills** (legal document to distribute someone's money and property) for the monks. Most monks have no material possessions to leave to anyone.

3. a. _____ Dr. Ahbar Ahmed put ______________________ **stress** (emphasis) on the importance of fasting to replenish the soul.

b. _____ According to Ahmed, fasting helps people pull back from their daily lives and thus have ______________________ **stresses** (worries).

4. a. _____ Monasteries sometimes produce ______________________ **works** (objects) of art which are commercially successful.

b. _____ The Spanish monks are well known for doing ______________________ spiritual **work** (activity) since they made it big in the music business.

5. a. _____ The nuns live in a dangerous, noisy, impoverished area of the city. So the sisters must put ______________________ **effort** (physical or mental energy) into maintaining their contemplative life.

b. _____ The area benefits from the nuns' food, blanket, and clothing distributions, in addition to ______________________ city-sponsored **efforts** (attempts) to improve the neighborhood.

6. a. _____ Wat Tham Krabok helps drug addicts from ______________________ different **faiths** (religions).

b. _____ Optimistic and determined, the Thai monks always have ______________________ **faith** (conviction, belief) in their treatment.

7. a. _____ The monks believe that regular and disciplined meditation replenishes the ______________________ **soul** (inner character).

b. _____ Many Buddhist monks perform good deeds so that after death their ______________________ **souls** (spirits) will return to a better life.

4 *Tibetan Buddhist nun Tenzin Palmo has frequently been interviewed as someone who has demonstrated spiritual genius. Her spiritual journey is the subject of two recent books.*

Work with a partner. Fill in the blanks with ***few, little, a few****, or* ***a little****. Then role-play the imaginary interview. Listen carefully, look at each other as much as possible, and say your lines like you mean them.*

Student A: You are the interviewer.

Student B: You are Tenzin Palmo.

INTERVIEWER: Ani-la,[1] I've come a long way to see you. Thank you for taking (1) ________________ time to talk to me. I am very grateful.

TENZIN PALMO: Thank you. It's a real pleasure to meet you. Tea?

INTERVIEWER: Yes, please. OK. Let's get started. You were the young English girl named Diane Perry, growing up in London's East End?

TENZIN PALMO: Yes, and I was your typical British teenager in the 1950s—rebellious, unfocused, and definitely having (2) ________________ or no interest in spirituality or religion.

INTERVIEWER: Then what happened?

TENZIN PALMO: Well, when I was 21 and a student at London University, I started to develop (3) ________________ interest in Eastern religions. I had become curious at university about Buddhism in particular, so I went to India on a spiritual quest. It was there I met my guru, my true mentor, Khamtrul Rinpoche. He spoke (4) ________________ words in English and had had (5) ________________ contact with Westerners.

INTERVIEWER: And then, is it true that within a month you broke up with your boyfriend, a man you had been engaged to for only (6) ________________ weeks?

(continued on next page)

[1]**Ani-la:** a special term that indicates full status as a Tibetan nun

TENZIN PALMO: Uh-huh . . . sad but true. My experience in India transformed me. I shaved my head, put on nun's robes, and entered a monastery. I was the only woman among 100 male monks.

INTERVIEWER: Other people had **(7)** ________________ faith that you could endure monastic life longer than a week, but you proved them wrong and stayed there for eight years, right?

TENZIN PALMO: Yes, until I went on my solitary retreat.

INTERVIEWER: Would you describe that retreat?

TENZIN PALMO: Sure. I lived alone as a hermit on a 13,000-foot (3,962-meter) mountain for 13 years. I ate very **(8)** ________________ food, mainly lentils and turnips. I slept upright on a small, wooden meditation box. I survived illness, wolves, freezing storms, even **(9)** ________________ very dangerous avalanches.

INTERVIEWER: **(10)** ________________ people, if any, could have survived not just the physical dangers, but the long periods of solitude. How did you do it?

TENZIN PALMO: I have **(11)** ________________ fear of death. The solitude awarded me a sense of infinite time and space.

INTERVIEWER: You have since built a convent school in northern India dedicated to girls, future nuns, who have had **(12)** ________________ opportunities for study and spiritual practice.

TENZIN PALMO: Yes, I run the school now and travel widely, speaking about girls' rights to achieve the same status as men in Tibetan Buddhism.

INTERVIEWER: I hope my book will bring you **(13)** ________________ publicity for your mission. Thank you, Ani-la, for speaking with me.

TENZIN PALMO: It's been a pleasure. Let's have more tea, OK?

C SPEAKING

PRONUNCIATION: Vowel Alternation

In some pairs of related English words, the vowel sounds shift or alternate. These words are pronounced quite differently.

1 CD 2 (22) *Listen to the difference between the underlined vowels in these pairs of words.*

divine–divinity	grateful–gratitude	compete–competitiveness
/ay/ /ɪ/	/ey/ /æ/	/iy/ /ɛ/

2 CD 2 (23) *Listen to the pairs of words, and repeat them.*

1. **a.** divine — divinity
   b. rite — ritual
   c. decide — decision
   d. write — written

2. **a.** grateful — gratitude
   b. explain — explanatory
   c. Spain — Spanish
   d. nation — national

3. **a.** compete — competitiveness
   b. keep — kept
   c. steal — stealth
   d. please — pleasure

3 *Work with a partner. Say the pairs of words. Circle only the pairs that have different vowel sounds. Say the circled pairs again. Write* **1** *if they alternate like* divine–divinity; *write* **2** *if the alternation is like* grateful–gratitude; *and write* **3** *if the alternation is like* compete–competitiveness.

_____ **1.** deal–dealt
_____ **2.** race–racial
_____ **3.** line–linear
_____ **4.** pervade–pervasive
_____ **5.** life–live
_____ **6.** nature–natural
_____ **7.** advise–advisor
_____ **8.** sleep–slept
_____ **9.** divide–division
_____ **10.** danger–dangerous
_____ **11.** sane–sanity
_____ **12.** faith–faithful

FUNCTION: Telling an Anecdote

Everyone loves to hear a good anecdote, or short story. Storytelling is one of the oldest, most basic methods for sharing information, knowledge, and experiences. In this short excerpt, the interviewer skillfully encourages William Claassen to share a few of his experiences visiting monasteries around the world.

1 CD 2 24 *Read the questions, then listen to the excerpt. Write short answers.*

1. What phrase does the interviewer use to encourage Claassen to tell his story?

   ____

2. Claassen uses the word *would* frequently while telling his story. How many times does he use *would*? Keep a tally:

   ____

3. What purpose does the repetition of *would* serve?

   ____

2 *Read the expressions to encourage someone to speak and to tell a story.*

ENCOURAGING SOMEONE TO TELL A STORY	TELLING THE STORY
• (Name), give me an idea of . . . • Why don't you talk briefly about . . . • Tell me . . . • I want to draw you out on the subject of . . . • Tell me about the time you . . .	• Well, I'll . . . • I remember when . . . • I don't remember all the details, but . . . • Let me begin. What I would do is . . . • Well, I'll pull in one example of the time . . .

3 *Prepare and tell an anecdote.*

1. Think of a story about a time you trained for something or disciplined yourself to accomplish a challenge over time.

   Examples

   training in martial arts, practicing a musical instrument, preparing for an exam, performing athletics, giving a big presentation

2. Make notes about the experience, and give your story a title. Rehearse your story by yourself. Use the expressions in the chart for telling a story. Use gestures, and practice good eye contact by looking in the mirror.

3. Work with a partner. Write down the title of your story and give it to your partner. Your partner will encourage you to begin your story using an expression from the left column. Then tell your story using expressions from the right column. When you are done with your story, encourage your partner to tell a story. Listen and take notes. Then tell your partner's story to another person in the class or to the whole class. Keep a tally of the number of times your partner uses the word *would*.

PRODUCTION: Group Discussion

In this activity, you will ***conduct a group discussion*** to debate the pros and cons of business expansion for a monastery. Try to use the vocabulary, grammar, pronunciation, and language for telling a story that you learned in the unit.*

Work in a small group. Read the information and case study, which are based on a real story. Then work in a small group, and follow the directions for the speaking activity.

BACKGROUND

Mepkin Abbey, located in the southeastern state of South Carolina, sits on 3,000 acres of beautiful country property. Since 1949, life there has been dedicated to the Trappist monastic traditions of solitude, prayer, work, and community. People who go on retreat to Mepkin learn the daily routine of the 45 monks who live there. However, retreats are not enough to keep the abbey financially stable. Economic renewal is proposed for the abbey—but are these plans at odds with a centuries-old way of ascetic life?

THE MONKS' SCHEDULE

3:20 A.M. Wearing hooded robes, the monks awaken in deep darkness. They gather in the church for two hours of prayer, chanting, singing, and meditation.

5:30 A.M. The monks greet the new day with more prayer, reading, breakfast, and simple chores.

7:30 A.M. They return to the church for more prayer.

8:30 A.M. The monks begin the morning work. Work includes:

- gathering eggs or making organic compost[1] for sale

[1]**compost:** a mixture of plants, leaves, etc., used to improve the quality of soil

(continued on next page)

*For Alternative Speaking Topics, see page 145.

- preparing food for the community of monks and guests
- working in the gift shop
- managing the hospitality–answering e-mail, updating the website, arranging for guests to visit Mepkin

Noon	Lunch is held in complete silence and is concluded by prayer and a reading.
1:45 P.M.	The monks rest.
3:30 P.M.	They work or study.
6:00 P.M.	They pray, meditate, or walk alone around the grounds.
7:35 P.M.	Closing prayer in the church is followed by sleep.

A New Abbot[2] Arrives

For many years, Mepkin Abbey was not well known. It is located in an obscure part of the state of South Carolina, notorious for its extreme heat, humidity, and abundance of snakes. The buildings and gardens were not maintained, and the chicken farm was outdated.

After decades of gradual decline, however, a new abbot assumed leadership, and over time things began to change. First he crafted a mission statement and a business plan. He convinced well-established financial institutions to contribute millions of dollars to Mepkin's renewal efforts. The result was the addition of a new chapel, library, air-conditioned dining room, and sleeping quarters for guests. Famous horticulturists created vibrant gardens, and zoologists humanely managed the snake population. Mepkin's chicken farm, before it closed under a cloud of controversy, generated annual revenues of more than $500,000, produced about 9 million eggs and 270 tons of organic compost. As a result of this outstanding performance, Mepkin had even won an award as the "Best Nonprofit of the Year."

As more and more people seek monastic retreats as a way to replenish hearts and minds, Mepkin's tourist business is catching on quickly. Mepkin now has more than 15,000 visitors a year who take advantage of its greatest resource: solitude and escape from the hectic outside world.

The Conflict

In spite of the highly successful tourist business, the abbot is now proposing another ambitious project, one that will require another $20 million in fundraising. He would like to build a state-of-the-art, revenue-producing retirement community on Mepkin land. The complex will support Mepkin's own aging community as well as provide limited housing to other elderly people wishing to live the contemplative life. The community will include an apartment building, 30 cottages, and a small health-care clinic with 80 beds.

The abbot's new notion has generated a great deal of debate. A group of monks within the Mepkin community, as well as some residents in the area, do not see eye to eye with the abbot. Some monks feel that the abbey is financially stable and should refrain from expanding. They feel that the fundraising will distract monks from their spiritual activities and foster materialism. These monks, as well as some local residents and farmers, worry that construction and possible overdevelopment will ruin the pristine

[2]**abbot:** a monk in charge of a monastery

landscape. They are urging the abbot to pull back on these development plans and instead take on beer- or bread-making industries successful in monasteries around the world.

The abbot and another group of monks feel the facility is needed. They believe that it will serve the retired monks and other elderly people, as well as help Mepkin become even better known and attract more visitors. A group of local business owners also supports the expansion because they hope it will bring more tourists and business activity to the area.

Speaking Activity

Divide into two groups: Those in favor of a retirement complex (Pro) and those against it (Con). Take on specific roles such as abbot, monk, resident, farmer, or business owner. List the pros and cons according to your character's point of view, and debate the issue. Use vocabulary terms from pages 131–132 and the quantifiers for count / non-count nouns on page 136. To illustrate your points, share anecdotes and encourage others to do the same, using the expressions on page 142.

Pro: ____

____

Con: ____

____

Example

I'm glad we're meeting today because there are **a lot** of concerns to discuss. Based on past experiences, I think there's **little** hope of improving our abbey by building a retirement community. **I remember one time** . . .

Discuss your reactions to the case with the entire class.

ALTERNATIVE SPEAKING TOPICS

Work in small groups. Read the introductions and the quotes on page 146. Work together to paraphrase the quotes, then discuss them. In your discussion, use ideas, vocabulary, grammar, pronunciation, and expressions for telling a story.

Expressions for Paraphrasing

In other words, . . .
The point she's trying to make is . . .
To put it another way, . . .
What he's trying to say is that . . .
What she means is that . . .

1. A modern doctor explains the spiritual practice of "quietude," intentionally remaining quiet, as a health-giving habit:

   "We have learned scientifically by carrying out the practices [of meditation, or prayer] for 10 to 20 minutes once or twice a day that the health—the mental health, the quietude—and the ability to deal with stress that the monks have can be captured by us within our busy lives."

   —Herbert Benson, MD, author of the book *Timeless Healing: The Power and Biology of Belief*

2. A famous monk focuses on "solitude," intentionally spending time alone, as spiritual renewal for anyone:

   "The aspect of solitude is important in every person's life; it's like a conversation or music. You've got to have space in between the notes, or it doesn't mean anything. The solitude is space between the notes."

   —Thomas Merton in his book *Thoughts in Solitude*

3. A writer describes her experience at St. Benedict's Monastery, where she lived for seven years:

   "I rose in the deep black of night—sometimes to blizzards, sometimes to shooting stars—to join the monks in chanting vigils, the night office. The monastic way of living slowly carves a crater in your heart."

   —Cynthia Bourgeault, journalist

4. A monk speaks about living in a monastery where a vow of silence is observed:

   "The battle . . . is defeating the noise inside you."

   —Father Michael Holleran, Carthusian monk

5. A fourth-century European monk explains the power of "common property" as a form of spiritual renewal in a monastic community:

   "No single man is sufficient to receive all spiritual gifts, but according to the proportion of the faith that is in each man the supply of the Spirit is given; consequently, in the common monastic life, the private gift of each man becomes the common property of his fellows."

   —St. Basil

RESEARCH TOPICS, see page 263.

UNIT 7 Workplace Privacy

1 FOCUS ON THE TOPIC

A PREDICT

1. Look at the cartoon. It shows employees arriving at their offices. The man says he is willing to give up civil liberties in order to gain security. However, he is worried that doing so might mean there will be few civil liberties left. Can you guess what he means by "civil liberties" and "security"?

2. What do you think of when you hear the word *privacy*? What does it mean to you? Brainstorm topics or words that may come up when discussing this issue, such as *snooping, confidential,* and *wiretapping.*

B SHARE INFORMATION

In a small group, discuss your answers to the questions.

1. Our ability to enjoy privacy often depends on the physical nature of the space we inhabit. Think about the home you grew up in and the home you are living in now. How does your sense of privacy compare in the two places? What factors make it easy or difficult to find privacy?
2. Think of different cultures you are familiar with. Comment on how the sense of privacy may differ. Think of home, school, and workplace. How much privacy do people expect? How is privacy protected?
3. When do you feel your privacy is being invaded? For example, would you feel your privacy was being invaded if ____?
   - **a.** an employer opened and read your office mail or e-mail
   - **b.** a colleague looked through your files, either on paper or on a computer
   - **c.** someone you just met asked your age, marital status, or salary

C BACKGROUND AND VOCABULARY

To keep up-to-date on workplace privacy and other important issues, many professionals write and read blogs (web logs) on the Internet. The following blog is a composite of information and opinion based on real blogs. On the blog, interested people bring up various aspects of workplace privacy, answering and raising questions. Readers then add their responses in order to conduct a public discussion.

CD2 25 *Read and listen to the blog and then match the boldfaced vocabulary with the definitions and synonyms that follow.*

http://albertohernandez.blogspot.com

THOUGHTS FROM A MANAGEMENT CONSULTANT
Alberto Hernandez

The views expressed here belong solely to the author and contributors.

Commentary and Discussion on Workplace Practice, Law, and Ethics

ABOUT ME

E-MAIL ME

CURRICULUM VITAE

DISCLAIMER

HOME

Workplace Privacy – News and Views

I thought I would spend time researching the latest news and views on the hot issue of workplace privacy and just share some of my findings with you, my loyal and intelligent readers. On Tuesday I will fly to Vancouver, British Columbia, in Canada, to deliver a speech at a conference focusing on international workplace privacy issues. Please read my summary below, and comment. I look forward to reading your thoughts.

First, let me briefly summarize the issue to date. Most **(1) employees**, from production line workers to managers, believe that an **(2) employer** has the right to **(3) keep an eye on** and evaluate the quality of their work. However, they feel that using cameras, computers, phone wiretaps, smart ID badges, or other forms of automated **(4) surveillance** is invasive and unnecessary. Furthermore, trying to control people's off-the-job behavior is clearly wrong. Employers argue that they need information about employees in order to make important decisions about quality and safety on the job.

So, what's the legal situation? In the United States, there are a few **(5) safeguards** to protect employees' privacy. The Fourth Amendment (1791) to the Constitution prevents the government from searching or removing things from one's home without proper permission. The Electronic Communications Privacy Act (ECPA) of 1986 prevents an employer from **(6) eavesdropping** on personal telephone conversations that take place during the workday. However, the act does permit **(7) legitimate** monitoring of business calls. The American Civil Liberties Union (ACLU) and other organizations are promoting ways to expand protections for Americans' privacy in the workplace.

Most countries have no laws about workplace privacy; others have a few protections. In France and Germany, for example, laws forbid the collection of information about an employee's political, religious, or union memberships. In Canada, employers must tell employees how personal information will be used. In Switzerland, employers must justify to employees any camera surveillance or monitoring of the workplace. In Hong Kong, there is a Privacy Commissioner for Personal Data to raise awareness of privacy issues for businesses and individuals. And in a recent survey, the people of Hong Kong ranked privacy the third most important social issue, behind air pollution and unemployment.

So, readers, what do you think? I look forward to hearing your thoughts, ideas, and experiences.

(continued on next page)

http://albertohernandez.blogspot.com/comments

ABOUT ME

E-MAIL ME

CURRICULUM VITAE

DISCLAIMER

HOME

Recent comments on this blog:

Marianne writes: ***15 hours ago***

Thanks, Alberto. Your blog is fantastic and so helpful. I just wanted to say that I have a sneaking suspicion that my employer is playing Big Brother.[1] My boss scans our office with video cameras, keeps **(8) a log** of all office phone conversations, tracks our location with cell phones and ID badges, and reads our incoming and outgoing e-mail. I think this surveillance has gone too far and is outside the **(9) scope** of a responsible business.

Marcel writes: ***12 hours ago***

In my company, we're forced to take drug tests **(10) willy-nilly**, without warning, and for no good reason. In this suspicious atmosphere, it's impossible to have a sense of pride and **(11) dignity** in my work. I feel **(12) demeaned** and disrespected. I can't understand what's **(13) driving** this increase in employee monitoring.

Roberto writes: ***6 hours ago***

I don't agree with Marcel or Marianne. There's nothing harmful or **(14) sinister** about these monitoring practices. As an employer, I have the right to know how my employees are using their time. On top of that, I use video cameras only to **(15) deter** theft. And I check employee e-mail to watch for any abusive language or **(16) racial slurs**. Come on—you know it's only for the employees' protection.

[1] **Big Brother:** a reference to George Orwell's novel *1984*, in which an all-powerful government controlled the minds and behavior of its citizens

_____ **a.** lawful; reasonable

_____ **b.** evil

_____ **c.** respectability, seriousness

_____ **d.** people who work for a company or organization

_____ **e.** listen to secretly

_____ **f.** prevent

_____ **g.** insulted

_____ **h.** the act of watching carefully or secretly

_____ **i.** insulting comments about a person's race

_____ **j.** causing

_____ **k.** unpredictably; without our choosing

_____ **l.** an official written record

_____ **m.** person or organization that you work for

_____ **n.** protections

_____ **o.** range

_____ **p.** watch closely and continuously

2 FOCUS ON LISTENING

A LISTENING ONE: Interview on Workplace Surveillance

You will hear an interview from the radio news program *Weekend Edition* that aired on NPR®. The interviewer, Elaine Korry, reports that workplace monitoring has increased dramatically in the United States.

CD2 26 *Work with another student. Predict the reasons you think workplace monitoring may be increasing. Then listen to the excerpt to check your list.*

_______________ _______________

_______________ _______________

LISTEN FOR MAIN IDEAS

CD2 27 *Read the questions. Then listen to Part One of the interview. Pause the audio and write short answers. Do the same for Parts Two and Three. Work with a partner, and compare your answers.*

Part One

1. How common is it for companies to monitor their employees at work?

____

2. What warning does Eric Greenberg of the American Management Association issue to employees?

____

3. According to Greenberg, what three things do employers have a right to know?

____

Part Two

4. According to Larry Finneran of the National Association of Manufacturers, what are some positive aspects of monitoring?

____

5. Why does Rebecca Locketz, a lawyer with the American Civil Liberties Union, oppose surveillance?

____

6. According to Locketz, what two safeguards should employees be entitled to?

____

(continued on next page)

Part Three

7. How does the 1986 Electronic Communications Privacy Act safeguard employee privacy?

____

8. According to some studies, what is the effect of electronic monitoring on worker performance?

____

LISTEN FOR DETAILS

CD 2 28 *Listen to Part One of the interview again. Read the sentences, and write **T** (true) or **F** (false) in the blank. Correct the false statements. Do the same for Parts Two and Three. Then compare your answers with those of another student.*

Part One

__F__ 1. Many attorneys believe that employees ~~should~~ do not give up their privacy rights when they go to work.

_____ 2. One-third of the 900 U.S. companies surveyed said they use surveillance methods to monitor their employees.

_____ 3. Greenberg is worried that 25 percent of companies spy on their work force without telling them.

_____ 4. In the last five years, the number of employees being monitored has increased by 50 percent.

_____ 5. Greenberg thinks workplace surveillance is morally wrong and should be stopped.

_____ 6. The U.S. Postal Service monitors the number of pieces of mail delivered correctly.

Part Two

_____ 7. The National Association of Manufacturers keeps a log of all employee phone calls for quality control purposes.

_____ 8. Sometimes employers listen in on phone calls to protect employees from sexual harassment and racial slurs.

_____ 9. Employees from the Chevron Corporation sued the company for sexual harassment.

_____ **10.** Locketz believes there are no legitimate reasons for workplace surveillance.

_____ **11.** The ACLU believes that employees don't have to be told when they are being monitored.

Part Three

_____ **12.** Few states allow surveillance in private places such as locker rooms or employee lounges.

_____ **13.** Under the Electronic Communications Privacy Act (ECPA), an employer cannot eavesdrop on an employee's personal phone calls.

_____ **14.** Under the ECPA, an employer cannot monitor the duration of an employee's phone call.

_____ **15.** According to attorney Penny Nathan Cahn, many employees are going to court to sue their employers if they think their privacy rights are being violated.

_____ **16.** Cahn believes that most juries are not going to be sympathetic or favorable toward companies that use surveillance methods without good reason.

MAKE INFERENCES

*Listen to four excerpts from the interview, in which the speakers express opinions on the topic of workplace privacy. Decide how strongly these opinions are expressed, and circle the corresponding number (**1** = not very strongly; **5** = very strongly). Then discuss your answers to the second question with a partner.*

CD 2 29

Excerpt One

1. Eric Greenberg warns that employees may be watched at any time. How strongly does Greenberg express his warning?	1 2 3 (4) 5
2. How do Greenberg's choice of words and tone of voice support your decision?	Choice of words: "Any employee," "anytime" Tone: Stresses "any," clear and decisive

(continued on next page)

Excerpt Two

3. Greenberg suggests that companies are acting like Big Brother when they do performance monitoring. How strongly does he believe this?	1	2	3	4	5

4. How does his choice of words support your decision?

Excerpt Three

5. Rebecca Locketz feels it's unnecessary to monitor employees' word processing output. How strongly does she believe this?	1	2	3	4	5

6. How do her choice of words and tone of voice support your decision?

Excerpt Four

7. Locketz believes there should be no monitoring in company rest areas. How strongly does Locketz express her opinion?	1	2	3	4	5

8. How do her choice of words and tone of voice support your decision?

EXPRESS OPINIONS

*Read the statements about the rights of employers and employees. Next to each statement, write **A** (agree) or **D** (disagree). Then, working in small groups, compare your answers with those of other students. Give reasons to support your opinions.*

An employer should have the right to _____.

_____ **1.** listen in on employees' work-related phone calls *without* telling them

_____ **2.** listen in on employees' work-related phone calls *but* tell the employees

_____ **3.** test employees for drug use if they hold *high-risk positions* such as airplane pilot, police officer, or firefighter

_____ **4.** test employees for drug use if they hold *low-risk positions* such as secretary, teacher, or computer programmer

_____ **5.** videorecord employees to monitor performance

_____ **6.** videorecord employees to prevent theft of equipment

_____ **7.** videorecord employees in rest areas such as locker rooms, employee lounges, and so on

_____ **8.** see employees' health records

_____ **9.** read employees' e-mail or office mail

B LISTENING TWO: Managers and Employees Speak Out

You are going to hear several people give their opinions on whether employers should monitor their employees while at work.

CD 2 33 *Listen to the four viewpoints on workplace monitoring. Listen again, and complete the chart as you listen. Then share your notes and reactions in small groups.*

POSITION	SUPPORTS OR OPPOSES	MAIN ARGUMENT	SUPPORTING ARGUMENTS	YOUR REACTIONS
1. *Owner of small data-processing company*	*Opposes*	*If employees are trusted, they will perform better.*	• *Surveillance causes loss of trust and morale.* • *People need freedom.* • *Happy people make happy, productive employees.*	Do you agree or disagree? Explain.
2.				How would you feel if you worked in this law firm?
3.				What's your position on making personal calls at work?
4.				Does an employer have the right to have access to your files and papers on your desk? Explain.

C INTEGRATE LISTENINGS ONE AND TWO

STEP 1: Organize

As you heard in the radio interview and the "person on the street" comments, there is a fine line between the employer's right to run a profitable business and the employee's right to privacy. Review Listenings One and Two and complete the chart.

TYPES OF SURVEILLANCE TOOLS	PROS	CONS	EXPLANATORY NOTES
Logging of personal calls	Cuts down on personal calls at work	Creates distrust or resentment toward employer	Some people might waste time on the phone, but some may work better if they can feel comfortable making calls at work.

STEP 2: Synthesize

Work in groups of three. You are members of an executive task force to develop a workplace privacy policy for a new software company with 300 employees. Consider each surveillance tool in the chart on page 156. Accept or reject it for the new company policy. Give reasons. Imagine your classmates are employees, and present the new policy to them.

3 FOCUS ON SPEAKING

A VOCABULARY

REVIEW

Work in groups of three. For each set of words, circle the two words that are related to the boldfaced word. Explain how the words in each group are related.

1. **scope** (range) (limit) importance

   These words relate to distance or measurement.
2. **legitimate** interesting legal justifiable

   ____
3. **concede** surrender meet give up

   ____
4. **morale** spirit confidence expectation

   ____
5. **surveillance** watching observing questioning

   ____
6. **demean** discourage disgust put down

   ____
7. **sinister** threatening evil illegal

   ____
8. **deter** discourage prevent distract

   ____
9. **drive** compel go along force

   ____

(continued on next page)

10. eavesdrop	show up	spy on	listen in on

____

11. willy-nilly	at random	quickly	haphazardly

____

EXPAND

The online Privacy Rights Journal *printed information on the Internet about a classic workplace privacy case at Nissan Motor Corporation. Working with another student, fill in the blanks in the newsletter with the correct form of the expressions from the box. Use the cues to help you.*

bug (v.)	keep tabs on	step up
cheap shot	leave . . . at the door	subject to
fine line	not have a leg to stand on	think twice about
foolproof	slippery slope	24-7
go that extra mile	snoop on	

Privacy Rights Journal—Cyberspace Issue **Volume 4** **Number 2** **Page 1**

Fact Sheet 27: Bourke v. Nissan Motor Corporation

WATCH OUT! Assume you are being observed in some way in anything that you do or say at your office!

That is the warning that Rhonda Hall and Bonita Bourke should have listened to five years ago. The two women worked as employee trainers at Nissan Motor Corporation. Traveling throughout the United States, they conducted training sessions for car dealers, sales staff, and mechanics. The women were competent, hard-working employees. Their supervisors had often commended them for ______________ (**1.** (making an extra effort)). They had handled a great deal of their business-related communication via e-mail. However, they did concede that at times, there was a(n) ______________ (**2.** (unclear distinction)) between business and personal matters. So, occasionally their online communications were chatty and informal, beyond the scope of business. They never really

______________________ sharing gossip or complaining about their boss.
3. (considered the problems with)

Their way of communicating was fine until doubts about the content of their e-mail were raised. Suddenly suspicious, their boss retrieved their passwords and began

______________________ their e-mail, which was full of insulting comments about him.
4. (secretly looking at)

Furious and offended, he immediately ______________________ his spying: He
5. (increased)

______________________ their phones and snooped around their offices. For
6. (put a secret listening device in)

several weeks he ______________________ them. He was confident that his surveillance
7. (observed carefully)

methods were absolutely ______________________ and that Hall and Bourke would be
8. (incapable of failing)

caught.

After three weeks of nearly ______________________ monitoring, Ms. Hall and Ms.
9. (constant)

Bourke were called in and fired. The news came totally out of the blue. Nissan claimed they were being fired for poor performance. Bourke and Hall immediately filed a formal complaint with top management. They said that the supervisor's surveillance was unfair, that it was "a(n) ______________________." They claimed they had reasonable
10. (unfair attack)

expectations that their e-mail would not be ______________________ monitoring. The
11. (open to)

women explained that eavesdropping practices create low morale among employees: "Workers can't just ______________________ their rights ______________________ when
12. (forget)

they come to work," said Bourke. Their lawyer insisted that Nissan's actions raised serious privacy concerns and that the company had started down a

______________________ towards civil rights violations.
13. (begun a process difficult to stop)

Nissan executives defended themselves by maintaining that the monitoring was legitimate because they owned the company system, and the employees' messages were written on company time. They said that when it comes to company e-mail privacy, the women ______________________.
14. (not stand a chance to win)

Unwilling to give up, the women sued Nissan Motor Corporation for invasion of privacy.

CREATE

1 *Work with a partner. Write the conversation that may have occurred when Ms. Bourke met with a senior manager at Nissan company headquarters to issue a formal complaint. Refer to the newsletter on pages 158–159. Assume the role of the Nissan manager or Ms. Bourke, and use the directions and vocabulary in the chart. Then give a dramatic presentation of the conversation to the class.*

DIRECTIONS, VOCABULARY	CONVERSATION
1. Nissan manager: Restate reasons for dismissal. **bug** **go that extra mile** **foolproof**	Manager: Good afternoon, Ms. Bourke. Please have a seat. As you know, . . .
2. Bourke: Express shock and surprise at monitoring. **snoop** **keep tabs on** **think twice about**	Bourke:
3. Nissan manager: State position on e-mail privacy. **24-7** **be subject to** **step up**	Manager:
4. Bourke: Express anger, and protest the policy. **cheap shot** **fine line** **leave at the door** **go down a slippery slope**	Bourke:
5. Nissan manager: Restate position more firmly. **not have a leg to stand on**	Manager:

2 *Work in a small group. Discuss what you think happened in the* Bourke v. Nissan *case. After you speculate, refer to page 258 for an explanation.*

B GRAMMAR: Verb + Gerund or Infinitive—Two Forms, Two Meanings

1 *Examine the sentences, and discuss the questions that follow with a partner.*

- When she found out she was subject to willy-nilly surveillance, she **stopped calling** her friends during office hours.
- When she realized how late it was, she **stopped to call** home and said she'd leave the office in 10 minutes.

1. What is the difference in meaning of the verb *stop* in the two sentences?
2. What other verbs can be followed by either a gerund or infinitive with a change in meaning?

VERBS FOLLOWED BY THE GERUND OR INFINITIVE WITH A CHANGE IN MEANING

Some verbs must always be followed by a **gerund** (base form of verb + *ing*). Other verbs must be followed by an **infinitive** (*to* + base form of verb). Others can be followed by either a gerund or an infinitive with no change in meaning.

However, certain verbs that can be followed by either a gerund or an infinitive do have a change in meaning. Sometimes the change is subtle; sometimes it is very obvious. Look at the verbs ***forget*** and ***stop***.

Verb	Meaning
***Forget* + gerund** He will never **forget having** his calls monitored. The experience was so demeaning.	To forget an experience—usually one that is particularly good or bad
***Forget* + infinitive** The manager was fired because he **forgot to write** a report about his staff's phone calls.	To forget to do something
***Stop* + gerund** She **stopped calling** her friends during office hours.	To stop doing something for an extended time
***Stop* + infinitive** When she realized how late she was working, **she stopped to call** home.	To stop doing something for a moment in order to do something else

NOTE: Some other verbs like this are ***mean***, ***quit***, ***regret***, ***remember***, and ***try***.

2 *Read the sentences. From the context, choose the best meaning of the boldfaced verb. Write the letter of the appropriate sentence next to the correct definition.*

1. **a.** To improve customer service, the company **tried** telephone monitoring for six months. Unfortunately it didn't work, so the company gave up.

   b. By keeping tabs on its employees' conversations with customers, the company **tried** to improve customer service.

   _____ experimented with

   _____ intended

2. **a.** The attorney convinced them to **stop** bugging employees' phones.

   b. The supervisor would **stop** to snoop on the new employee's calls every few hours.

   _____ finish in order to do something else

   _____ quit

3. **a.** I can't **forget** finding the wiretap on my phone.

   b. I **forgot** to complain about the static on my phone.

   _____ forget about something unpleasant

   _____ forget to do a task or duty

4. **a.** In court, he told the judge that he **remembered** having sent the e-mail message, but he didn't remember what was in it.

   b. Before leaving, he **remembered** to send his colleagues an e-mail message about the project.

   _____ remembered to do something (task or duty)

   _____ recalled

5. **a.** He **regretted** suing his employer because he'd worked there for 20 years. Getting fired was a cheap shot.

   b. The judge **regretted** to inform him that employees leave their privacy rights at the door.

   _____ regretted to tell someone something or do something

   _____ regretted something that happened in the past

6. **a.** His company stepped up surveillance every year, and after three years he **quit** working there.

   b. Things weren't going well at her job. Her morale was low, so she **quit** to travel around the world.

   _____ stopped

   _____ stopped in order to do something else

7. **a.** The employees knew that their top-secret work **meant** intense monitoring from the boss.

   b. The bosses **meant** to monitor only for security.

   ____ intended; planned

   ____ signified; involved

3 *For this role play, work with a partner. Fill in the blanks with the correct form of the word in parentheses. Then choose roles.*

Student A: You are a television news reporter interviewing a workplace privacy expert on the issue of pre-employment testing and workplace privacy.

Student B: You are Rebecca Locketz, legal director of the Workplace Privacy Project.

Read the conversation aloud. Listen to each other carefully, look up as much as possible, and say your lines like you mean them. Be dramatic.

Putting Job Seekers to the Test

REPORTER: Thanks for taking the time to speak to me, Ms. Locketz. I've heard that more and more businesses today are turning to pre-employment tests to try ______________ (**1.** match) workers to jobs.

MS. LOCKETZ: No problem. I'm glad to be here. Yes, that's right. The employee-testing business is booming. Employers are scared. They don't want to regret ______________ (**2.** hire) the wrong person.

REPORTER: Yes, actually, I remember ______________ (**3.** read) about Lori Miller, director of Boeing Aircraft's Child Care Center, a while ago. Miller had to hire 40 childcare workers in three weeks. This monumental task meant ______________ (**4.** test) and ______________ (**5.** interview) 200 candidates. Do you know this story?

MS. LOCKETZ: Yes, I do. I spoke to Miller at that time. She said the test was meant ______________ (**6.** provide) her with insight into the candidates. She worried she would forget ______________ (**7.** ask) certain questions.

(continued on next page)

REPORTER: Uh-huh, that's right. The test really simplified the hiring process. She didn't have to remember ________ (8. question) specific details about the applicant's background.

MS. LOCKETZ: Exactly. In Miller's case, the tests were used fairly. However, in some cases, pre-employment testing violates workers' privacy rights. So, our organization is now trying ________ (9. make) tests legal.

REPORTER: Are you suggesting employers stop ________ (10. administer) the tests completely?

MS. LOCKETZ: No. You misunderstood me. What I am suggesting is that they stop ________ (11. apply) the tests willy-nilly and ________ (12. ask) highly personal and inappropriate questions.

REPORTER: So, would you suggest that applicants simply quit ________ (13. take) pre-employment test if certain questions make them feel uncomfortable?

MS. LOCKETZ: Absolutely. If they don't, I guarantee they will soon regret ________ (14. reveal) information that could later be used against them. These tests are an invasion of privacy.

REPORTER: OK, thanks for the information, Ms. Locketz. We appreciate your taking the time to be on our show today.

MS. LOCKETZ: My pleasure.

4 *Work with a partner. Discuss: Have you ever been faced with a pre-employment test? How would you feel if you had to take a test before getting a job?*

C SPEAKING

PRONUNCIATION: Stress on Two-Syllable Words

Certain two-syllable words are stressed on the first syllable when they are used as nouns and on the last syllable when they are used as verbs.

1 *Listen to the statements. As you listen, place a stress mark (´) over the stressed syllable of the boldfaced words.*

- Companies **recórd** service calls.
- They keep **récords** of personal phone calls made by employees.
- The **object** of installing the surveillance equipment was to create a topnotch security system.
- I don't understand why any employee would or should **object** to that.

2 *Work with a partner. Take turns reading. Mark the stress (´), and write* **N** *(noun) or* **V** *(verb) after the boldfaced word. Then listen to the sentences to check your answers.*

1. The American Civil Liberties Union director was shocked by the **increase** (_____) in monitoring and was afraid that surveillance would continue to **increase** (_____).
2. We decided to **conduct** (_____) a comprehensive survey to evaluate employee **conduct** (_____).
3. The **object** (_____) of my presentation is simply to **object** (_____) to the use of secret surveillance.
4. The boss **suspects** (_____) that she is the only **suspect** (_____) in the case involving the stolen computer files.
5. She got a special **permit** (_____) that would **permit** (_____) her to see confidential employee information.
6. You have to keep a special **record** (_____) of every personal call you **record** (_____).
7. Why do you always **insult** (_____) me with all those **insults** (_____)? Just tell me how to fix the mistakes.
8. We're pleased with your **progress** (_____) in the job so far, but you'll have to **progress** (_____) even further before getting promoted.
9. As hard as I tried to settle the **conflict** (_____) with my boss, our opinions continued to **conflict** (_____) over certain key issues.
10. The company **projects** (_____) big profits from these **projects** (_____).

3 *Work with a partner. Look at the columns on page 166.*

Student A: Cover the right column. Use the cues to form a statement or question. Use the underlined word in the form indicated (verb or noun), being careful to clearly stress the appropriate syllable.

*Student B: Cover the left column. Listen to the statement or question. Mark the stress (´) of the key word. Then decide whether the word was used as a noun or a verb, and write **N** or **V** on the line. Then switch roles after statement 5.*

Student A

1. Question: conduct (verb) / survey / computer needs?

   Do you plan to conduct a survey to check the computer needs of the employees?

2. Statement: increase (noun) / theft / employee monitoring
3. Question: boss / suspect (verb) / bug the phones
4. Question: insult (verb) / in front of everyone
5. Statement: make / progress (noun) / protect / privacy

Now switch roles.

6. Statement: employees / object (verb) / video surveillance / locker rooms
7. Question: manager / permit (verb) / personal phone calls / company time?
8. Question: boss / keep / record (noun) / long-distance calls / a log?
9. Statement: lawsuit / conflict (verb) / privacy issues

Student B

1. condúct: V
2. increase: _____
3. suspect: _____
4. insult: _____
5. progress: _____
6. object: _____
7. permit: _____
8. record: _____
9. conflict: _____

FUNCTION: Framing an Argument

Speakers use special expressions to introduce their main ideas and to frame or focus their key arguments. Framing your argument makes it stronger and more sophisticated. Notice that these expressions are more interesting than "I think . . ." or "In my opinion . . ."

- **The real question is,** if we're not doing anything wrong, what do we have to worry about?
- **I mean, you would have to agree that** when you're in the office, you're not conducting your private life.
- **The point I want to make** has to do with trust.
- **Let me just pose a question here**: Isn't it a fact that we all take work home once in a while?
- **I would say specifically that** most employees have no idea their bosses are snooping on them.
- **The thing we need to look at is** the fact that balancing privacy and security is really a delicate matter.

Work with a partner.

Student A: Cover the right column. Ask Student B the question.

Student B: Cover the left column. Answer Student A's question. Argue your point, using the cues listed. Add your own ideas. Using several of the expressions on page 166, frame your argument. Then switch roles after question 3.

Student A	**Student B**
1. Should employers have the right to snoop into employees' e-mail?	**1.** Of course. E-mail _____. • systems belong to the company • monitoring discourages gossip • is really like a postcard **I would say specifically that** e-mail systems belong to the company. I wouldn't care if my boss snooped in my e-mail. I have nothing to hide, anyway. If we all know that our e-mail may be read, we wouldn't be likely to gossip or write love letters. **I mean, you would have to agree that** e-mail messages are really just like postcards.
2. Should employers have the right to monitor employees' off-the-job activities such as smoking, drinking, eating junk food, and engaging in dangerous hobbies like skydiving?	**2.** Definitely. These activities _____. • affect the health of the employees • cause employees to miss work • lead to high insurance rates
3. Should employers be allowed to have employees wear an "active badge," a small electronic card that is clipped onto the employees' clothing to keep track of their movements?	**3.** Sure. Why not? The badge will _____. • allow workers to use time better • tell supervisors where an employee is at all times • eliminate the need to look for workers if necessary

Now switch roles.

Student A	**Student B**
4. Should employers be allowed to install computer software that enables them to monitor employees' computer work?	**4.** I don't think so. Electronic searches create an atmosphere of _____. • "Big Brother is watching" • mistrust and fear • stress
5. Should employers do legitimate monitoring?	**5.** Absolutely. It's necessary to _____. • deter theft • control quality • enhance profits

PRODUCTION: A Debate

In this activity, you will ***debate a controversy*** over the use of biometrics. Try to use the vocabulary, grammar, pronunciation, and the language for framing an argument that you learned in the unit.*

Read the transcript below of an imagined interview that could have appeared in a local newspaper. Then refer to the transcript as you prepare a debate.

Background

Biometrics refers to a method of personal identification based on unique characteristics such as face recognition, fingerprint readings, or retina (eye) scanning. For years, we have only just imagined the role biometrics could play in our lives through spy thrillers, detective stories, and science fiction. However, now biometric technology is a reality, and it is used increasingly to monitor the actions of employees in the workplace, visitors to Disney World, children at day care centers, or college students in their "workplace"—the university campus. The use of biometrics is not without controversy. It raises serious privacy concerns because of the method and amount of data collection.

One university in the United States, the University of Georgia, relies on this technology for both student and employee identification.

BIG BROTHER IS WATCHING YOU!

University of Georgia enters the Orwellian world. Big Brother is Watching You! University of Georgia installs biometric identification for students and employees. Administrators hail the new system as a huge technical advance. Students and workers cry: "Invasion of privacy!"

Star Daily reporter Marylyn Rice interviews the president of the University to hear his views on the system.

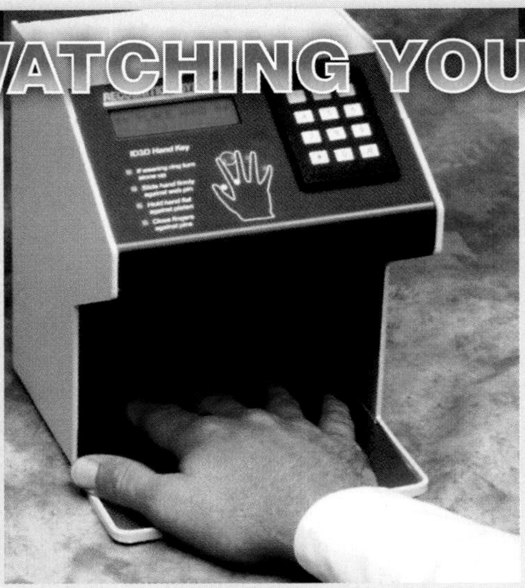

Rice: Sir, I appreciate your taking the time to meet with me.

President: My pleasure.

Rice: The university's use of biometrics for students and staff has received a great deal of media attention recently. Can you explain what kind of technology you are actually using?

President: Yes. We are using hand geometry to scan the students' and employees' hands. The system measures the length, width, thickness, and surface area of each hand. The students don't need pin cards or ID cards or

*For Alternative Speaking Topics, see page 170.

any other form of identification to gain access to science and computer labs, gymnasiums, dining halls, etc. The scanners are also used for our food service workers who punch in and out of their work shifts with the scanner.

Rice: Why did you initiate this system?

President: Well, it provides a greater degree of accuracy and security. We can safeguard our campus data more efficiently by controlling access to our computers and networks. If students are on the "all you can eat" meal plan, they cannot share their plans with students who may be on more limited plans. In addition, this saves time and money because students are always forgetting or losing their passwords and meal cards.

Rice: Has the system been successful?

President: Yes. We have been using it for several years now with over 30,000 students.

Rice: Well then, why all the opposition? The campus newspaper has been publishing highly critical articles claiming that hand scanning is a violation of privacy. They have even organized themselves into a group called SSAB, Students and Staff Against Biometrics. Have you heard about this?

President: Yes, I have, and I am interested in having an open debate and discussion with this group.

Rice: OK, well, are you aware of their concerns?

President: Of course. Basically, they claim that the use of hand geometry is a violation of privacy because it captures very personal data which can be used or abused. They also harbor a number of fears: 1) The system could create an electronic history in which all activities and locations could be tracked; 2) Students' biometric measurements would be recorded and saved and then used for other purposes in the future; 3) Hand geometry could lead to the use of other biometric measures such as eye prints. I heard that one of the food service employees was upset and said his body, including his hand, is private and belongs to him. I understand all these points and would welcome the chance to ease students' and employees' fears and discuss them with the group.

Rice: Hmmm … are you at all worried that the use of biometrics could lead down a slippery slope?

President: Not really. The thing I worry about the most is campus efficiency and security.

Rice: It sounds like there are many unanswered and complicated questions. I appreciate your speaking with me, sir. Thank you very much.

President: You're welcome.

Situation and Roles

1. Divide into two teams, and debate the controversial biometric system.

Team A: The president and campus security officials
Team B: Members of SSAB (Students and Staff Against Biometrics)

2. Working in your teams, analyze the interview for arguments. Add additional arguments, using information from the entire unit.

Team A: Supporters of the System	Team B: Opponents of the System
necessary for accuracy	*invasion of privacy*
__________	__________
__________	__________
__________	__________
__________	__________

3. Begin with two-person debates. Practice your arguments.
4. Start the whole class debate. Frame your arguments, using expressions from the Function section on page 166. Try to use the gerunds and infinitives from the Grammar section on page 161.

ALTERNATIVE SPEAKING TOPICS

Discuss the questions with the class. Use ideas, vocabulary, grammar, pronunciation, and the language for framing an argument.

1. Describe the amount and stated purpose of employee monitoring in your workplace or in workplaces you know. To what extent does the employer monitor computer, phone, or e-mail use? How do you feel about this? Refer to the cartoon on page 147.
2. Some workplaces implement surveillance devices (such as video cameras or telephone monitoring) for security reasons. How can companies balance the need for security with the individual's right to privacy? How would you feel about losing some of your privacy for the sake of security?
3. As an employee, how much and what kinds of monitoring would you be comfortable with?
4. As part of overall wellness programs and efforts to reduce the number of days employees are out sick, companies worldwide are initiating programs to protect both nonsmokers' and smokers' health. Many companies now prohibit smoking on company property or provide a "smokers only" area. One company in Michigan has even gone so far as to ban employees entirely from smoking even in their own homes. There is no law preventing the company from doing this. What do you think about this policy? What are the pros and cons? Can companies require employees to maintain a certain level of health, fitness, or weight? Why or why not?

RESEARCH TOPICS, **see page 263.**

UNIT 8

Warriors without Weapons

TODAY THERE ARE 4 GENEVA CONVENTIONS
THEY PROTECT:
THE WOUNDED AND SICK IN THE FIELD
THE WOUNDED, SICK AND SHIPWRECKED AT SEA
PRISONERS OF WAR
CIVILIANS IN TIME OF ARMED CONFLICT

1 FOCUS ON THE TOPIC

A PREDICT

1. Work in a small group, and look at the sequence of drawings and the title of the unit. What do you know about the International Committee of the Red Cross (ICRC) or local Red Cross organizations? What do you think the Geneva Conventions might be?
2. ICRC volunteers have been referred to as "warriors without weapons," or unarmed warriors. In your group, discuss why you think they are referred to in this way.

B SHARE INFORMATION

ICRC

The International Committee of the Red Cross now has three symbols that it uses internationally: the Red Cross, the Red Crescent, and the Red Crystal.

Read the information. Then work with a partner. Check (✓) the statements that are true for you or for someone you know. Then discuss the experiences.

Almost everyone recognizes the original symbol of the ICRC. It looks like the Swiss flag. Although the Red Cross was started by a Swiss citizen and its headquarters are in Geneva, the organization has no official ties to Switzerland. It is not related to the United Nations (UN), either. It is a completely independent organization which is funded by donations from public and private agencies and from governments. The ICRC is also the oldest humanitarian relief organization in the world.

Have you ever given blood or taken swimming lessons through a Red Cross-sponsored program? These are the best-known peacetime activities of the organization. The Red Cross also aids refugees and victims of such disasters as floods, fires, and famines.

Have you ever _____? If not, do you know someone who has _____?

_____ **a.** done volunteer work

_____ **b.** given or received first aid (temporary medical treatment given in an emergency)

_____ **c.** witnessed or experienced suffering caused by disasters such as fire, flood, famine, earthquake, hurricane, typhoon, tornado, or volcanic eruption

_____ **d.** fought in a war or lived in a country during wartime

C BACKGROUND AND VOCABULARY

CD 3 2 *Read and listen to the information presented on a well-known news site. Then, working with a partner, match each boldfaced word in the passage to the synonym or definition on page 174. Discuss your reaction to the neutrality idea.*

http://www.abouttheicrc.org

Brief History

Geneva Conventions

Neutrality

Search

International Committee of the Red Cross: A Brief History

In 1862, the wealthy Swiss businessman Jean-Henri Dunant proposed an international volunteer organization to care for the wounded on both sides of a battle. He wanted an international agreement that would give protection and **(1) legitimacy** to these tireless volunteers. Dunant had been inspired by the **(2) devastating** scene of thousands of dead Austrian, French, and Italian soldiers in a **(3) volatile** regional conflict of the time. He witnessed firsthand the horrific battlefield: bloody corpses, severed body parts, and wounded and dead horses. Shocked by the **(4) barbarism and savagery** he had witnessed, Dunant wrote a book, *A Memory of Solferino*, in which he explained his ideals and the need to care for war's sick and wounded without discrimination.

With his influence, Dunant persuaded the Swiss government to organize an international meeting to discuss his proposals. In 1864, representatives of 12 governments met and **(5) ratified** an agreement. It was the first version of the Geneva Conventions, the "rules of war," and represented the first attempt to **(6) institutionalize** guidelines for wartime behavior. Dunant's rules launched the beginning of the modern humanitarian law movement whose purpose is to civilize conflict.

Geneva Conventions

The original 1864 Conventions **(7) prevailed** until 1949, when several more were added to **(8) spare** the lives of wounded soldiers, prisoners of war, and of civilians during wartime. Now more than 190 countries **(9) subscribe to** the Geneva Conventions. The Red Cross devotes a great deal of effort to **(10) disseminating** information about the conventions.

COMITE INTERNATIONAL GENEVE
ICRC

(continued on next page)

Brief History

Geneva Conventions

Neutrality

Search

ICRC's Position on Neutrality

Dunant's ideas were met with skepticism and controversy. Some people thought his beliefs were **(11) counterintuitive**, going against a natural way of thinking. Critics did not believe that **(12) codes**, or laws of war, could help **(13) restrain** soldiers during conflicts. Yet Dunant argued that these laws are basic **(14) human universals**, with roots in every culture.

The ICRC's dedication to neutrality continues to provoke controversy today. Committed to aiding the wounded and sick on both sides of an armed conflict, the ICRC believes war should and can be controlled, but not abolished. Other humanitarian relief organizations disagree with the Red Cross's position. Instead of promoting the neutrality principle and the laws of war, these human rights organizations promote the UN's Universal Declaration of Human Rights (1948). If people's human rights are violated—as in torture, slavery, or lack of freedom of speech or religion—then these human rights organizations do not remain neutral. Instead, they denounce the abusers and help the victims. Among the best known of the human rights organizations are Amnesty International, Doctors Without Borders, and Human Rights Watch.

_____ **a.** likely to explode; tense

_____ **b.** communicating widely

_____ **c.** rules

_____ **d.** signed; officially approved

_____ **e.** save

_____ **f.** support and follow

_____ **g.** moral and legal acceptability

_____ **h.** existed; lasted

_____ **i.** values shared by all human beings

_____ **j.** completely destructive

_____ **k.** cruel and extremely violent behavior

_____ **l.** make generally acceptable; establish

_____ **m.** control

_____ **n.** illogical; unexpected

2 FOCUS ON LISTENING

A LISTENING ONE: Warriors without Weapons

You will hear an interview from a radio program, *Fresh Air with Terry Gross*, that aired on NPR® in the United States. Gross interviews Michael Ignatieff, author of a magazine article, "Unarmed Warriors," and a book, *The Warrior's Honor.*

CD 3 *Work with a partner. Predict what topics Ignatieff might deal with in this interview about his work. Make a list of the topics. Then listen to Gross's introduction to check your predictions.*

______________________ ______________________

______________________ ______________________

LISTEN FOR MAIN IDEAS

CD 3 (4) *Look at the key phrases. Then listen to Part One of the interview. When you hear the key phrases, add information about these topics. Do the same for Parts Two and Three. Share your notes with a partner.*

Part One

1. volatile regional wars: how war is changing—what that means for relief workers
2. controversies: ______________________________
3. two traditions in the humanitarian movement: ______________________________

Part Two

4. Geneva Conventions: ______________________________
5. the Gulf War[1], for example: ______________________________
6. standards of decency: ______________________________

Part Three

7. warrior tradition: ______________________________
8. men have to be trained: ______________________________
9. war and morality: ______________________________
10. warrior's honor: ______________________________

[1]In the Gulf War (August, 1990–February 1991) a coalition force of 35 nations authorized by the United Nations fought against Iraq following the Iraqi invasion of Kuwait.

LISTEN FOR DETAILS

Read the statements below. Then listen to each part of the interview, and circle the letter of the correct answer. Compare your answers with those of another student.

Part One

1. Ignatieff reported on the safety of _____.
   a. Red Cross workers
   b. regional armies
   c. civilians in war zones

2. Ignatieff wrote about the Red Cross because he wanted to _____ humanitarian relief work.
   a. understand
   b. get involved in
   c. recruit volunteers for

3. The tradition of the "laws of war" and the tradition of "international human rights" are _____.
   a. the same
   b. slightly different
   c. very different

4. The humanitarian movement does *not* include _____.
   a. laws of war
   b. human rights
   c. workers' rights

5. The Red Cross wants to enforce the "laws of war tradition," which means that the Red Cross _____.
   a. opposes war
   b. accepts war if fought with rules
   c. accepts only traditional war

Part Two

6. The Geneva Conventions have been ratified by _____ countries.
   a. 100
   b. more than 100
   c. fewer than 100

7. The Geneva Conventions do not protect _____.
   a. combatants who are not injured
   b. prisoners of war
   c. civilians

8. During the first Gulf War, the United States _____ the Geneva Conventions.
   a. did not follow
   b. followed
   c. questioned

9. Ignatieff refers to universal human values, which he believes you can find in _____.
   a. only European cultures
   b. all cultures
   c. only cultures with warrior traditions

10. To educate people about the Geneva Conventions, the Red Cross uses many methods. One thing it does *not* do is _____.
    a. tell the story in comic books
    b. read the Conventions on the radio
    c. translate the Conventions into many languages

Part Three

11. According to Ignatieff, in all societies the warrior's primary responsibility is to protect his _____.
    a. community
    b. traditions
    c. honor

12. In the tradition of warrior's honor, warriors are trained to _____.
    a. wound, not kill
    b. kill aggressively
    c. kill selectively

13. According to Ignatieff, many people in the modern world think war is _____ moral.
    a. sometimes
    b. never
    c. always

14. The warrior's honor is one of the oldest moral traditions in the world. The Red Cross wants to use this tradition to get combatants to _____.
    a. stop fighting completely
    b. fight with honor
    c. fight with control

MAKE INFERENCES

Read the statements. Then listen to the excerpts from the interview with Terry Gross, where Michael Ignatieff speaks about complex, abstract ideas such as war, warriors' honor, and human rights.

*Decide whether Ignatieff would agree or disagree with the statements. Write **A** (agree) or **D** (disagree) next to each statement. Then write a short explanation for your answer below the statement.*

CD 3 6 **Excerpt One**

_____ 1. Upholding the international human rights tradition is more important to the Red Cross than promoting the rules of war.

____

_____ 2. It is common knowledge that there are two equal traditions to the humanitarian movement.

____

CD 3 7 **Excerpt Two**

_____ 3. Waging a civilized war according to "rules" is an absurd idea.

____

CD 3 8 **Excerpt Three**

_____ 4. Standards of decency in warfare exist both inside and outside Western European culture.

____

CD 3 9 **Excerpt Four**

_____ 5. The Red Cross is using an element of warrior tradition, which is restraint, to reduce the negative humanitarian impact of war.

____

EXPRESS OPINIONS

1 *In the interview, Ignatieff discusses important controversies surrounding the ICRC. Recall the issues he discusses. Then read the statements, and decide whether you agree or disagree. Write **A** (agree) or **D** (disagree) next to each statement. Then, working in small groups, discuss your opinion about these statements.*

_____ 1. In order to do his or her job, a relief worker cannot take sides in a conflict.

_____ 2. War involves killing. Killing is morally wrong. Therefore, war cannot be made civilized by any codes.

_____ 3. The Geneva Conventions sound good on paper; however, they are impossible to enforce. A soldier's aggression cannot be restrained, controlled, or disciplined.

_____ **4.** The ICRC should be working toward abolishing war, not civilizing it.

_____ **5.** "War should always be waged with a view to peace." –Hugo de Groot, seventeenth-century Dutch scholar and diplomat

2 *Think of places in the world currently coping with conflict. What are the challenges of international relief organizations there? What do you think their role should be?*

B LISTENING TWO: Michael Ignatieff's Views on War

Listening Two is from the second part of the interview with Michael Ignatieff. Here he discusses how his study of the ICRC affected his personal views on war.

*Listen to four more excerpts from the interview. As you listen, mark the statements **T** (true) or **F** (false). Then compare your answers with those of another student.*

CD 3 10 Part One

Michael Ignatieff _____.

_____ **1.** protested against the Vietnam War during the 1960s
_____ **2.** was drafted into the Vietnam War
_____ **3.** changed his views on war after witnessing the Red Cross in action

CD 3 11 Part Two

In the Red Cross's approach, Ignatieff discovered that war _____.

_____ **4.** is necessary to human culture
_____ **5.** is never a good way to solve conflicts
_____ **6.** can sometimes free oppressed people

CD 3 12 Part Three

The rules that the Red Cross enforces are that armies must not _____.

_____ **7.** capture prisoners
_____ **8.** shoot at civilians
_____ **9.** kill anyone
_____ **10.** torture prisoners

CD 3 13 Part Four

Michael Ignatieff believes that the Red Cross's rules of war are _____.

_____ **11.** too simple and unrealistic
_____ **12.** barbaric because war itself is barbaric
_____ **13.** moral

C INTEGRATE LISTENINGS ONE AND TWO

STEP 1: Organize

Review Listenings One and Two. In Listening One, Ignatieff outlines the basic principles supporting the work of the ICRC. In Listening Two, he expresses his views on these principles. Fill out the chart with four key principles from Listening One and Ignatieff's view of them from Listening Two.

ICRC PRINCIPLES	IGNATIEFF'S VIEW OF PRINCIPLES
1. War must be fought according to certain rules.	ICRC must enforce these rules—don't shoot prisoners, make war on noncombatants, etc.
2.	
3.	
4.	

STEP 2: Synthesize

Imagine that your local university hosted a three-day conference on international humanitarian law. Michael Ignatieff gave the keynote address.

Work with a partner. Review the information in the organizing section and create a brief speech summarizing Ignatieff's keynote address. Include the principles of the ICRC and his views. Present your summary of the first two principles to another pair of students.

The other pair of students will check to see that you have included key points and views and give you feedback. Then they will present the last two principles and opinions to you and your partner, and you will give them feedback.

3 FOCUS ON SPEAKING

A VOCABULARY

REVIEW

Read the open letter that Dr. Sandra Martino wrote to the Star Daily. *A physician with the ICRC, Dr. Martino has been working in Africa for the past three months. After you read the letter, match each boldfaced word with a synonym or definition.*

To the Editor:

Thanks for your article on the ICRC. It's important that people all over the world be aware of its valuable work. For years, I had been **(1) drawn to** the idea of doing relief work. So, last year, after receiving my medical degree, I joined the International Committee of the Red Cross.

As I had grown up in a wealthy San Francisco suburb, I wondered whether I could do the job. Could I truly relate to and **(2) identify with** the **(3) devastating** misery of victims in war-torn regions? I questioned my ability to **(4) do without** the comforts of home and family that I took for granted. But more important, could I truly **(5) live by** the principles of the ICRC, especially the principle of neutrality?

My parents were firmly opposed to my decision to join the ICRC. My father had been a **(6) draft evader** and had participated in many antiwar demonstrations in Berkeley, California, during the 1960s. Raised as a pacifist, my mother has always **(7) equated** war with barbarism and believes that war has no **(8) legitimacy** whatsoever.

My parents had advised me to join the group Doctors Without Borders, a human rights group which provides medical relief to populations in need, including in **(9) volatile** war zones. However, I had studied the ICRC and the Geneva Conventions in college and was fascinated by the **(10) alternative ethic** of neutrality. What I'd like to **(11) get at** here is that the Red Cross is not just trying to help people in need but also remind people that during times of conflict, it is not honorable to **(12) unleash** aggression against innocents. The Geneva Conventions emphasize that we all share one moral tradition: the warrior's honor. In other words, "warriors" in all human societies must be trained to **(13) tame** and discipline their aggression. The **(14) codes** of the ICRC, the Geneva Conventions, are really simply **(15) house-and-garden** rules that remind people to follow the tradition of the warrior's honor.

In the ICRC, my role is not only to provide medical services but also to **(16) disseminate** information in a clear, meaningful way. I firmly believe that more people should know about what this organization does; more young doctors should sign up for service with it, too.

Sandra Martino, M.D.

_____ **a.** potentially violent

_____ **b.** follow

_____ **c.** express

_____ **d.** rules

_____ **e.** completely destructive

_____ **f.** attracted to

_____ **g.** release

_____ **h.** understand

_____ **i.** live without

_____ **j.** legal acceptability

_____ **k.** distribute; spread

_____ **l.** common-sense

_____ **m.** different moral principle

_____ **n.** strongly associated

_____ **o.** someone who avoids the military

_____ **p.** control

EXPAND

1 *Read the following statements, and then read about confusing pairs of words.*

- "There's a distinction between war and barbarism. And we should keep to that distinction and struggle to **ensure** it, and that's what the Red Cross tries to do."
  —Michael Ignatieff
- The Red Cross volunteer **assured** the families that food and water would be coming soon.

Ensure and ***assure*** are words that are often confused. To ***ensure*** means to make sure or certain that something happens. To ***assure*** means to tell someone that something will happen to lessen their worries.

CD 3 14 *Below are some confusing pairs. Some differ in pronunciation; others do not. Listen to the pairs, and repeat each one.*

1. accept / except
2. access / excess
3. advice / advise
4. affect / effect
5. assure / ensure
6. council / counsel
7. disinterested / uninterested
8. eminent / imminent
9. imply / infer
10. principal / principle

2 *Read the sentences. From the context, identify the meaning of each boldfaced word. Then write the letter of the appropriate sentence next to each definition.*

1. a. The volunteer **advised** his friend not to go into that volatile war zone.

b. Although she felt she should have gone onto the battlefield, she took her colleague's **advice** and her life was spared.

_____ an opinion about what someone should or shouldn't do

_____ give an opinion about what someone should or shouldn't do

2. a. Red Cross workers must **accept** the ICRC's position of neutrality.

b. Some people support all the ICRC's ideas **except** the principle of neutrality.

c. Jean-Henri Dunant, founder of the ICRC, **accepted** the Nobel Peace Prize in 1901.

_____ apart from

_____ receive

_____ agree to

3. a. According to the Geneva Conventions, the ICRC must remain a **disinterested** group in any conflict.

   b. In law school, she was **uninterested** in studying international codes of law.

   _____ impartial

   _____ not curious about

4. a. The **principal** reason that Ignatieff wrote about the ICRC was to understand its controversial position on neutrality.

   b. The ICRC is based on universal human **principles**.

   c. The **principal** insisted that all the teachers in the school receive some basic first aid training.

   _____ beliefs

   _____ main

   _____ director of a school

5. a. The aid workers had no **access** to that volatile zone because it was blocked by soldiers.

   b. Civilians and aid workers are thrilled to receive any **excess** food or medical supplies.

   _____ additional; extra

   _____ way to enter

6. a. The ICRC has a duty to **ensure** respect for international humanitarian law.

   b. The president **assured** the ICRC that the Geneva Conventions would prevail.

   _____ make sure or certain that something happens

   _____ tell someone something to lessen their worries

7. a. Ignatieff **implies** that he has become wiser since his antiwar days.

   b. From the interview, we can **infer** details about Ignatieff's past.

   _____ form an opinion; derive meaning

   _____ suggest indirectly

(continued on next page)

8. **a.** The original ICRC consisted of a small **council** of five Swiss citizens.

   b. The ICRC volunteer **counseled** the civilians not to drink the water until the wells were cleaned.

   c. The prisoner of war asked for some legal **counsel**.

   _____ give an opinion

   _____ opinion

   _____ official group

9. **a.** Traveling in war zones **affected** Ignatieff's views on war.

   b. He didn't realize that the experience would **effect** such a huge change in his thinking.

   c. Critics believe that the Geneva Conventions will have little **effect** on the conduct of warfare in the twenty-first century.

   _____ influence

   _____ cause to happen

   _____ consequence

10. **a.** On October 15, 1999, the **eminent** director of Doctors Without Borders, Dr. James Orbinski, accepted the Nobel Peace Prize on behalf of his organization.

    b. Once the terrorists attacked the water-treatment plant, everyone in the region knew that war was **imminent**.

    _____ threatening to happen soon

    _____ outstanding

3 *Work with a partner.*

Student A: Ask Student B a question. Check Student B's answer by referring to the correct answer in the parentheses.

Student B: Cover the left column. Answer Student A's question using the cues provided. Choose the correct word provided and use the correct form of it. Spell it if necessary. Add additional words to the cues when necessary. Then switch roles after question 5.

Student A

1. I heard you got typhoid shots before you went to Africa. How did you react to them? (Fine. They didn't affect me at all.)
2. What did your parents call you about? (They advised me not to go into that volatile war zone.)
3. What did the Red Cross workers tell the civilians? (They counseled them to stay inside until further notice.)
4. What drew you to the ICRC? (I respected the principle of neutrality.)
5. Did you hear about the demonstrations planned by Doctors Without Borders and UNICEF[1]? (Yes. I heard the protest against women's rights violations was imminent. It will happen tomorrow.)

Now switch roles.

6. Did she take sides in the negotiations? (Absolutely not. She remained disinterested.)
7. Have you completed all the necessary first aid training? (I finished everything except the part about treating snake bites.)
8. Why was the reporter angry? (He couldn't get access to the ICRC files. They were top secret!)
9. Do the Geneva Conventions prescribe exactly how to enforce the rules of war? (Not exactly. The rules themselves are clearly stated, but governments usually infer from the rules how to behave in a given situation.)
10. What did the Red Cross worker tell the prisoner of war? (He assured him that his message would be delivered.)

Student B

1. Fine. They didn't (affect / effect) me at all.
2. They (advice / advise) me not to go into that volatile war zone.
3. They (council / counsel) them to stay inside until further notice.
4. I respected the (principal / principle) of neutrality.
5. Yes. I heard the protest against women's rights violations was (imminent / eminent). It will happen tomorrow.
6. Absolutely not. She remained (disinterested / uninterested).
7. I finished everything (accept / except) the part about treating snake bites.
8. He couldn't get (excess / access) to the ICRC files. They were top secret!
9. Not exactly. The rules themselves are clearly stated, but governments usually (imply / infer) from the rules how to behave in a given situation.
10. He (ensure / assure) him that his message would be delivered.

[1]**UNICEF:** The United Nations Children's Fund

CREATE

1 *Another* Star Daily *reader, Dr. David Chan, responded "on air" to Dr. Martino's letter on page 181 in a radio call-in show. Work with a partner.*

Student A: Read the first half of Dr. Chan's "on-air" letter to your partner. Pause or say "blank" when you come to a blank space. Wait for your partner to say the missing word. Check Student B's answers with the correct answer in parentheses. Give your partner a hint if necessary.

Student B: Cover the letter. Listen to Student A, and fill in the on-air letter as Student A reads it. Choose from the words in the box. Then switch roles after the first half of the letter.

Student A

www.stardaily.com/lettertotheeditor

To the Editor

I would like to respond to Martino's comments from a different perspective. As a physician working for the organization Doctors Without Borders, I too have seen the _________ (devastating) effects of war going on in _________ (volatile) war zones. I agree with the ICRC in that soldiers must try to obey "_________ (codes) of honor," or rules of war. I do not _________ (equate) war with _________ (barbarism) and savagery. However, we members of Doctors Without Borders disagree with the ICRC in an important way.

Student B

barbarism
codes
devastating
equate
volatile

Now switch roles, and continue reading the letter.

We do not believe that a soldier's aggression can always be _________ (tamed) and controlled, since war by its nature _________ (unleashes) instincts and behavior that cannot always be restrained. It's simply unrealistic to think that soldiers will strive to _________ (live by) "rules of war," simple _________ (house-and-garden) rules that tell them how to behave. Therefore, we do much more than just _________ (disseminate) basic health-care information or bandage up the wounded. As doctors, there are times when we are forced to denounce human rights violations.

disseminate
house-and-garden
live by
tamed
unleashes

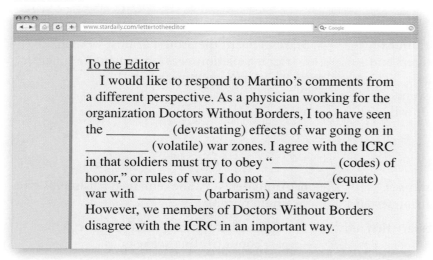

2 *Work with a partner. Ask and answer the questions.*

1. Which of Dr. Chan's ideas can you *accept*?
2. What does Dr. Chan *imply* about Dr. Martino? What can you *infer*?
3. What is a *principal* concern for Dr. Chan? What are his *principles*? Which *principles* of the ICRC do you most agree with? Most disagree with?
4. How would Dr. Chan *advise* a new doctor choosing between ICRC and Doctors Without Borders? What *advice* might he give him or her about doing international aid work?

Médecins Sans Frontières, known in English-speaking countries as Doctors Without Borders, is an international medical humanitarian organization. It was founded by doctors and journalists in France in 1971.

5. How might personal experience doing international aid work *affect* someone's viewpoint?
6. In order to be an international aid worker, what kind of training would a prospective candidate need *access* to?

B GRAMMAR: Direct and Indirect Speech

1 *Examine the passage, which includes both direct and indirect speech. Then answer the questions that follow.*

The interviewer, Terry Gross, asked Michael Ignatieff why he wanted to write about the ICRC. He replied, "As a group I was very drawn to them because I thought they could take me into the whole world of what involves people into that kind of humanitarian relief work." Terry wondered if he had always believed in the ICRC's principle of neutrality. He responded, "I was very involved in the anti-Vietnam protests that were centered in Toronto during the '60s."

Michael Ignatieff

1. Why do you think some of the statements have quotation marks and some do not?
2. What do you think are some of the differences between the direct quotations and the other statements?

DIRECT AND INDIRECT SPEECH

To add variety and interest when you tell a story or report information, use a combination of direct and indirect speech. **Direct speech** is a quotation of someone's exact words. **Indirect speech** reports or tells what someone said without using the person's exact words. When you use indirect speech, try to vary the reporting verbs. Choose expressive verbs such as ***complain***, ***mention***, ***remark***, ***answer***, ***reply***, ***predict***, ***deny***, ***explain***, ***wonder***, ***question***, ***add***, ***respond***, ***comment***, ***observe***, and ***continue***.

Look at the rules and examples for changing direct speech to indirect speech.

Rules	Direct Speech	Indirect Speech
Statements		
Shift tense back (for example, from past to past perfect). Make appropriate pronoun and adverb changes.	Dunant remarked sadly, "Yesterday we lost another 50 soldiers right here."	Dunant reported, with sadness, that on the previous day, they had lost another 50 soldiers in that place.
Questions		
Yes / No questions: Do not use ***say***. Use ***if*** or ***whether***.	Ignatieff asked the ICRC representative, "Can I record my interviews with the volunteers?"	Ignatieff asked the ICRC representative if he could record his interviews with the volunteers.
Wh- questions: Do not use ***say***. Use statement word order.	Ignatieff asked the volunteer, "How did you survive the tough Red Cross training?"	Ignatieff asked the volunteer how he had survived the tough Red Cross training.
Commands		
Use ***not*** + **infinitive** with negative commands or other imperative verb forms.	Dunant warned the soldier, "Don't shoot!"	Dunant warned the soldier not to shoot.

2 *Work with a partner.*

Student A: Read silently Part One of the conversation between an ICRC volunteer and the prisoner of war (POW) whom he is visiting in a detention camp. Then retell the story to Student B using direct and indirect speech and a variety of reporting verbs. (See previous page.)

Student B: Read Part Two of the conversation silently. After Student A has finished retelling Part One, retell the second part of the story using direct and indirect speech and a variety of reporting verbs. (See previous page.)

Then switch partners and roles.

Part One

VOLUNTEER: Hello. How are you doing? I'm here to collect your messages for your family.

POW: Thanks so much. But I have a question. Can I attach photos to my message?

VOLUNTEER: Yes, you can. However, let me warn you: Do not attach more than two photos, and be sure to protect them with something so they don't get damaged.

POW: Oh. Then, does that mean I can staple a little plastic bag to the message?

VOLUNTEER: Well, this is the first time anyone has ever asked me this question. Let me think. Yes, I guess it's all right with me. I can't imagine the prison censor would object.

Part Two

VOLUNTEER: But where did you get the plastic bag? You know, plastic bags are against prison rules.

POW: I traded ten cigarettes with the prison cook.

VOLUNTEER: Hmm. Well, what exactly are you going to put into this bag?

POW: Please, please, trust me. Don't worry. But I have to tell you: It's not for photos. It's for something more special than that.

VOLUNTEER: What do you mean?

POW: You see, I've been working in the prison gardens this year. I grew the most lovely azaleas in the world. I want to send some of the seeds to my wife. It's as simple as that.

C SPEAKING

PRONUNCIATION: Vowels

1 CD 3 15 *Look at the diagrams of the mouth, and listen to the words.*

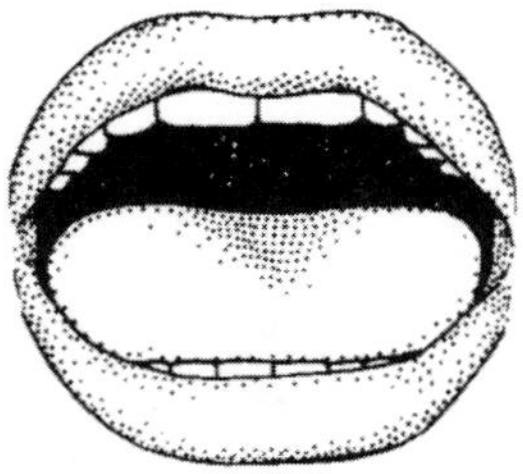

/æ/ cat

Your mouth is open.

Your lips are spread.

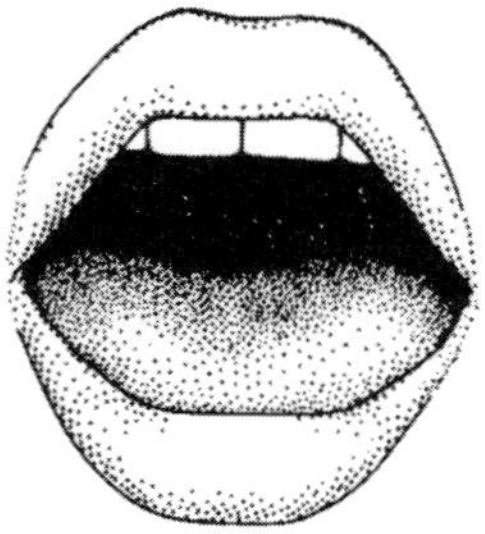

/ɑ/ cot

Your mouth is open wide.

Your lips are not spread.

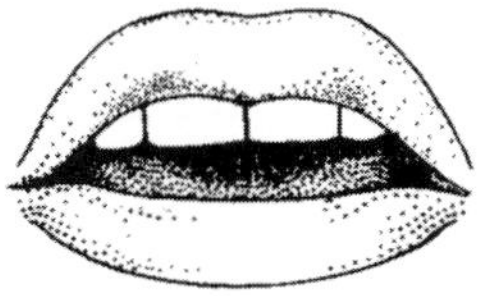

/ə/ cut

Your mouth is almost closed.

Your lips are not spread.

2 CD 3 16 *Listen to the words, and repeat them.*

	/æ/	/ɑ/	/ə/
1.	cat	cot	cut
2.	cap	cop	cup
3.	lack	lock	luck
4.	Nat	not	nut
5.	hat	hot	hut
6.	lag	lock	lug

3 CD 3 17 *Listen to the words from Exercise 2, and circle the words that you hear.*

4 *Work in pairs.*

1. Choose a set of words from Exercise 2, and say them to your partner. Your partner will check the shape of your mouth with the diagrams at the top of the page.
2. Say any word from Exercise 2. Your partner will point to the word. Then switch roles.

5 CD 3 18 *Listen and repeat the phrases. Then, working with a partner, write the phrase under the correct vowel pattern in the chart below.*

a bloody battle	floods and famines	natural disasters
a bloody struggle	government funding	a practical discovery
a challenging task	gun shots	public controversy
combatants' conduct	lack of money	savage attack
cultural values	love of country	a tough job

CUP–CUP /ə/–/ə/	CAP–CAP /æ/–/æ/	CUP–COP /ə/–/ɑ/	CUP–CAP /ə/–/æ/	CAP–CUP /æ/–/ə/
government funding				

6 CD 3 19 *A* tongue twister *is a phrase with many similar sounds that is difficult to say quickly. Listen to these tongue twisters. Practice saying them as quickly as possible.*

1. A block from the gun battle, the cops found a black bottle full of gasoline.
2. A lack of love and trust made him lock the clock in the closet.
3. Nat did not eat the nuts.
4. The big black bug bled black blood.

FUNCTION: Responding to Complex or Controversial Questions

Sometimes people ask complex or controversial questions that require thought before they are answered. To respond, use expressions to signal that the answer is complex and that you need time to think, and / or to give a partial answer.

In the interview, Terry Gross and Michael Ignatieff discuss complex issues such as war, neutrality, humanitarian law, and human rights. In this imaginary exchange between Gross and Ignatieff, notice the expressions he uses to respond to her questions. He uses an *opening phrase* to buy time, and then *follow-up phrases* to explain his answer.

TERRY GROSS: Michael, why is the ICRC spending so much time and money these days educating people about the Geneva Conventions?

IGNATIEFF: Well, Terry, **there's no simple answer to that. You might** say they are doing that to let people know how important their work is. **But you could also say** they feel they must inform people about the "rules of war" in order to lessen the amount of violence in certain conflicts.

Here are additional expressions you can use:

OPENING PHRASES	FOLLOW-UP PHRASES
Well, there's no simple answer to that ...	You might say ... (but you could also say ...)
Well ... that's a complicated issue ...	One way to look at it is ... (another way ...)
Hmm ... that's a tough one ...	You could think that ... (but perhaps ...)

Work with a partner.

Student A: Ask Student B the complex or controversial question.

Student B: Answer the question, using an opening phrase to buy time and follow-up phrases to answer. Then switch roles after question 4.

Student A

1. Do you think soldiers can really follow "rules of war"?
2. How can Red Cross workers witness horrible, unjust scenes and not take a stand?
3. Should the ICRC allow its volunteers to work in highly volatile and dangerous areas?
4. Working for the ICRC is so risky. Why would anyone want to do it?

Student B

1. Well . . . that's a complicated issue.
2.
3.
4.

Now switch roles.

5. Can people really learn about the Geneva Conventions and the "rules of war" through comic books, radio soap operas, or posters?

5. Hmm . . . that's a tough one.

6. Shouldn't ICRC workers be allowed to carry weapons as a form of self-defense?

6.

7. Don't you think the ICRC should work harder to eliminate war and not just limit war?

7.

8. The ICRC says it's not concerned with "justice," but simply "good treatment." What does this really mean?

8.

PRODUCTION: A Public Service Announcement

Public Service Announcements (PSAs) are short messages broadcast on television and radio. Their purpose is to inform the public of important health and safety issues. Generally, in the United States, nonprofit organizations produce public service announcements, and television and radio stations are required to broadcast them.

> In this activity, you will ***create a public service announcement about blood donation***. Try to use the vocabulary, grammar, pronunciation, and language for responding to complex or controversial questions that you learned in the unit.*

1 CD 3 20 *Listen to the American Red Cross's PSA about blood donations. The announcement is about a gift that would "go over really big," or be highly appreciated. Work with a partner, and discuss the questions:*

1. What is the message and tone of this PSA?
2. What title would you suggest for the PSA?

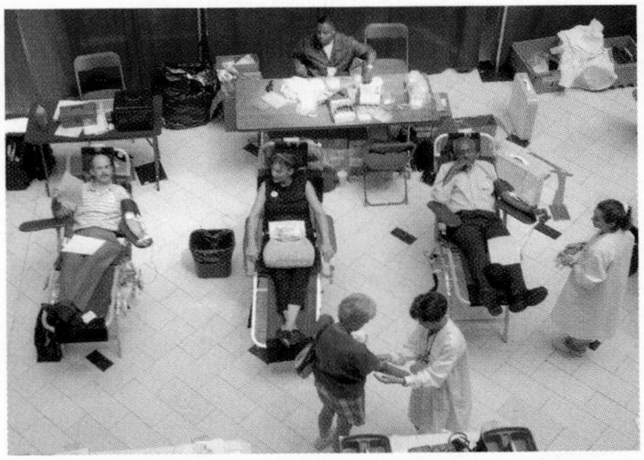

People donating blood at a blood drive

*For Alternative Speaking Topics, see page 195.

2 CD 3 21 *Listen again. Then fill out the outline of the PSA.*

Purpose: ______________________________

Sound effects: ______________________________

Opening line (used to grab the listeners' attention): ______________________________

____

Reasons for giving blood: ______________________________

____

Suggested action: ______________________________

3 *Work in groups of two or three. Write and present your own PSA about blood donations.*

1. Decide on a target audience, such as college students, first-time donors, or business people.
2. Write your PSA. Use the outline of the Red Cross PSA from the previous section as a guide. Include some of the following facts about blood donations in the United States in your announcement:
    - Fewer and fewer people are donating blood.
    - Blood is needed every day, not only for emergencies.
    - There are 40,000 units of blood needed daily.
    - The Red Cross **always** needs donations since there is a serious world shortage of blood.
    - If donors gave twice a year, there would be no blood shortages.
    - Some people donate blood in order to get cookies, candy, or doughnuts that are given after the blood is drawn.
3. Select music and sound effects to fit your target audience. Record your PSA.
4. Present your PSA to the class. Ask the other students to listen and discuss how effective its message is for your target audience.

ALTERNATIVE SPEAKING TOPICS

Working in a small group, discuss the answers to the questions. Use ideas, vocabulary, grammar, pronunciation, and phrases for responding to complex or controversial questions.

1. The ICRC strictly adheres to the principle of absolute neutrality. It takes no sides in a conflict; it makes no judgments, and its sole concern is the welfare of war's victims. On the other hand, Doctors Without Borders, another international human rights organization, will not assist countries or groups that violate basic human rights. If you were going to join one of these groups, which would you join and why? Discuss your reasons for your decision.
2. Should the ICRC be involved in helping both sides of a terrorist conflict?
3. Can people be taught about the "rules of war" through comic books and radio soap operas? What would be another effective means of education?
4. What would motivate someone to join the ICRC? What qualities, experience, background, or education do you think a new recruit should have? To check your guesses, go to www.icrc.org, and look for information about jobs with the ICRC.
5. Doctors Without Borders speaks out about human rights violations. Dr. James Orbinski, former head of that organization, said, "We don't know for sure whether words save lives, but we know for sure that silence kills." What does this mean? Do you agree or disagree? Support your ideas with specific examples.

RESEARCH TOPICS, **see page 264.**

UNIT 9

Boosting Brain Power through the Arts

"When I listen to Mozart, the numbers just seem to crunch themselves."

1 FOCUS ON THE TOPIC

A PREDICT

Look at the title of this unit. The *arts* refers to all the arts, including music, painting, sculpture, theater, dance, and so on. Look at the cartoon. To crunch numbers is a popular idiom meaning "to calculate." Why do you think listening to Mozart might make this man's job easier? Do you think this cartoon is funny? Why or why not?

B SHARE INFORMATION

1 CD 3 (22) *Some scientists have suggested that listening to classical music, particularly music composed by Mozart, may improve our ability to perform certain tasks. Listen to the excerpt from a piano sonata by Mozart, and discuss the question with a partner.*

What skills or abilities (for example, doing math) may be helped by listening to such music?

2 *Work in a small group, and discuss your answers to the questions.*

1. Think back. Did you have music and art lessons in primary and secondary school? How often? How important were they in the overall school program? Did you like them? Why or why not?
2. Outside of school, what other music or art training have you had?
3. What role do music and art play in your life today?

C BACKGROUND AND VOCABULARY

Scientists in many parts of the world are conducting experiments to explore the relationship between art and music, and intelligence. You are going to learn about three of these studies. Three important terms will be used in the descriptions of the studies:

- *control group:* a group studied in a scientific experiment; this group's behavior is not changed
- *experimental group:* another group studied in a scientific experiment; this group's behavior is changed and compared to the standard, the control group
- *spatial reasoning:* the ability to understand how things fit together in space and time (for example, putting together a puzzle)

1 CD 3 (23) *Step One: Divide into groups of three. Each student should choose one of the three scientific studies on pages 199–200. Read the study and take brief notes on a separate piece of paper. Then close your books, and use your notes to summarize the study to the group.*

Step Two: Listen to all three experiments. Write the appropriate number of the boldfaced word next to the definition on page 200.

Check your answers with your group.

Experiment 1 (Alpine Experiments)

Maria Spychiger and Jean-Luc Patry conducted the so-called Alpine experiments in Switzerland and Austria. The subjects were children, ages 7 to 15. Approximately 1,200 children were involved in the study, which lasted three years. The researchers wanted to investigate the ways in which music might (1) **enhance** math and language (2) **proficiency**.

Control group: Children received one or two music lessons per week and seven or eight math and foreign language lessons per week.

Experimental group: Children received five or six music lessons per week and only two or three math and foreign language lessons per week.

The researchers found that even though the experimental group received fewer math and foreign language classes, those children scored just as well as the control group children on certain math tests which required (3) **abstract reasoning**. More surprising, in spite of the reduction in language instruction, the experimental group scored better at foreign languages. In follow-up interviews with the researchers, the media reported that the children displayed greater (4) **self-esteem** and worked more cooperatively with each other, (5) **underscoring** the notion that exposure to music might have beneficial effects beyond math and languages.

Experiment 2 (University of California, Irvine)

Frances Rauscher, from the University of Wisconsin, Oshkosh, has been conducting studies for years examining the impact music has on the (6) **neurological** connections in the brain. Originality has been a (7) **hallmark** of Rauscher's groundbreaking work.

In one study,[1] she worked with 79 college students, ages 18 to 22, for two years. She wanted to find out if listening to the music of Mozart would affect the students' scores on tests of spatial reasoning. She used only one group in three sessions: two control sessions and one experimental session.

Control session 1: Students listened to a recorded message suggesting they imagine themselves relaxing in a peaceful garden.

Control session 2: Students sat in silence for 10 minutes.

Experimental session: Students listened to 10 minutes of Mozart's Sonata for Two Pianos in D Major.

After each 10-minute period, the students took a standard IQ (intelligence) test of spatial reasoning. Rauscher discovered that the students scored much higher on the spatial reasoning IQ test when they took it after listening to Mozart's music. Still, Rauscher says that it is difficult to design a program to improve brain functioning, to set up a precise (8) **sequential** order for such tasks. For that reason, she says there is still a great deal more to be done.

(continued on next page)

[1]Dr. Rauscher led this study while a professor at the University of California in Irvine.

EXPERIMENT 3 (UNIVERSITY OF CALIFORNIA, IRVINE)

In another study Frances Rauscher and her colleague Gordon Shaw worked with 19 three-year-olds for eight months. They wanted to study the effect of music, singing, and piano on spatial reasoning abilities. They had one control group and two experimental groups, which had well-defined (9) **interventions.**

Control group: Children received the regular (10) **curriculum**, which included a (11) **well-rounded** offering of many subjects, including some music and art.

Experimental group 1: Children received 30 minutes of singing lessons each day.

Experimental group 2: Children received 30 minutes of piano lessons each day.

At the end of the study, the children in the experimental groups scored 35 percent better on a spatial reasoning test than the children in the control group did.

The studies looking at this relationship have become the (12) **building blocks** for a solid, comprehensive analysis of the connection between music and the brain. However, the research also showed them that "music is a window to higher brain function."

_____ **a.** parts; pieces

_____ **b.** related to nerves

_____ **c.** confidence

_____ **d.** list of subjects taught

_____ **e.** special activities to prevent bad results

_____ **f.** improve

_____ **g.** emphasizing

_____ **h.** in a particular order

_____ **i.** ability to understand general concepts that cannot be immediately seen or felt

_____ **j.** complete and varied

_____ **k.** ability and skill

_____ **l.** outstanding feature

2 *In your groups, discuss your answers to the questions.*

1. Which results were the most surprising? Interesting? Explain.
2. In the University of California studies, the researchers chose the music of Mozart because it is repetitive and structured.
   a. Do you agree with the choice of Mozart? Why?
   b. What other composer or style of music could have been chosen? Why?
   c. What kind of music would not fit these criteria? Why?

2 FOCUS ON LISTENING

A LISTENING ONE: Does Music Enhance Math Skills?

You will hear an interview from the radio news program *All Things Considered*, which airs on NPR® in the United States.

CD 3 24 *Work with a partner. Brainstorm some answers to the question "Why do you think music may enhance mathematical skills?" Make a brief list. Then listen to a short segment of the interview to check your answers.*

______________________ ______________________

______________________ ______________________

______________________ ______________________

LISTEN FOR MAIN IDEAS

CD 3 25 *Read the questions. Then listen to Part One of the interview, and circle the letter of the correct answer to each question. Do the same for Part Two. Compare your results with those of another student.*

Part One

1. According to a recent study, music and art education can _____.
   a. increase students' appreciation of nature
   b. improve reading and math skills
   c. improve math but not reading skills

2. The purpose of the special arts program in Rhode Island was to _____.
   a. help students appreciate the arts
   b. make students' education more well-rounded
   c. investigate the impact of arts training

3. The special arts program in Rhode Island took advantage of children's natural inclination to master skills in _____.
   a. sequencing
   b. testing
   c. building

4. At the end of the test period, the researchers checked the children's _____.
   a. attitude
   b. test scores
   c. attitude and test scores

Part Two

5. Children who benefit from arts training are those with _____.
   a. involved parents
   b. artistic talent
   c. no special talent
6. Scientists have made some guesses as to how music may enhance mathematical skills. One factor *not* mentioned is that arts training _____.
   a. increases self-esteem
   b. relaxes nervous students
   c. teaches students how to learn new things
7. Scientists and educators are now more aware that a rich learning environment can help children _____.
   a. learn more
   b. become more artistic
   c. become more musical

LISTEN FOR DETAILS

CD 3 26 *Listen to the interview again. As you listen, fill in the chart on page 203 with the information about the two experiments described.*

		PART ONE	PART TWO
Researcher's Name			
Experiment Location			
Research Subjects (age/number of subjects)			
Purpose of Study			Impact of arts education on math ability
Frequency of Classes	Control Group	Standard curriculum music: _____ x/month art: _____ x/month	
	Experimental Group	Special arts classes _____ x/week	
Style of Instruction	Control Group	music lessons were: [check (✓) one] _____ active _____ passive	
	Experimental Group	arts program was: [check (✓) one] _____ active _____ passive	
Skills Taught: Art and Music	Control Group	Check (✓) two items: _____ went to concerts _____ listened to concerts _____ played music _____ talked about music	
	Experimental Group	Check (✓) two items: _____ sang together _____ sang alone _____ drew portraits _____ drew shapes	
Results		**1.** **2.** **3.**	**1.** **2.**

MAKE INFERENCES

*Work in a small group. Review the chart on page 203. Then listen to the excerpts about the two experiments. Based on these studies, researchers have given suggestions to schools and parents on ways to enhance children's brain power. For each excerpt, infer how you think these researchers might rank the items below in order of importance. Use the number **1** as the most important and **6** as the least important. Then discuss your judgments with students in your group.*

CD 3 27

Excerpt One

1. **What would researchers recommend?** If schools want to apply the Rhode Island research, they should _____.

_____ **a.** offer more music and art classes than math classes in the curriculum

_____ **b.** offer intensive music and art classes in kindergarten (age five)

_____ **c.** organize art and music exhibitions

_____ **d.** encourage parents to arrange for private music lessons

_____ **e.** invite visiting artists and musicians to lecture to the children

_____ **f.** have students write reports about famous musicians

CD 3 28

Excerpt Two

2. **What would researchers recommend?** If parents want to apply the results of Rauscher's research, they should _____.

_____ **a.** have pregnant mothers listen frequently to Mozart's music

_____ **b.** provide intensive music and art classes for children under age five

_____ **c.** provide computer lessons along with music lessons

_____ **d.** sing with their children

_____ **e.** give at-home tutorial math instruction

_____ **f.** take their children to recitals, operas, and concerts

EXPRESS OPINIONS

Follow the steps for noting and summarizing opinions.

Step 1: Look at the questions in the left-hand column. Quickly jot down your answers in the second column. Then circulate in the classroom and find two other students. Write their names in the top row, ask the questions, and take notes on their answers. Spend no more than three minutes with each of your classmates.

QUESTIONS	YOU	STUDENT 1	STUDENT 2
What new or surprising information did you find out from the interview with Michelle Trudeau?			
Besides art and music, what other things can boost intelligence? Food? Games? Meditation? Yoga? Why?			
In your opinion, in addition to increasing intelligence, how else might art and musical experiences help children?			
The research results indicate the importance of arts education in schools. However, most schools around the world emphasize reading and math proficiency over art and music. In your view, is arts and music education only a "frill," a supplementary activity to be added only if there's time and money?			

Step 2: Find two other students with whom you didn't speak and summarize your results.

B LISTENING TWO: Music, Art, and the Brain

Listening Two focuses on studies of babies. Here, David Alpern and Warren Levinson, hosts of the weekly radio broadcast *Newsweek on Air,* interview Sharon Begley, *Newsweek* magazine's science editor, about the relationship between music and art and the brains of very young children.

Listen to Part One of the interview. As you listen, take notes on a separate piece of paper about the ideas and examples expressed. Then rephrase the main idea in your own words. Do the same for Parts Two through Four. Share your summary statements with a partner.

CD 3 29 **Part One**

Things a Baby Is Born With

Example

beating heart

Restate: Basically, Sharon Begley is saying that when a baby is born, it has a beating heart but is still a work in progress.

CD 3 30 **Part Two**

The Relationship between Music and Math

Restate: So, in short, ______________________________

____

CD 3 31 **Part Three**

Warren's and Sharon's Reactions to the Research

Restate: In other words, Sharon and Warren feel that ______________________________

____

CD 3 32 **Part Four**

Things to Do with Your Child

Restate: In other words, Sharon suggests that ______________________________

____

C INTEGRATE LISTENINGS ONE AND TWO

STEP 1: Organize

Listening One contains reports on scientific studies of school-age children and young adults. Listening Two focuses on studies of babies.

Review your notes on pages 205 and 206 and fill in the chart.

	SCHOOL-AGE CHILDREN	VERY YOUNG CHILDREN (BIRTH–36 MONTHS)
Kind of intervention	More music and arts instruction, tapes, listening to music, discussions of music	
Effect of intervention		
Explanation of effect		

STEP 2: Synthesize

Work in groups of three. Conduct a discussion about the proposals. Take the roles below.

Student A: Education adviser to the mayor of a large city. The mayor wants to enhance music education in the preschools and elementary schools in your city. You have called a meeting with two experts to help you understand the benefits of music education. You will ask their opinions about the mayor's proposals.*

Student B: Expert in music education for school-age children. Based on research, comment on the proposals.

Student C: Expert in music education for babies and very young children. Based on research, comment on the proposals.

Mayor's Proposals

- Distribute free classical CDs to all families of newborns.
- Give out books about and music by Mozart to all families with children under the age of four years.
- Require 15 minutes of Mozart's music to be played prior to any standardized statewide examination.
- Offer free, once-a-week private piano or violin lessons for every two- or three-year-old child, for one year.
- Require all public preschools and day care centers (schools with children under the age of five) to play 30 minutes of classical music each day.

* Some of these are actual ideas and have already been implemented.

3 FOCUS ON SPEAKING

A VOCABULARY

REVIEW

Work with a partner. Match the boldfaced words in the sentences with a similar expression from the list on page 209. Write the corresponding letter in the blank.

_____ **1.** Scientists are **advancing** slowly toward an understanding of brain development in children.

_____ **2.** The students' intensive preparation in reading and vocabulary helps **boost** their test scores.

_____ **3.** The university applied the new rules to the student body **as a whole**, not just to the first-year students.

_____ **4.** After the accident, he fell behind in piano studies and never **caught up to** the level of the other children in his group.

_____ **5.** Many parents hope that their musical training has **primed** their children's brain circuitry to excel on mathematics exams.

_____ **6.** The parents of the young cellist want to buy the best instrument available, **regardless of** the price.

_____ **7.** A painter's **work in progress** often reveals more about the creative process than the finished painting does.

_____ **8.** Playing piano **did more for** the young woman's self-esteem than getting good grades in school.

_____ **9.** The student insisted that the wrong notes **had nothing to do with** lack of practice. The piece had sounded much better at home.

_____ **10.** The music and publishing industries **reaped benefits** from the media's overblown attention to the "Mozart Effect."

_____ **11.** A Stanford University study **found** that musical training can improve the reading ability of children who have certain reading problems.

_____ **12.** The Stanford study concluded that musical learning and mastery **enhances** the regions of the brain responsible for processing sounds.

_____ **13.** The **hallmark** of the M.I.N.D. curriculum is the effect of piano keyboard and computer training on standardized math scores. More than 13,000 students in more than 67 schools have seen dramatic increases in test scores.

a. benefited

b. didn't involve

c. entirely

d. increase

e. progressing

f. reached

g. unfinished product

h. without considering

i. concluded from data

j. got advantages

k. prepared

l. improves

m. outstanding feature

EXPAND

1 *Work with a partner. Read the sentences. Put an **L** next to the sentence if the boldfaced word or expression is being used in a **literal** way, and put an **F** next to the sentence if it's being used in a **figurative** way. Then, using the context clues, explain what the expression means in the sentence.*

1. a. __F__ Early interventions might be having some effect in children knowing how to **attack** new material (Andrea Halpern, Listening One)

Explanation: **Attack** is used in a non-physical way. It's not a literal attack. The word creates a picture in your mind. In this sentence, attack means "set to work on" or "approach."

b. __L__ The army **attacked** the opposing forces.

Explanation: **Attack** is used in a physical way. Here, it is a literal attack. It means "used violence against."

2. a. _____ After the performance, the audience gave the singer **a big hand**.

Explanation: ______________________________

____

b. _____ The pianist's **big hands** allowed him to play the difficult chords in romantic music.

Explanation: ______________________________

____

3. a. _____ The composer **orchestrated** his pieces for only string and brass instruments.

Explanation: ______________________________

____

(continued on next page)

b. _____ The museum director **orchestrated** the contract with intelligence, skill, and persistence. Her strategy was successful.

Explanation: ____

____

4. a. _____ The **wiring** in this lamp is so old it could start a fire.

Explanation: ____

____

b. _____ Warren Levinson said that the **wiring** for music and math is in the same part of the brain, right next to each other.

Explanation: ____

____

5. a. _____ When speaking to the architects who were designing her art studio, the artist said that she needed many **windows** in order to see color in natural light.

Explanation: ____

____

b. _____ According to Warren Levinson, the notion that so many **windows** in the child's brain are closed so early may be frightening for parents.

Explanation: ____

____

6. a. _____ Levinson and Begley both felt that parents may have already **blown** it if their children have not been introduced to music and art by the age of seven.

Explanation: ____

____

b. _____ While she was practicing the electric organ, the electricity went out. The instrument may have **blown** a fuse.

Explanation: ____

____

7. a. _____ Parents will sometimes **blow up** at their children when they misbehave.

Explanation: ____

____

b. _____ Police suspect that the terrorist group may **blow up** another car.

Explanation: ____

____

8. a. _____ The pianist's hand was **scarred** after he burned it.

Explanation: ____

____

b. _____ The father forced his child to practice eight hours a day. That experience was painful and **scarred** the child for life.

Explanation: ____

____

2 *Work with another student.*

Student A: Ask Student B questions 1 through 4.

Student B: Cover the left column. Answer Student A's questions. Respond in as much detail as possible, using the cues given and incorporating figurative language as much as possible. Then switch roles after question 4.

Student A	**Student B**
1. When was the last time you went to a concert or show and gave the performers **a big hand**? Describe the performance.	**1.** Hmm. Let me see, . . .
2. Have you ever **orchestrated** anything? A party? A meeting? A sports event? What did you have to do?	**2.** Yes, I remember . . .
3. What is your strategy for **attacking** new material in English?	**3.** Well, one idea I have . . .
4. Were you interested in the fact that the **wiring** for both music and math is in the same area of the brain? Why?	**4.** Yes, because . . .
Now switch roles.	
5. Do you agree with Warren Levinson that it's a bit scary to find out that **windows** for learning close so early in life? Why?	**5.** Well, maybe . . .
6. Have you ever **blown** an important test, presentation, job interview, business deal, etc.? Describe what happened.	**6.** Of course. One time . . .
7. When was the last time you **blew up** at someone? What happened?	**7.** Hmm. I'm not sure I remember all the details, but...
8. Very scary movies often frighten young children out of their wits. Do you think these experiences **scar** them for life? Why or why not?	**8.** Let me see . . .

CREATE

Form teams of two to four players. All teams will play the game described below.

WORD GAME: CLEAN THE BOARD

Object of the game: To be the first team to "clean the board," or remove all cards from the large piece of paper, the "game board."

How to Play the Game

1. Each team copies the game board onto a larger piece of paper. It should have two columns and three rows as shown in the picture on the left below.
2. Each team chooses six words from the list and writes each one on a small card. Place them face up over a different box on the game board. Each team may choose different words or expressions.

advance	boost	have to do with
attack	catch up to	orchestrate
be primed to	do more for	reap benefits
a big hand	enhanced	regardless of
blow	found	windows
blow up	hallmark	work in progress

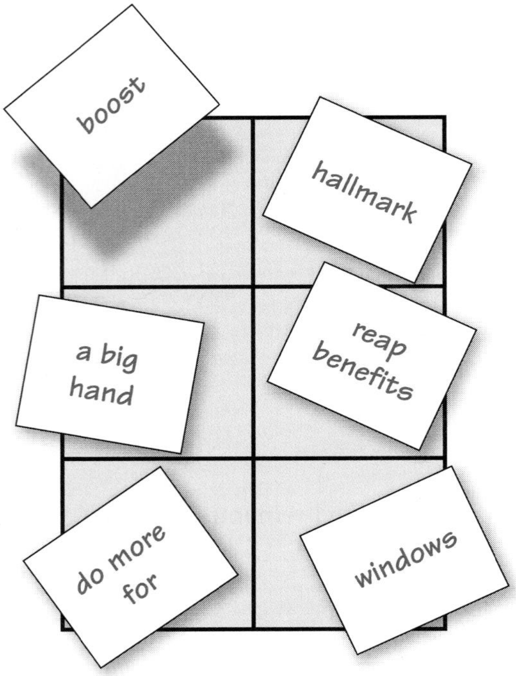

Game board

3. All teams play at the same time. The object is to clean the board as quickly as possible. This is how a team works to clean the board: One student on each team asks the teammate(s) a question and tries to get his or her teammate(s) to answer it using one of the words on the board. If the teammate(s) choose a correct word to answer the question, the card from the board is removed.

Example

Teammate One: "How do you feel about winning the Best Young Writer's Award?"

Teammate Two: "Great! It *boosted* my self-esteem."

A correct word, *boosted*, was chosen, so Teammate One removes the word from the board.

4. The winning team is the one that cleans the board (removes all its cards) first.
5. Play again. Start over using different words from the list.

B GRAMMAR: The Passive Voice and the Passive Causative

1 *Work with a partner. Examine the sentences, and discuss the questions that follow.*

- In one study, a group of three-year-olds **was given** singing lessons while another group **was given** piano lessons.
- A lot of the brain research **has been done** on animals.
- A mistake **was made** in the printed program. The sonatas by Mozart **will not be played**.
- Before the concert, we had the piano **tuned** and **got** the lights **repaired**.

1. In each sentence, why do you think the speaker chooses the passive voice for the verbs?
2. In the last sentence, who is performing the action?

THE PASSIVE VOICE AND THE PASSIVE CAUSATIVE

How to Form the Passive Voice

The **passive voice** is formed by using a form of the verb ***to be*** plus the past participle of the main verb. The verb *to be* can be used in any tense, as illustrated below.

Subject	Form of the Verb *To Be*	Past Participle	Complement
The students	**are**	**given**	a well-rounded education.
His self-esteem	**was**	**enhanced**	by the new arts curriculum.
Intervention	**will be**	**needed**	if things don't improve.
The curriculum	**is going to be**	**improved**.	
The pieces	**must be**	**practiced**	before the performance.
The neurons	**might have been**	**stimulated**.	
Spatial reasoning	**is being**	**improved**.	

(continued on next page)

When to Use the Passive Voice

The passive voice is used when you:

- Want to emphasize the object of the action, not the actor
- Do not know the actor
- Want to avoid mentioning who performed the action or to avoid blaming anyone
- Want to report an idea or fact

Passive Causative

The **passive causative** is used to speak about services arranged.

It is formed by the verbs **get** or ***have*** and the past participle of the main verb.

- Ms. Diaz is organizing an art exhibition of her students' work. With special funds collected for this purpose, she **had** the paintings **mounted** on special paper. She also **had** the works **framed**. Finally, she **got** the school lobby **cleaned** and **set up**.

2 *Complete the paragraphs with the appropriate forms of the verbs provided. Choose active or passive forms, including passive causative. Keep in mind that some verbs cannot be used in the passive voice. Then discuss your reaction to the study.*

Piano or Computer: Which Boosts Intelligence?

There is exciting new research about the effects of musical training on intelligence. Currently the effects of piano lessons on young children <u>are being researched</u> (**1.** research) by Frances Rauscher of the University of Wisconsin.

Whether children can learn more from a piano keyboard or a computer keyboard __________ (**2.** study). Last week, a report on this research __________ (**3.** appear) in the journal *Neurological Research.* It said that certain aspects of a child's intelligence __________ (**4.** can / enhance) by musical training, particularly by piano study. Spatial reasoning skills __________ (**5.** can / improve) by work on a piano keyboard, but not on a computer keyboard.

In one of Rauscher's recent studies, 78 young children __________ (**6.** involve). They __________ (**7.** divide) into four groups of

subjects. Some of the children ______________________ piano keyboard lessons,
8. (receive)

some computer lessons, and others group-singing lessons. No special training ______________________ for the fourth group. By the end of six months, the piano
9. (provide)

keyboard children ______________________ instruction in muscle coordination,
10. (give)

simple compositions, and musical literacy. Rauscher claimed that the children ______________________ enough training to be able to play simple pieces, like Beethoven's "Ode to Joy."
11. (give)

The final step in the research ______________________ of a test of analytical
12. (consist)

reasoning skills. Rauscher ______________________ the results ______________________ by research assistants. Then she
13. (collect)

______________________ the data ______________________ by a highly
14. (analyze)

sophisticated computer program. An important finding ______________________.
15. (emerge)

The children who ______________________ in piano keyboard training scored
16. (instruct)

significantly higher on the test than the children in the other three groups.

Therefore, Rauscher ______________________ that, regardless of the fact that a
17. (conclude)

keyboard ______________________ for the computer group, the children who used
18. (use)

a piano keyboard still ______________________ higher on the test.
19. (score)

The research underscores the fact that the piano ______________________ to
20. (seem)

be the critical ingredient. In musical training, the brain circuits ______________________ in such a way that certain nerve pathways
21. (may / stimulate)

______________________. These pathways ______________________ to be the
22. (strengthen) 23. (appear)

same ones that ______________________ when spatial reasoning tasks
24. (fire)

______________________. Nevertheless, in order to confirm these results, Rauscher
25. (perform)

______________________ the study ______________________ by other researchers.
26. (repeat)

3 *Work with a partner.*

Student A: You are a reporter for Music Times Newsletter. *You are writing a story about a child who displayed extraordinary talent at a very young age. The prodigy is Tanya Moreno, a 13-year-old violinist who could play works by classical composers at the age of four. You are interviewing Tanya's mother. Cover the right column. Read the questions in the left column. Change the boldfaced verbs to the passive voice as you read.*

Student B: You are Ana Moreno, Tanya's mother. You have dedicated your life to supporting your daughter's musical training. Cover the left column. Read the responses in the right column. Change the boldfaced verbs to the passive voice as you read.

Listen carefully, look at each other as much as possible, and read your lines with feeling.

Student A	**Student B**
1. Thanks so much for taking the time to speak with me.	**1.** Oh, it's my pleasure.
2. So, how **be** Tanya's interest in violin **spark**?	**2.** I'm not really sure. She **might / inspire** when she **give** a violin at the age of two.
3. **Be** she **push** to **play**?	**3.** Absolutely not! She **encourage**, but not **push**. In fact, she had been playing for over two years before she **identify** as a gifted musician.
4. Do you mean it took two years to identify her talent?	**4.** Unfortunately, yes. It **should / notice** earlier, but I just wasn't paying attention.
5. I **told** that at the age of four, you **have** a tape **make** of a recital and this tape **send** to a famous school in New York City. Is that correct?	**5.** Yes, it is. Then she immediately **ask** to enter the school at the age of five.
6. Have you been guiding and supporting her career, or **have** that **do** by her teachers?	**6.** No, her teachers only teach. All other details **handle** by me alone. Before a concert, we sometimes have to **have** her violin **repair**. We always **get** her dress **dry-clean** and **have** photos **take**. There's so much that **must / do**.
7. I hear now that she may **have / be / choose** to participate in a concert at the Royal Academy Hall in London.	**7.** Yes, at this time she **consider** for the position. If she **be / choose**, she'll be the youngest performer ever to **have / invite**.
8. Good luck to you both. I'm sure she **will / select** and then her picture **will / print** in newspapers all over the world.	**8.** Thanks for interviewing me. I hope you'll hear Tanya play sometime soon.

C SPEAKING

PRONUNCIATION: Joining Final Consonants

Words that end in final consonants join to following words in different ways.

- When the next word starts with a vowel: Join the final consonant and vowel clearly.

  Self‿esteem works‿in progress

- When the next word starts with the same consonant or sound: Hold one long consonant. Do not say the consonant twice.

  Art teachers enhance skills

- When the next word starts with a different consonant: Keep the final consonant short. Hold it, and then immediately say the next word.

  Crunch numbers attack problems

1 CD 3 33 *Listen, and repeat the phrases. Then practice saying them with a partner. Pay attention to how you join the two words together.*

1. music appreciation
2. art education
3. critical ingredients
4. parental involvement
5. music class
6. top performance
7. math theories
8. abstract topics
9. math proficiency
10. reap benefits
11. research findings
12. geometric shapes

2 CD 3 34 *Listen, and repeat the phrases. Using the rules for joining consonants, mark each phrase: ‿ or ⁀‿ or). Then complete the sentences with the correct phrases. Compare your answers with those of a partner. Take turns saying the sentences.*

art classes	an interactive approach	self-esteem
boost brain power	logical thinking	standard curriculum
a critical ingredient	research challenge	typical lesson

1. In most music classes around the country, listening to CDs or a lecture is really the ______________________.
2. The researchers found that music has a general effect of improving a child's self-image and ______________________.
3. Just how and why music and art enhance certain mathematical skills continues to be a ______________________.
4. Some classes got the special arts curriculum; others received the ______________________.
5. The children learned to draw shapes and deal with colors and forms in the ______________________.
6. Arts education seems to be ______________________ in improving analytical reasoning.
7. Studies done in the past seven years indicate that studying music and art can significantly ______________________.
8. Communication, discussion, and involvement are hallmarks of ______________________ to education.
9. Neuroscientists believe the brain works similarly when people perform tasks requiring spatial reasoning and ______________________.

FUNCTION: Expressions That Link Sentences or Ideas

Notice the boldfaced words or phrases in the sentences.

- Students listened to tapes and concerts and talked about music in class. **In contrast**, the special arts classes met twice weekly and got students involved.
- Music appears to stimulate certain brain cells involved in logical thinking and spatial reasoning. **Likewise**, mathematics seems to activate these same brain cells.
- Three experiments done by the psychologist are **similar in that** in all three, spatial reasoning proficiency was enhanced. They are **different, however, in that** one involved 18- to 22-year-olds and the other two involved preschool children.

The boldfaced phrases are common expressions used to make **transitions of similarity and contrast** that link sentences and ideas. When we speak, it's important to use these transitions to show how ideas are similar or different.

Similarity	**Contrast**
Likewise,	In contrast,
Similarly,	However,
. . . is similar to . . . in that	. . . is different from . . . in that

Working with a partner, examine the chart on the next page. It summarizes four studies. Make statements about the information under each heading. Compare and contrast the experiments using the transitional expressions above. Share your responses with each other.

Example

The Hong Kong study **is similar to** the Providence study **in that** it included six- and seven-year-old children.

The Hong Kong study used children—5- to 15-year-olds. **In contrast**, the Harvard study used adults.

EXPERIMENT LOCATION	RESEARCHER'S NAMES	AGE OF RESEARCH SUBJECTS	LENGTH OF STUDY	PURPOSE OF STUDY	RESULTS OF STUDY
#1 Switzerland Austria	Maria Spychiger and Jean-Luc Patry	7 to 15 years old	3 years	Effect of music on math and language ability	Math and language skills improved.
#2 Hong Kong	Agnes Chan and colleagues	5 to 15 years old	6 years	Effect of music training on the ability to remember a list of words	Ability to remember lists of words improved.
#3 Providence, Rhode Island, USA	Martin Gardiner	6 to 7 years old	7 months	Effect of arts education (music and art) on math and language ability	Math and language skills improved.
#4 Harvard University, Cambridge, Massachusetts, USA	Christopher Chabris	18 to 22 years old	8 months	Effect of Mozart's music on intelligence	Spatial reasoning skills did not significantly improve.

PRODUCTION: A School Board Meeting

In this activity, you will ***conduct a school board meeting*** about the role of arts education in a public school and the funding for it. Try to use the vocabulary, grammar, pronunciation, and language for linking sentences and ideas you learned in the unit.*

*For Alternative Speaking Topics, see page 223.

Follow the steps.

Step 1: Read the background information and case study based on a real news report.

Background

In the United States, public schools are administered and financed by local governments. Each local district has a school board, a group of citizens who are elected by the voting residents of the town. One of its most significant responsibilities is to determine the local school budget, the yearly financial plan of how the school district will spend money allocated for the local school.

Money to support public school education comes from a variety of sources: local taxpayers, state governments, and the federal government. In recent years, many public schools have had to deal with smaller and smaller budgets. The cost of services is rising, and the state and federal governments are contributing less financial support. Therefore, many districts are struggling to maintain a high-quality educational program.

Case Study: School Board Proposes Drastic Cuts in Arts Program

One school district in Illinois is in the process of developing its yearly budget. However, this year the district must work with 30 percent less money than it has had in the past. The state of Illinois has severely cut back on the amount of money it usually gives to the local districts. In order to save money, the local school board has already decided on a number of actions: (1) mandatory early retirement for 17 teachers, (2) elimination of physical education classes in the middle school and high school, and (3) elimination of foreign language instruction in the elementary school (kindergarten through sixth grade).

However, now the board is saying that these cuts are not enough. Now they have proposed the elimination of all art and music classes from the elementary school curriculum.

Parents are outraged. Angry discussion can be heard everywhere throughout the town: on downtown streets, in supermarkets, at the YMCA and soccer fields, and so on. Parents are demanding that the board reconsider its decision.

Because of all the complaints, the board has agreed to hold open forum meetings to discuss the proposal. It has invited representatives from three groups to attend the meetings: (1) parents, (2) art and music teachers, and (3) school board members.

Step 2: Prepare for the meeting. Everyone in the class should choose a role: parent, teacher, or school board member. Divide into groups of students all playing the same role. In your role groups, study the descriptions that follow, and brainstorm other supporting arguments. Write your arguments on separate pieces of paper.

Parents

- want to keep art and music classes in the school curriculum
- do not wish to pay extra to provide private art or music lessons
- feel art and music instruction inspires appreciation of the arts and provides a break from academic instruction

Art and Music Educators

- believe in the research findings from California and Rhode Island
- feel that it's important for children to have many ways to express themselves
- feel that arts instruction can improve perceptual skills and motor coordination

School Board Members

- feel that art and music instruction is a frill, a non-academic extra
- feel the arts do not have the rigor or importance of math, science, or reading
- think parents should be responsible for this instruction

Step 3: Conduct the meeting. During the meeting, all students should use the passive voice and expressions of similarity and contrast whenever appropriate. One student leads the meeting. This leader:

- opens the meeting by introducing the participants and explaining the purpose
- conducts the meeting by eliciting comments and questions from the participants
- asks a representative from each group to present a two-minute summary of the group's position
- closes the meeting by presenting a short summary of the meeting; asks for a vote on the issue of cutting school funding for arts

Step 4: Summarize the issue. Write an editorial letter to the local newspaper voicing your concerns about the cuts to the arts education program. Emphasize the important role that art and music play in the lives of all children.

ALTERNATIVE SPEAKING TOPICS

Work with a partner. Read the quotes by great artists and thinkers from the last three centuries. Follow the steps.

Step 1: Paraphrase the quotes (use different words to express the same ideas).

Step 2: Select your favorite quote and explain what it means to you. Use expressions that link sentences and ideas.

Step 3: Select a quote as a slogan for encouraging arts in education. Explain your choice.

1. "Art is both creation and recreation."
—Lin Yutang, Chinese writer and inventor

2. "Art enables us to find ourselves and lose ourselves at the same time."
—Thomas Merton, Catholic monk, philosopher, and author

3. "I once had the nerve to ask Picasso the question 'What is art?' He answered, 'Art is a lie which makes us see the truth.' "
—James Dickey, American poet

4. "Art evokes the mystery without which the world would not exist."
—René Magritte, French artist

5. "Art and the approach to life through art, using it as a vehicle for education and even for doing science is so vital that it is part of a great new revolution that is taking place."
—Jonas Salk, American biologist and physician

6. "The veracity of 'art for art's sake' is more accurately expressed as 'art for our sake.' "
—Ché Baraka, African-American painter

7. "Art is a necessity—an essential part of our enlightenment process. We cannot, as a civilized society, regard ourselves as being enlightened without the arts."
—Ken Danby, Canadian artist

8. "Art knows. Art sees beyond . . . Art points us in new directions that make us think and question."
—Warren Criswell, American artist and animator

RESEARCH TOPICS, see page 264.

UNIT 10

Microfinance: Changing Lives $50 at a Time

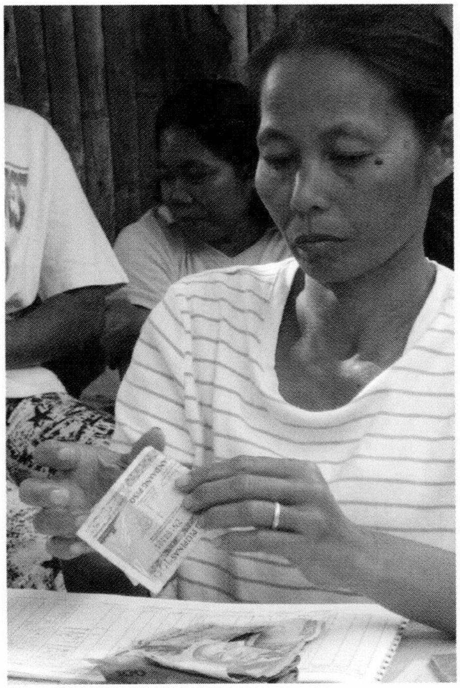

1 FOCUS ON THE TOPIC

A PREDICT

1. Three billion people—roughly half the world's population—live on less than two dollars a day. Why are so many people poor? Why is it so difficult for people to escape from poverty?

2. The photos above show one approach to fighting poverty: establishing small businesses through microfinance. Based on the information in the photos, what do you think microfinance is? How effective do you think it might be?

B SHARE INFORMATION

Governments, organizations, corporations, religious groups, and private individuals have tried for years to find the best way to lift people out of poverty. There is a great deal of debate over which approach to alleviating poverty is the most effective.

Work with a partner. Look at the chart. It presents a variety of programs designed to tackle the problem of poverty. Evaluate and classify each approach as **Most Effective**, **Somewhat Effective**, *or* **Least Effective**. *Give reasons for your views.*

APPROACH / PROGRAM	DESCRIPTION	MOST, SOMEWHAT, OR LEAST EFFECTIVE	REASON FOR YOUR VIEW
Government-based loans (World Bank, International Monetary Fund, HPIC Initiative)	Governments work together to provide loans to poor countries for economic development or for projects such as education, housing, and agriculture. They may also reduce debt payments of poor countries to increase the government's chances of helping people move out of poverty.		
Government-based aid (direct aid)	Rich countries give a percentage of their national income to poorer countries.		
Global businesses (Wal-Mart)	Large trans-national corporations open factories and employ thousands of local people.		
Microfinance	Organizations or small banks provide tiny loans to poor people to help them start or expand small businesses.		

Anti-poverty campaigns championed by famous celebrities (Bill Gates's and Bono's projects)	Celebrities raise money for direct aid to countries, as well as urge canceling of international debts.		
Private agencies and organizations (Oxfam, Heifer International)	Agencies raise private money and donate to poor countries or individuals to improve education, health, and agricultural resources. They may also provide livestock or agricultural training to support sustainable agricultural growth.		
Personal loans / gifts	Individuals loan or give money or aid directly to people in need.		

C BACKGROUND AND VOCABULARY

1 CD 3 35 *Read and listen to this website interview with the director of a microfinance institution (MFI) to learn some of the basic concepts and vocabulary of microfinance. Transformation International is a fictional organization, but it is based on characteristics of many real organizations. Discuss your reactions to microfinance.*

www.TransformationInternational.org

10 Questions for Sylvia Otero

Director of leading microfinance institution Transformation International, Sylvia Otero discusses microfinance and her bold efforts to raise the poor out of poverty.

What exactly is Transformation International? *Edward Montgomery, Kansas City, Kansas*

Sylvia Otero: Well, like other international microfinance institutions, our mission is to provide financial services to the very poor. We believe that many people are poor because they have no control over capital—meaning money or property (buildings, equipment, machines, tools, etc). Now, without capital, the poor do not have any way to make money and businesses can't start or grow. So, what we do is we offer loans or credit to people who have **no** access to traditional financial services. We do **not** give charity or handouts.

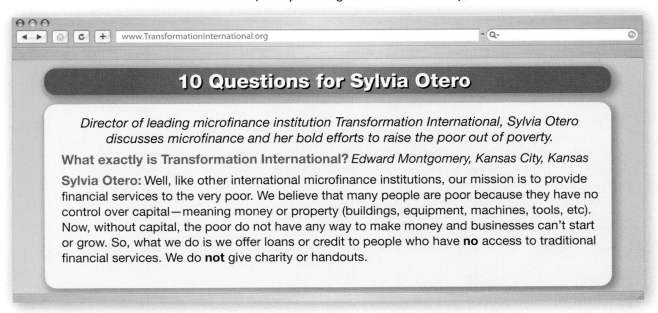

Your motto is "Changing Lives $50 at a Time." What does that mean?
Maria Orozco, Bogotá, Colombia

SO: Well, basically our key service is microcredit. And, it is a simple idea: "The smaller the loan, the greater the impact." So, basically we give tiny loans of $40 to $100 to very poor people, mostly women, in developing nations. Each woman uses the money to open or expand a small, simple business, a cottage industry, such as making textiles, opening a small food shop, or raising cows to produce dairy products to sell. And once the original loan is paid off, the women can get additional, larger loans, which are leveraged[1] by their businesses.

I've heard that microlending interest rates can be 40 percent or more. Why are they so high, and doesn't this victimize poor clients? *Jeon Do-yeon, Seoul, Korea*

SO: Good question. Though these rates are higher than those on traditional loans, they are considerably lower than what people in poverty commonly pay to informal village lenders, and they are necessary to cover the high operational costs of lending in undeveloped areas. Fortunately, as MFIs become more efficient, they are able to operate with lower interest rates.

What is your mission? *Lida Stepanek, Czech Republic*

SO: Well, we are committed to the four themes set forth by the international microfinance movement:

1) empower women
2) reach the very poor
3) build financially stable and sustainable incomes and institutions
4) create positive, measurable impact

How do you respond to skeptics who say that poor people are not likely to repay a debt? *Ali Faramawi, Dubai*

SO: Well! We respond by publicizing the facts. As you know, poor people are generally excluded from traditional banking services because many are illiterate, lack collateral[2] to get a loan, or feel intimidated. Banks readily point out potential pitfalls of loaning money to the poor. Basically, they fear that the poor could easily get overextended and fail to repay their loans. Yet the fact is that the rate of global repayment of microcredit loans is between 97 and 99 percent. Those numbers are quite compelling. Our thousands of microcredit success stories disprove the characterization of poor people as unmotivated and a credit risk. Indeed, we see success at the bottom of the economic pyramid.

Is it true that most microcredit borrowers are women? *Natalia Bruzoni, Junín, Argentina*

SO: Yes, as a matter of fact, it is. Internationally, 85 percent of microcredit clients are women because they are the ones who usually bear the brunt of poverty. We lend mainly to women because they repay loans at a higher rate than men. In addition to that, if a woman's business is undercapitalized,[3] she will apply for a new loan, reinvest, and stick with the business instead of spending whatever she's made on alcohol or girlfriends. And finally, microcredit institutions know that women are the best investment because the impact can reach in perpetuity, benefiting their children and future generations. In this way, we diminish poverty long-term.

---

[1]**leveraged:** structured so that the original value can potentially multiply
[2] **collateral:** money or property offered as a guarantee to repay a loan
[3] **undercapitalized:** not having enough money to operate effectively

Do you ever see a backlash from men who may be jealous of their wives' success? *Reka Randell, Auckland, New Zealand*

SO: Well, you might think so, but actually we don't see this because it's not a zero-sum[4] situation: The wife's accomplishments don't take away from her husband's success. Most families are just happy to have food on their plates and a safety net in case of health emergencies.

How and why did you start the foundation Transformation International? *Eser Vural, Denizli, Turkey*

SO: Well, I joined the Peace Corps in 1976 and, being of Haitian ancestry, I specifically requested to do my volunteer service in Haiti, the poorest country in the western hemisphere. Hurricane Jeanne hit Haiti in 2004, and it wiped out hundreds of small coastal villages, and killed over 3,000 people, including some very close friends and relatives.

A week after the hurricane, I decided to quit my high-paying job as a biotech consultant to start a foundation which would provide long-term economic support to the poor in Haiti and help rebuild the devastated country. Overnight, I became an activist for the poor as well as the founder and CEO of Transformation International.

Have you ever actually met Muhammed Yunus, the recipient of the 2006 Nobel Peace Prize and the so-called "Father of Microfinance"? *Kami Pipoblabanan, Chiang Mai, Thailand*

SO: As a matter of fact, yes. The charismatic Muhammed Yunus spoke to the Haitian Peace Corps volunteers in the late '70s. He had just started the Grameen Bank in Bangladesh and wanted to share his crazy, revolutionary microcredit idea with the world. He told us the story of how in 1976, distraught over the poverty and famine he witnessed in Bangladesh, he decided to lend $27 to 42 bamboo weavers there. The weavers quickly repaid the loans, started their own small businesses, and were on their way to escaping poverty. Microcredit was born. Today the Grameen Bank and other MFIs like it serve well over five million clients—10,000 families a month. Now, many supporters see microcredit as a panacea to ease the poor out of poverty.

Don't you think microcredit could be seen as a fad, just another popular idea in the world of global poverty relief? *Luc Berry, Montreal, Canada*

SO: Oh, no, not at all. I am committed to the revolutionary words of the author, Victor Hugo: "An invasion of armies can be resisted, but not an idea whose time has come." Microcredit's time has come. It is time to create a new kind of bank, one that builds on the labor and imagination of small groups of motivated people.

QUOTE OF THE DAY:
When asked what his strategy was in forming the Grameen Bank, Muhammed Yunus said:

"Well, I didn't have a strategy. I just kept doing what was next. But when I look back my strategy was, whatever banks did, I did the opposite. If banks lent to the rich, I lent to the poor. If banks lent to men, I lent to women. If banks made large loans, I made small loans. If banks required collateral, my loans were collateral free. If banks required a lot of paperwork, my loans were illiterate-friendly. Yes, that was my strategy of whatever banks did, I did the opposite."

[4]**zero sum [game]:** a situation in which success on one side is balanced by loss on another side

2 *Find these words underlined in the interview on pages 227–229. Circle the best synonym or definition for the word as it is used in the reading.*

1.	cottage industry	=	home-based business	OR	home-building business
2.	sustainable	=	able to continue	OR	very large
3.	pitfalls	=	dangers	OR	costs
4.	overextended	=	owing too much money	OR	having too much money
5.	compelling	=	interesting	OR	upsetting
6.	characterization	=	personality	OR	description
7.	bear the brunt	=	suffer the worst	OR	accept the fact
8.	in perpetuity	=	for all future time	OR	in old age
9.	diminish	=	ignore	OR	lessen
10.	backlash	=	violent action	OR	negative reaction
11.	safety net	=	equipment for work	OR	help in times of trouble
12.	wiped out	=	cleaned	OR	destroyed
13.	overnight	=	sudden	OR	tireless
14.	panacea	=	solution	OR	option

2 FOCUS ON LISTENING

A LISTENING ONE: Microfinance

You will listen to a radio interview on the benefits and pitfalls of microfinance. The host, Ross Reynolds, interviews three leaders in the field: Alex Counts, president and CEO of Grameen Foundation USA; Raj Shah, Director of Financial Services and Agriculture with the Bill and Melinda Gates Foundation; and Matt Flannery, co-founder of Kiva.org, a website that connects lenders with people in need of microloans.

People living in extreme poverty—less than a dollar a day—are unable to meet their basic needs for survival. Those living in moderate poverty—one to two dollars a day—can just meet their basic needs but have no safety net in case of misfortune. People in microfinance like to study the outcomes of the move from extreme poverty to moderate poverty.

CD 3 36 *Work with a partner. Predict what basic needs might be met when a family moves from extreme to moderate poverty. List them here. Then listen to the excerpt to check your predictions.*

____

____

____

LISTEN FOR MAIN IDEAS

CD 3 37 *Read the items. Then listen to the interview. Complete the sentences to express the main idea(s) of each segment from the interview. Add an additional sentence if necessary. Compare your sentences with those of another student.*

Part One: Alex Counts, Grameen Foundation USA

1. According to Alex Counts, 60 or 70 dollars can make a huge difference in the life of a poor person because ____

   ____

Part Two: Raj Shah, Bill and Melinda Gates Foundation

2. According to Raj Shah, the biggest outcome of moving from extreme to moderate poverty is ____

   ____

Part Three: Matt Flannery, Kiva.org

3. According to Matt Flannery, microfinance is more beneficial than direct charity programs because ____

   ____

Part Four: Alex Counts

4. According to Alex Counts, the biggest impact of microcredit is _______________

   ____

LISTEN FOR DETAILS

CD 3 38 *Listen to the interview again. As you listen, fill in the outline with information from the interview.*

I. ROSS REYNOLDS, interviewer and host of the radio show

A. Credit has two pitfalls:

1.

2.

B. The poor are disadvantaged in two ways:

1.

2. no safety net

C. The poor have two options:

1.

2.

D. Challenges originally faced by Bengali woman:

1. couldn't afford more than three chickens

2.

E. Possible outcomes of the $60–$70 investment:

1.

2. send child to school

3.

II. RAJ SHAH, Bill and Melinda Gates Foundation

A. Impact on the kids when parents have benefited from microfinance investments:

1.

2. better school attendance

3.

B. Number of clients who move out of poverty: ____________________

III. MATT FLANNERY, founder of Kiva.org website

A. Microfinance is sustainable; it's "a _____ that can keep on __________."

IV. ALEX COUNTS, president of the Grameen Foundation USA

A. Drawbacks:

1.

2.

B. Examples of going from extreme poverty to moderate poverty:

1.

2.

MAKE INFERENCES

Read the following questions. Then listen to each excerpt from the interview. Circle the correct answer and provide an explanation for your choice. Discuss your answers with a partner.

CD 3 39

Excerpt One

1. Why does the host ask the question: "Is credit always a good thing?"

a. To encourage the speaker to agree with him
b. To get the speaker to explain microcredit
c. To allow the speaker to establish his expertise

Explain: ______________________________

CD 3 40

Excerpt Two

2. What is the speaker's attitude about the poor?

a. They are unable to take action to help themselves.
b. They must take action to help themselves.
c. They should have the chance to take action to help themselves.

Explain: ______________________________

CD 3 41

Excerpt Three

3. When the host asks if microfinancing is "zero sum" and brings up the topic of other charities, he is asking Alex Counts to _____.

a. justify microfinancing over direct charitable giving
b. realize that there are enough charities already
c. admit that loans won't help people in deep poverty

Explain: ______________________________

(continued on next page)

Excerpt Four

4. What assumption does Alex Counts make about the radio audience? They are _____.

   a. disappointed in microfinancing's ability to make a big impact
   b. not part of the extremely poor or moderately poor populations
   c. aware of the different levels of poverty around the world

   Explain: ______________________________

Excerpt Five

5. Why does Alex Counts tell the story of the chicken farmer?

   a. To demonstrate how well chicken farming can work in Bangladesh
   b. To show how skillfully the woman built her business
   c. To illustrate how transformative a small loan can be

   Explain: ______________________________

EXPRESS OPINIONS

Work in small groups. Read the quotes related to Listening One and microfinance. Paraphrase the quotes and then decide if you agree or disagree with the author of the quote. Explain reasons for your opinions.

Muhammed Yunus

1. *Muhammed Yunus, 2006 Nobel Peace Prize winner:*

   a. "One day our grandchildren will go to museums to see what poverty was like."
   b. "Charity is not the answer to poverty. It only helps poverty to continue. It creates dependency and takes away the individual's initiative to break through the wall of poverty."

2. *Alex Counts, president of Grameen Foundation USA:*

   "I've always felt that the greatest threat to world peace was the global poverty crisis—seeing the competition for resources and how it leads to tension and violence."

3. *Milton Friedman, 1976 Nobel Prize in Economic Sciences winner:*

   "The poor stay poor not because they are lazy, but because they have no access to capital."

B LISTENING TWO: Interview with a Microfinance Director

Listen to a microfinance expert, Will Bullard, tell the story of a woman in a village in Honduras, Central America. This real story illustrates how a local lending organization, or "assembly," works—the benefits and pitfalls.

CD 3 44

Part One: Maria Jose's Story

Check (✓) the true statements. Correct the false statements.

_____ **1.** Maria Jose Perona had nine children, all of whom were malnourished.

_____ **2.** The women in the assembly decide who gets the loan.

_____ **3.** The women did not vote to grant Maria Jose Perona the loan because they thought she would spend the loan on food, not on the business.

_____ **4.** The women finally agreed and gave her a loan of 25 dollars.

_____ **5.** Maria Jose Perona had to take a test to get the 25 dollars.

_____ **6.** Maria Jose Perona bought flour and cooking supplies with her loan.

_____ **7.** She created a small meat pie business in front of the school.

_____ **8.** Although she paid her friend back, she was not allowed into the assembly.

_____ **9.** She finally became successful and was then allowed into the assembly.

_____ **10.** She built a concrete house and became president of the assembly.

CD 3 45

Part Two: Non-Monetary Benefits of Microfinance

Check (✓) the non-monetary benefits (other benefits not related to money) that the speaker mentions or implies.

_____ **11.** sales and marketing skills
_____ **12.** education
_____ **13.** confidence
_____ **14.** risk-taking ability

CD 3 46

Part Three: Business Training

Check (✓) the phrases that complete the statement accurately.

The speaker believes that business training is important because the women _____.

_____ **15.** find the loans too small
_____ **16.** don't know how to manage their money carefully
_____ **17.** sell very similar things
_____ **18.** should sell things that bring them more money

C INTEGRATE LISTENINGS ONE AND TWO

STEP 1: Organize

Review Listenings One and Two. In each listening, speakers refer to three major benefits of microfinance. Work with a partner. Complete the chart by identifying specific examples of these benefits from each listening.

BENEFITS OF MICROFINANCE	EXAMPLES: LISTENING ONE	EXAMPLES: LISTENING TWO
Financial changes		
Non-monetary changes		
Sustainability		

STEP 2: Synthesize

Work in groups of three. Each person will choose one of the benefits listed in the chart above. Review the related examples from Listening One and Listening Two. After two minutes, close your book and present a one-minute summary to the group. Use examples.

3 FOCUS ON SPEAKING

A VOCABULARY

REVIEW

A journalist for *Economic Daily,* Pedro Martinez, broadcast an "audio postcard" about his recent trip to La Ceiba, Honduras.

1 *Read the transcript of Martinez's report. Fill in the blanks with the appropriate word or expression from the list. Use the phrases under the blanks to help you.*

anecdote	had faith in	panacea	took a hit
compelling	hit a ceiling	pitfalls	wiped out
diminish	kicker	sustainable	the world over
elaborate	malnourished		

www.TransformationInternational.org

Greetings from La Ceiba, Honduras. First, I must tell you that this little speck on Earth is just unbelievably gorgeous—beautiful, lush, with breathtaking cloud formations hugging spectacular green mountains.

Still, on the drive from the airport to my lodge I witnessed the pervasive poverty we see ______________________ **1.** (in every area of the world): skinny, ______________________ **2.** (sick or weak due to lack of food) children standing next to houses and shops still not rebuilt since Hurricane Mitch ______________ **3.** (destroyed) much of the country in 1988. Already the second poorest country in Latin America, Honduras ______________________ **4.** (was negatively affected) and never recovered. To research my article, I set out to visit microfinance institutions as well as meet the microcredit client to whom I had lent money from my laptop in Mexico City, where I live.

Kiva.org is a nonprofit microcredit organization that allows individuals with access to the Internet to fight global poverty in a ______________________ **5.** (able to continue long-term) way by making a direct personal loan to poor entrepreneurs anywhere in the world. On the Kiva website I came across the ______________________ **6.** (so interesting or exciting that you have to pay attention) photo and story of Julia Marta Mendez, a fascinating Honduran widow in her late thirties with six children, to whom I

had lent 50 dollars. I ______________________ her and just knew she would stick with her
7. (believed in; trusted)
goals and use the money well.

With this tiny loan, Julia opened a small shop in which she sold delicious coconut bread made from a unique family recipe. After three months, she was able to leverage the initial investment to expand her business to include other savory Honduran foodstuffs, such as baleadas, special Honduran tortillas.[1] I wish there were time to ______________________________ on these
8. (give more details or information)
specialties, describing their delicate aromas and flavors.

And I wish you all could witness the non-monetary benefits of the loans—no challenge, no obstacle, nothing can ______________________________________ Julia's enthusiasm, sense of confidence, and
9. (make something smaller or less important)
hope for her future. But here's the real ______________________________________ which
10. (unexpected and surprising remark or fact)
you might find difficult to believe! In spite of Julia's outstanding success so far, she worries that her business may already have ___________________________. A competing shop
11. (reached the limit of success)
has opened next to hers, so she now feels she needs training in marketing and advertising to fuel future business growth. Indeed, I realize that money alone is not a total ______________________________________. We all know that when it comes to
12. (something thought to eliminate a problem)
alleviating poverty, there is no such thing as overnight success. Truly, one of the biggest ________________________of microfinance is the need for business training. Listen again
13. (problems or difficulties)
for tomorrow's story—an ____ from my visit
14. (a short story based on personal experience)
with Julia.

[1] **tortilla:** a piece of thin, flat bread made from wheat or corn

2 CD 3, track 47 *Now listen to the audio postcard to check your answers. Work with a partner, and discuss the questions.*

1. What might be the pros and cons of lending money to microborrowers on a website like Kiva.org? Would you be interested in doing so?
2. Why do you think microfinancing institutions don't focus more heavily on job training for the microborrowers?

EXPAND

After hearing Mr. Martinez's audio postcard, several listeners called the radio station to voice their reaction. Following is a transcript of those comments.

Read the listener comments and match the boldfaced words or expressions with a similar expression on page 240. Compare your answers with those of a partner.

• **Jiseon Park, barista at Starbucks, Seoul, Korea, August 20**

Wow . . . Pedro Martinez's story was so inspirational. Just amazing how this woman Julia could actually **(1) make do** with a single small loan to get her business off the ground. Raising six children alone on two dollars a day, Julia really does **(2) bear the brunt** of poverty. Loaning money **(3) as opposed to** just giving charity or a handout clearly is a better way to help the very poor fulfill their dream of **(4) upward mobility**, or at least building a **(5) safety net** in case of emergency.

• **Susana, English teacher, São Paulo, Brazil, August 21**

I heard Martinez's broadcast the other day and even though I found it interesting and moving, I have mixed feelings about microcredit. The way I see it, microcredit only tells half the story. Even if Julia repays her initial loan, reinvests future loans, and lives a slightly better life, she'll still be at the **(6) bottom of the** economic **pyramid**. Of course, she may enjoy some **(7) non-monetary** benefits from her microcredit enterprise. But, I hate to say it, ultimately her business will only generate very slim **(8) profit margins**. Research shows it takes years for even the most ambitious microlending entrepreneurs to **(9) pull themselves up by their bootstraps**.

• **Dr. Nguyen Anh Tuan, physician, Hanoi, Vietnam, August 21**

Thank you for airing Mr. Martinez's audio postcard yesterday. It reminded me of a visit I made to a family in a small village 30 kilometers from Hanoi two years ago. I knew the family well because I had treated a poor peasant woman's son who had been fighting a very serious intestinal illness. For years, **(10) top-down aid** from international organizations had never reached this rural community. Struggling with deep debts and worry caused by her son's illness, Le Thi Tran was desperate. One day she heard about the Tao Yeu May[1] Fund, a microfinance organization with local, **(11) grassroots** support in Vietnam, and with a single loan of $40 she purchased six chickens. She reinvested her earnings, creating a **(12) niche market** famous for the tastiest chickens in the area. Her son is doing fine now; all debts have been paid off, and Le Thi lives in a brand-new house. Truly, TYM gave her the **(13) gift that keeps on giving**.

[1] **Tao Yeu May:** I love you (literal translation)

_____ **a.** assistance from higher levels

_____ **b.** a gift that continues to grow and benefit its recipient

_____ **c.** suffer the worst

_____ **d.** not related to money

_____ **e.** manage

_____ **f.** related to ordinary people

_____ **g.** moving toward a better position

_____ **h.** improve their situation through hard work

_____ **i.** specific or specialized market

_____ **j.** compared to

_____ **k.** lowest economic level

_____ **l.** the difference between business expenses and income

_____ **m.** plan or arrangement to help in case of problems or difficulties

CREATE

Work with a partner. Role-play a conversation between two students discussing microfinance.

Student A: Read the comments 1 to 8 on page 241 to Student B.

Student B: Listen to the comments. Paraphrase each comment using one of the vocabulary words in your list below.

Student A: If Student B's paraphrase isn't correct, give a clue from the sentence. Clues are in italics. The answers are in parentheses.

Switch roles after item 8.

Vocabulary for Student B	Vocabulary for Student A
compelling	anecdote
grassroots	as opposed to
make do	bear the brunt
pitfalls	bottom of the economic pyramid
sustainable	elaborate on
take the biggest hit	hit a ceiling
upward mobility	top-down
the world over	wipe out

Example

Student A: Microcredit loans are simply not a *cure-all* for poverty. (panacea)
Student B: So, you mean it's clear that these loans are not a **panacea** for poverty.

1. It's really painful to see how some people in Lagos, Nigeria, are forced to *manage* on $2 a day. (make do)
2. Although microfinance offers a promising solution, there are still a number of potential *problems and dangers* in the approach. (pitfalls)
3. A poor, illiterate person cannot create a *healthy, lasting* business on a $50 microloan without access to job training and education. (sustainable)
4. Living in slums or tiny rural villages, many poor people do feel there's no real *ability to move to a better position.* (upward mobility)
5. Kiva.org lenders have said that loaning money directly to a small entrepreneur is a *powerful* form of philanthropy. (compelling)
6. When natural disasters strike, the "poorest of the poor" are the ones who *are most severely affected.* (take the biggest hit)
7. Microfinancing is always established at the *local* level. The women in each borrower's group are responsible for managing and repaying the group's loans. (grassroots)
8. It's been proven *everywhere* that women will repay loans at a higher rate than men. (the world over)

Now switch roles.

9. It is a myth that the very, very poor can leave poverty behind. The reality is that poor women in developing countries will always *suffer the worst* of poverty. (bear the brunt)
10. There are limits to growing a business through microcredit. It's clear that, after moving from extreme to moderate poverty, many people *reach a limit.* (hit a ceiling)
11. Unfortunately, a single natural disaster can suddenly *destroy* a microborrower's business and savings. (wipe out)
12. I'd say a *large-scale, high-level,* government-led approach focused on overall economic health leads to greater poverty alleviation than microcredit does. (top-down)
13. I was moved by the *story* of the Thai woman who rebuilt her peanut business in three months after it had been destroyed by the tsunami. (anecdote)

(continued on next page)

14. In order to get their loans, the five women in the borrower's group were required to *speak in detail about* their business plans. (elaborate on)

15. Microfinance institutions require small, frequent loan repayments *rather than* more traditional large, long-term loans. (as opposed to)

16. Unfortunately, women are most often stuck at the *lowest economic level,* since they usually have less education than men and they take primary responsibility for their children. (bottom of the economic pyramid)

B GRAMMAR: Unreal Conditionals—Present, Past, and Mixed

1 *Work with a partner. Examine the statements and discuss the questions that follow.*

- If Maria Jose weren't a successful micro-entrepreneur, her children couldn't attend school.
- If Maria Jose's friend hadn't had faith in her, she wouldn't have given Maria Jose her first 25 dollar loan.
- If Maria Jose hadn't invested the initial loan, she wouldn't be such a successful micro-entrepreneur today.
- If the microfinance organization offered job training, she might have enjoyed larger profit margins from the get-go.[1]

1. Which sentences express conditions in the past? In the present? Both?
2. How do the tenses in the last two sentences differ from those in the first two? What is the difference in meaning?

Conditional sentences express ideas about things which happen or don't happen because of certain situations. They consist of an "*if* clause" and a "result clause." Use unreal conditionals to express ideas which are contrary to fact in the present, past, or both.

Remember:

- Not all conditional clauses use *if.*

  They wish they could provide more training in marketing.

- When there is an *if* clause, it can come before or after the result clause.

  If the women make enough money, the children can go to school.

  The children can go to school *if* the women make enough money.

Note: There is a comma after the *if* clause when it comes before the result clause.

[1]**from the get-go:** from the beginning

PRESENT UNREAL CONDITIONALS

Use present unreal conditionals to discuss situations in the present which are contrary-to-fact.

Real Situation	Conditional	
	***If* Clause**	**Result Clause**
	If + subject + verb (past form)	subject + *could* / *would* / *might* + verb (base form)
She doesn't have any savings, so she can't afford medicine when her children get sick.	**If she had** some savings,	**she could afford** medicine when her children get sick.
Microcredit is not truly a panacea, so the poverty rate is high.	**If microcredit were** truly a panacea,	**the poverty rate wouldn't be** as high as it is.

PAST UNREAL CONDITIONALS

Use past unreal conditionals to discuss situations in the past which are contrary-to-fact.

Real Situation	Conditional	
	***If* Clause**	**Result Clause**
	If + subject + verb (past perfect form)	subject + *could* / *would* / *might* + *have* + verb (past participle form)
Mrs. Du Ying got a loan, so she could buy raw silk for her rug-making business.	**If Mrs. Du Ying hadn't gotten** the loan,	**she couldn't have bought** the raw silk for her rug-making business.
She repaid the loan, so the other women in her group weren't responsible for it.	**If she hadn't repaid** the loan,	**the other women in her group would have been** responsible for repaying it.

MIXED UNREAL CONDITIONALS

Sometimes, present and past unreal conditionals are mixed if the times of the "*if* clause" and the "result clause" are different.

- Past result of a present condition:
  If microfinance weren't so successful, Yunus wouldn't have won the Nobel Peace Prize.
- Present result of a past condition:
  If the epidemic hadn't killed her cows last year, she wouldn't be so poor today.

Real Situation	Conditional: *If* Clause	Conditional: Result Clause
	Past *If* + *had* + verb (past participle form)	**Present** subject + *would* / *could* / *might* + verb (base form)
	Present *If* + verb (past form)	**Past** subject + *would* + *have* + verb (past participle form)
Hurricane Mitch wiped out her home and village in 1998, so she is poor today.	**If Hurricane Mitch hadn't wiped out** her home and village in 1998,	**she wouldn't be** so poor today.
She has low profit margins, so she applied for a second loan.	**If she had** higher profit margins,	**she wouldn't have applied** for a second loan.

NOTE: The present progressive tense is often used with mixed conditionals:
If I had known about the Grameen Bank 10 years ago, I'd be working for the bank now.

2 *Discuss real and unreal situations with a partner. Imagine the opposite of the statements that follow.*

Student A: Cover the right column. Read the sentence which reviews information on microfinance.

Student B: Cover the left column. Using an unreal conditional (present, past, or mixed), comment on the information, imagining the opposite condition. Use the cues provided.

Then switch roles after item 8.

Student A	Student B
1. Many of the world's poor have no access to capital, so they cannot start or grow a business.	**1.** That's true. If the world's . . .
2. Matt and Jess Flannery were determined to make a difference in the world, so they started the Kiva.org website.	**2.** Yes, I know. If they . . .
3. I heard a compelling broadcast about Kiva on the radio last month, and now I am a microlender. (mixed)	**3.** Oh, I see. So, if you . . .
4. Julia Mendez's husband died a year ago, and she struggles to support her six children alone. (mixed)	**4.** Hmmm . . . but I think even if her husband (not) . . .
5. Julia did not even have 50 dollars to buy the cooking supplies she needed, so she couldn't start her business.	**5.** Yes, if she . . .
6. I had faith in Julia, so I decided to lend money to her.	**6.** Yes, of course. If you . . .
7. Julia repaid her initial loan this week and is now feeling really confident. (mixed progressive)	**7.** Uh-huh. You know, if she . . .
8. She has some money now, so her children are in school.	**8.** Do you mean if she . . . ?
Now switch roles.	
9. Muhammed Yunus lent 27 dollars to 42 stool makers and came up with the idea of microfinance.	**9.** Yes, I'm sure if he . . .
10. The traditional banks refused to participate in Yunus's microcredit scheme, so he started his own bank, the Grameen Bank.	**10.** Hmmm . . . I suppose that if . . .

(continued on next page)

11. Yunus is a charismatic leader, so he was able to persuade many people to believe in his vision. (mixed)	**11.** True. Some people think that if Yunus . . .
12. Yunus listens to critics who mention the pitfalls of microfinance, and he continues to improve the system.	**12.** That's good. If he . . .
13. In general, men are not good risks as borrowers, so they are approved less often for microloans.	**13.** Really? So do you think that if men . . .
14. One microborrower didn't repay her loan, so her group members can't approve any further loans.	**14.** That's too bad. If she . . .
15. The microborrower had no literacy or job skills, and so her business hit a ceiling.	**15.** Yes, that is common. If she . . .
16. Three of the five borrowers in the group failed the exam on the banking policies, so they can't join the microfinance program. (mixed)	**16.** That's unfortunate. If they . . .

3 *Work with a partner. Discuss unreal situations.*

Student A: Ask your partner questions 1 through 4.

Student B: Answer Student A's questions using unreal present, past, and mixed conditionals. Use the information from the unit and your own opinions and imagination.

Then switch roles after question 4.

What if . . .

1. . . . Muhammed Yunus hadn't started the Grameen Bank?

2. . . . Yunus hadn't won the Nobel Peace Prize?

3. . . . there weren't a microfinance rule that each woman in a solidarity group has to approve the members' loans?

4. . . . there really were a poverty museum?

Now switch roles.

5. . . . traditional banks also operated like microfinance institutions and gave out tiny loans to the poor?

6. . . . governments outlawed begging on the streets?

7. . . . microfinance organizations required all borrowers be literate in their native language and pass a business training course?

8. . . . microfinance institutions began to target more men as potential borrowers?

C SPEAKING

PRONUNCIATION: Stress in Two-Word Units Used as Nouns

CD 3 48 Meaningful units composed of two words are stressed on the first word when the unit is a noun. Pitch is also high on the first word. Listen to the phrases and sentence.

cóttage ìndustry rúg-màking páthwày póverty cỳcle

A **cottage industry** like **rug-making** can become a **pathway** to break the **poverty cycle**.

TWO-WORD NOUNS	EXAMPLES
Noun-noun units (compounds)	cóttage ìndustry páthwày póverty cỳcle
Adjective-noun units	grándchìldren lívestòck bláckbòard
Preposition + Verb used as a noun	íncòme óutgròw bácklàsh
Other sequences	hóusehòld rúg-màking mícrolòans

1 CD 3 49 *Listen to the phrases and repeat them. Pronounce the first word with heavy stress and high pitch.*

1. microcredit
2. interest rates
3. aid agencies
4. Peace Corps
5. drawback
6. business growth
7. debt payment
8. cottage industry
9. pitfall
10. household

2 *Work with a partner. The words in the box can be combined with the words under the blanks into two-word expressions that match the definitions. Read the definitions. Then make two-word expressions from the words in the box and write them in the blanks.*

back	broad	live	profit	safety

1. A negative or critical reaction to a program or policy: ____________ (lash)
2. The difference between the money a business earns and the money it spends: ____________ (margin)
3. Information made public, usually by radio or television: ____________ (cast)
4. Farm animals: ____________ (stock)
5. A source of help during difficult times: ____________ (net)

3 *Look at the three categories below. Add more examples to each category. If you include a two-word noun unit, circle it. Then share your lists with the class.*

Drawbacks to Microlending	Safety Nets for Poor People	Cottage Industries
high interest rates	aid agencies	selling eggs
____________	____________	____________
____________	____________	____________
____________	____________	____________

FUNCTION: Supporting Ideas with Details and Examples

To clarify and support ideas, speakers need to offer details. There are many expressions for introducing details and examples. Use a variety of expressions when you are speaking.

- Building on this idea, . . .
- What we've witnessed time and time again is . . .
- Another thing to keep in mind is . . .
- To illustrate this point, . . .
- The story of X shows . . .
- One figure / statistic that supports this idea is . . .

The first Microcredit Summit was held in Washington, D.C., in 1997. At that time, more than 2,900 delegates from 137 countries created concrete goals to reach 100 million of the world's poorest families, especially women, through microcredit.

Each year, Muhammmad Yunus, Alex Counts, and other key leaders in microfinance speak at local microcredit summits designed to educate people the world over about the ways in which microcredit can help alleviate poverty. This year, the microfinance institute—the Tao Yeu May Fund—is hosting a conference in Vietnam. Student delegates from universities around the world are attending.

Work with a partner to role-play a discussion between conference attendees.

Student A: You are a student delegate to the conference. You are going to ask the two questions on page 250 to a microfinance director who is serving on a panel called "The ABCs of Microfinance."

Student B: You are the director of the Tao Yeu May Fund. According to the panel rules, you must answer the student delegate's questions in less than one minute. Respond using the notes on the right and the expressions on page 248 for supporting ideas with details and examples.

Switch roles after question 2. *(See page 251.)*

STUDENT A	STUDENT B	
Delegate Questions	**Director's Main Ideas**	**Supporting Details**
1. Why does the Grameen Bank, the original MFI, give credit without providing business training?	People come with innate skills.	• salesmanship • practical abilities (sewing, cooking, etc.) • charisma
	Poor can be immediately successful without training.	Beatrice, 35, mother of four: • $50 loan started business selling goat milk and cheese • in one year, gained seven goats and got new tin roof
	The cost is prohibitive.	Increases operating expenses by up to 10%
2. Why are women such reliable people to loan money to?	Women bear the brunt of poverty, feel the most pain, and are the most motivated.	• 70% of people in extreme poverty are women • highest numbers of illiteracy, maternal and infant mortality, malnutrition, and HIV/AIDS
	They feel the responsibility for taking care of the family, especially children who are victims of poverty.	• no choice—either borrow money or watch children die • 30,000 children die every day because of extreme poverty • about 90% use profits from microcredit business to pay school fees
	Women show a higher repayment rate than men.	• female repayment rate = 95–100% male repayment = 60–70% • less mobile—won't run away • more responsive to peer pressure to repay

Now switch roles.

STUDENT B	STUDENT A	
Delegate Questions	**Director's Main Ideas**	**Supporting Details**
3. What are some of the criticisms of microfinance?	Microfinance isn't a panacea.	• 55% of Grameen households still can't meet nutritional needs • clients become dependent on loans • increases womens' burden—make money and raise a family
	MFIs have high costs and never have enough money to be financially self-sustainable.	• charge high interest rates (12–40%) to cover costs • compete with other aid agencies for donations and grants
	MFIs do not provide enough support programs, leaving clients vulnerable.	• lack of business training = clients hit a ceiling • not enough savings programs: Yasmin, 40, grows chiles: business wiped out by drought and illness; without savings, can't pay loan • poorest women are the least healthy and are in most need of health care
4. Why is the solidarity group model so effective?	"Social collateral" is a very effective way of getting the women to repay their loans.	• knowing applicant's reputation eliminates risk early on • group must pay back loan if member defaults, then member is excluded from future loans • minimizes bank risk
	The group functions as a resource for information and informal training.	• education on health, family planning, women's rights • members compare business experience and share knowledge
	It fosters community and helps raise confidence and self-esteem.	• participation is broad; literacy is not required • as Yunus says: "Each individual person is very important. Each person has tremendous potential. She or he alone can influence the lives of others within the communities, nations, within, and beyond her or his own time."

PRODUCTION: Simulation

In this activity, you will compete for a contract to help the Brazilian Ministry of Health / Finance build a program to alleviate poverty in the country. Representing an anti-poverty agency, ***present recommendations*** for tackling this problem. Try to use the vocabulary, grammar, pronunciation, and language for supporting ideas with details and examples you learned in the unit.*

Follow the steps.

Step 1: As a class, complete the first row of the chart on page 253 with information about microfinance.

Step 2: Work in a small group. You will be assigned to one of the following agencies:

Group 1: Microfinance Institution
Group 2: World Bank
Group 3: Global Business
Group 4: Ministry of Health / Finance

Groups 1–3: Read the information in the chart. Pay particular attention to the agency you represent.

Group 4: Read the information in the chart.

Step 3: Groups 1–3: Prepare a plan for alleviating poverty. Then decide how to present your plan to the ministry. Acknowledge the challenges of your plan, but be sure to explain how the potential benefits outweigh them. Refer to the other agencies' plans in order to illustrate how yours is superior.

Group 4: Create challenging and provocative questions to assess the viability of each agency's plan.

Step 4: Groups 1–3: Present your plan to the ministry and the class.

Group 4: At the end of each presentation, pose your questions to the agency.

*For Alternative Speaking Topics, see page 254.

AGENCY / DESCRIPTION	EXAMPLES	BENEFITS	CHALLENGES
Microfinance Institution			
World Bank • Wealthy member nations provide loans and grants to poor countries. • Programs aim to boost economic growth and improve living conditions by fixing major government institutions (highways, schools, public services).	• help countries create programs to stop disease • fund education • build roads, bridges, power plants	• provide long-term, low- or no-interest loans • require recipients to take steps to fight disease, grow economy, etc. • can offer huge resources	• leave countries in debt • establish programs that may not consider unique needs of that culture • may introduce corruption and bias • may cost a lot to administer program, no direct benefit to the poor
Global Business Provides jobs to people in developing countries	• retail stores (Wal-Mart, Home Depot) • food companies (Dole, Chiquita) • auto makers (Toyota)	• can offer factory jobs with pay to lift workers out of poverty • create competition between businesses—drives up local wages • bring wealth of developed nation, not limited by local economy • provide jobs for people who are not entrepreneurs • offer stability	• might have bad working conditions in "sweatshops" or fields • may introduce child labor • require relocation of villagers to the city • raise environmental concerns about shipping goods around the globe

ALTERNATIVE SPEAKING TOPICS

Work in small groups. Discuss your answers to the questions. Use ideas, vocabulary, grammar, pronunciation, and language for supporting ideas with details and examples.

1. Microcredit has been tried in developed countries such as the United States, but it has not been as successful there as it has been in poorer, developing countries. For example, 37 million Americans (one out of eight) live below the official poverty threshold, which is 19,971 dollars a year for a family of four. One microcredit experiment, The Good Faith Fund in Arkansas, failed miserably when it hit a low repayment rate of 48 percent. Why do you think this methodology is not as successful?
2. Grameen gives interest-free loans of 15–35 dollars to beggars, who are encouraged to buy small trinkets or food to take door to door to sell. Even beggars who cannot walk can take part in the program. They can keep "some soft drinks, some bananas, some cookies" next to the begging bowl, Yunus explained, and "people have a choice whether they want to throw a coin or buy a banana." The program is growing rapidly. According to Yunus, "All we need to do is put a roof on top and she turns into a businesswoman right there. Just because one cannot move doesn't mean one is totally incapable." Do you agree or disagree with this program? Explain your opinion.
3. Muhammed Yunus predicts that microfinance will prove to be so effective that the number of people living in poverty will be reduced by 50 percent by the year 2015. Do you agree or disagree with this prediction? Explain your opinion.
4. One of the positive consequences of microlending is that women have gained the financial means to leave abusive husbands or relationships. They can own a home in their own name, live longer, have improved nutrition, take better care of their children, and so on. When asked about these changes to women's status and lifestyle, Yunus has commented, "I am destroying the culture, yes . . . culture is a dynamic thing. If you stay with the same old thing over and over, you don't get anywhere." Do you agree or disagree with Yunus? Explain your opinion.

RESEARCH TOPICS, see page 266.

STUDENT ACTIVITIES

UNIT 2: Honesty Is the Best Policy

PRODUCTION, page 43

Trading a Lemon

- A 25-year-old man bought a brand new car.
- He put the car into reverse and the car crashed into a pole across the street.
- He had the paint and dent fixed, and then he took the car into two different mechanics. Both said there was nothing wrong.
- He knows something is wrong and doesn't want to keep the car. He wants to trade it in for a new car.
- Even though both mechanics think nothing is wrong, the man is sure something is wrong.

Video Piracy

- A woman's son watches pirated, illegally recorded videos at a neighbor's house.
- Even though the neighbor has bought the videos, they are pirated.

A Doctor's Debate

- A 65-year-old man comes to his physician with complaints of persistent, but not extreme pains in his stomach.
- Tests reveal that he has cancer of the pancreas.
- The man has just retired from a busy professional career, and he and his wife are about to leave on a round-the-world cruise that they've been planning for over a year. His wife doesn't want him to know that he's dying.

Turtle Trouble

- A woman sees a man with two children walking a turtle down a path with a fishing line around the turtle's throat.
- The man's kids are dragging the turtle up and down the path.
- The woman is horrified because she feels it is cruel.
- The woman tells the man that she is a biologist at the university and that turtles are dangerous because they produce a poisonous fluid which will make the man's children deathly ill.

UNIT 5: Feng Shui: Ancient Wisdom Travels West

Exercise 1, page 100

ASPECTS OF THE ENVIRONMENT	FAVORABLE FENG SHUI	UNFAVORABLE FENG SHUI	REASON
an aquarium	✓		If placed correctly, aquariums invite the kind of chi that brings wealth.
plants and flowers	✓		Live plants are best, and fake plants are fine. Depending on where they are placed, plants invite good luck and wealth. Dead or dried flowers and plants are not good—they invite bad luck.
the colors red and purple	✓		Red is the color of energy—divine energy, the energy of the sun and life, joy, excitement, and sexual desire, richness and luxury. If used too much, though, it can bring destructive energy. Purple is excellent for physical and mental healing and is associated with spiritual awareness.
mirrors	✓		If placed properly, a mirror brings an energy like the calming and refreshing energy of water. Mirrors can invite beneficial chi into a space, or shift the chi in that space.
a desk facing a view	✓	✓	The view should not be direct. If possible, have the light come in from the right if you are right-handed, the left if you are left-handed. The light from the view should not cast a shadow on your work surface. It should invite creative and financial opportunities.

ASPECTS OF THE ENVIRONMENT	FAVORABLE FENG SHUI	UNFAVORABLE FENG SHUI	REASON
a room full of windows		✓	There should not be too many windows in any room or office. If there are too many windows, good luck and energy can flow out easily. The proper ratio is three windows to every door.
living near a cemetery		✓	Cemeteries have a "dark" energy that throws off the balance in the surrounding area.
living on a quiet dead-end street		✓	Living at the end of the dead-end street, or the "T" of two streets, is unfavorable because the shape of the street traps the sha (negative or low energy).
an odd number of dining room chairs		✓	Odd numbers represent loneliness. An even number of chairs represents balance and togetherness (pairing).
pictures of bats on the walls	✓		Bats invite happiness and good luck.
a tiger statue outside an office door	✓		The white tiger is one of the best symbols of protection and guards against getting "stabbed in the back."

UNIT 6: Spiritual Renewal

SHARE INFORMATION, page 124

1. Most monks and nuns are quiet, introverted people.

   Myth: The personality of monks and nuns around the world is as diverse as the personality of human beings around the world. There are monks and nuns who have all kinds of temperaments: quiet, gregarious, aloof, friendly, reserved, and so on. Because monks and nuns do live in a community with others, it is necessary that they enjoy being with other people.

2. Monks and nuns never retire and generally work until they die.

   Fact: There is a saying among one group of monks called the Trappists: "Live, work, and die in place." Monks and nuns are expected to work hard and rest while being vitally interested in everything. Becoming a monk or a nun is a lifelong commitment that must be nurtured by work and play.

3. Since they devote themselves to the spiritual world, monks and nuns have made few contributions to the outside world.

   Myth: Monks and nuns throughout history have excelled in scientific research, healing arts, agricultural development, architecture, politics, poetry, and social work. Community service is a major part of the work of many monasteries throughout the world.

4. Monks and nuns are chosen from birth to become monks and nuns by the family or the community.

   Myth: Most monks and nuns are people who respond to a spiritual calling as young adults or adults.

5. It is necessary for monks and nuns to be vegetarians, shave their heads, or wear special robes called "habits."

   Myth: Some monasteries are vegetarian only; some groups of monks, particularly in Asia, must shave their heads, and many monks do wear habits. However, these practices vary widely from monastery to monastery throughout the world.

6. Although most monks and nuns follow strict daily schedules, most monasteries are open to outside visitors.

   Fact: Many monasteries welcome the public in order to sell things they produce; others have retreat programs that address the spiritual needs of people in the surrounding community or people from far away.

Unit 7: Workplace Privacy

Exercise 2, page 160

The court ruled in favor of Nissan, saying that the electronic mail system is owned by the company. In addition, the e-mail messages were written on company time. Therefore, management has the right to read anything created on that system.

The judge in the case, however, recommended that Nissan come up with a privacy policy that informs employees of the fact that their e-mail may be monitored from time to time without notice.

RESEARCH TOPICS

UNIT 1: The Internet and Other Addictions

Research Internet addiction using the quiz.

Step 1: Read the quiz used to diagnose Internet addiction. Test yourself or a friend.

http://www.onlinesurvey.com/hookedonthenet?

HOOKED ON THE NET?

LET'S FIND OUT

Take this quiz to see if your passion for the Net has become an all-consuming addiction. Check the appropriate boxes. Remember—be honest!

YES	NO	
○	○	1. Do you check your e-mail more than six times a day?
○	○	2. Do you lose track of the time because you are on the computer?
○	○	3. Do you dream about surfing the Net?
○	○	4. Have you ever missed class or called in sick to work because you were too busy online?
○	○	5. Do you introduce yourself by immediately giving out your e-mail address?
○	○	6. Do you neglect your pets because you are online and forget to feed and walk them?
○	○	7. Does your family constantly complain that you are spending too much time in front of the computer?
○	○	8. Have you forgotten to do your usual chores around the house?
○	○	9. Do you talk more to your friends around the world via e-mail than you do to your neighbors?
○	○	10. Do you feel uncomfortable at the thought of going on vacation without your computer?

SCORING

If you answered YES to . . .

0 to 4 questions—Don't worry! You can get a bit carried away, but it's just a fun hobby.

5 to 8 questions—You may be getting hooked. Try to cut down on the number of hours you're on the Net.

9 to 10 questions—Watch out! Stop cold turkey now, and run to the nearest support group.

Step 2: Work with a partner. Choose one of the "other addictions" such as compulsive shopping, workaholism, compulsive eating, compulsive gambling, exercise addiction, and so on. Using the Internet survey as a model, design your own survey to diagnose the addiction you chose. You may use the same scoring system as in the model.

Step 3: Use your survey to interview a friend or a classmate.

Step 4: Share the results with the class or in small groups.

UNIT 2: Honesty Is the Best Policy

Choose a topic and research it.

TOPIC 1

Lying in Movies

There are a number of movies in which the theme is truth, deception, or concealment. Some examples of these are *Goodfellas*, *Shattered Glass*, *The Man Who Never Was*, *The Good Shepherd*, *Catch Me If You Can*, *The Hoax*, and *Liar, Liar*. Watch one of these movies. Summarize the plot and the theme to the class. Analyze the movie using concepts and language that you have learned in this unit.

TOPIC 2

Different Kinds of Lying

Choose one of the following areas of research and present a short report on the topic to your class: lying in the animal world, political lies and deception, scientific fraud, cheating.

TOPIC 3

Stories about Lying

Interview several friends, neighbors, or family members. Ask them to tell you the best whopper they have ever told in their life. Present their stories to your class.

UNIT 3: The Bold and the Bashful

Follow the steps to research the topic.

Step 1: There are many things that people can be afraid of. Choose one or two phobias from the box on the next page. You may also choose to present another phobia you come across in your research.

acrophobia: fear of heights
agoraphobia: fear of leaving the house
ailurophobia: fear of cats
arachnophobia: fear of spiders
aviophobia: fear of flying
claustrophobia: fear of closed spaces
glossophobia: fear of public speaking
testophobia: fear of taking tests
technophobia: fear of technical devices—computers, etc.
triskadekaphobia: fear of the number 13

Step 2: Research one or two of these phobias on the Internet or in the library. Organize your research into three parts:

1. Definition and statistics, particularly from different countries
2. Examples from research and personal experience
3. Treatment options

Step 3: Present your research to the class.

UNIT 4: The Tipping Point

Choose a topic and follow the steps for researching it.

TOPIC 1

Starting or Stopping a Trend

Step 1: Can you start or stop a trend? Work in a small group. Decide on a trend you would like to start or stop. You can choose a trend from the list or think of your own.

- You want your university to be car-free and have all students ride bikes on campus or take the campus shuttle bus.
- You want your office to start recycling paper to cut down on paper use and cost.
- You want people in your community to start running groups and run each weekend.
- You want to stop cell phone use on commuter trains and in restaurants.

To get more ideas, you may also conduct research on the Internet, in your community, or in your school to find out what things people would like to see changed in their environment.

Step 2: Prepare a strategy using all three components of Gladwell's model in order for your trend to "tip," or happen, as soon as possible.

- Law of the Few: mavens, connectors, and salesmen
- Power of Context: small environmental changes can trigger larger changes
- The Stickiness Factor: memorable messages help make an idea "sticky," or successful

Step 3: Present to the class. Describe your strategy—one that illustrates how your group intends to get your trend to tip. Use visual and sound aids. Be creative!

TOPIC 2

Researching a Successful Product

Step 1: Contact a company in your area. Find out which of its products has been extremely successful recently. Interview a manager from the company to find out what helped make the product suddenly successful. Was it powerful connectors? Contextual changes? Sticky advertising?

Step 2: Prepare a short research summary and present it to the class.

UNIT 5: Feng Shui: Ancient Wisdom Travels West

Choose a topic and follow the steps for researching it.

TOPIC 1

Exploring Other Ancient Traditions That Have Traveled West

Besides feng shui, other traditional Eastern practices have become popular in the West. Examples are tai chi, yoga, reiki, shiatsu massage, karate, and tae kwon do.

Step 1: Conduct an interview. Try to find someone who practices one of these arts. Look for either a professional or an amateur. Ask friends or neighbors, or look in the telephone book or business directory.

Step 2: Work with a partner. Brainstorm a list of questions that you would like to ask the practitioner. For example:

- How did you get into this practice?
- How and why did this art become popular in the West?
- How is it practiced differently here?

Step 3: Interview the person, and take notes.

Step 4: Report your findings to the class.

TOPIC 2

Web Research

In the past few years, the popularity of feng shui has skyrocketed all over the world. Many people are studying feng shui and applying its principles in order to improve their lives. However, some people think these principles are being exploited for commercial reasons. For example, a cosmetics company recently launched a new line of makeup called "feng shui makeup." Company representatives claim that this new makeup contains the right feng shui "balance" of colors and texture to guide the user through a smooth or rocky passage as her face ages.

Step 1: You can find many of these kinds of products on the Internet. Do research on the Web to find the most unusual applications of feng shui. What is your opinion of them? Take notes.

Step 2: Prepare a short research summary and report your findings and opinions to the class.

UNIT 6: Spiritual Renewal

Choose a topic and follow the steps for researching it.

TOPIC 1

Researching a Topic Related to Monasticism

Step 1: Work with a partner. Research a topic related to monasticism on the Internet or in the library. Choose one topic from the box or think of your own. You can also use the information from the documentary *Into Great Silence* in your research.

Thomas Merton	New Skete monasteries
Tenzin Palmo	Meditation
Mt. Athos	Fasting
Trappist monasteries	Vows of silence
Buddhist monasteries	

Step 2: Prepare a 5- to 10-minute presentation. If possible, use pictures or illustrations in your presentation.

Step 3: Present your findings to the class.

TOPIC 2

Field Research

Step 1: Work with a partner. Research a spiritual retreat center or monastery in your area. Write, call, or visit for more information.

Step 2: Prepare a research summary and present your findings to the class.

UNIT 7: Workplace Privacy

Follow the steps on the next page to research the topic.

In this activity, you will play a roving reporter and interview several people about their opinions on the topic of workplace privacy.

Step 1: Choose two different workplaces, and try to arrange interviews with both employees and employers. If you cannot, interview people you know who work or run businesses.

Step 2: Work with a partner. Brainstorm a list of questions that you would like to ask in your interview. For example:

- Are you aware of any monitoring practices done in your company?
- Does your company have a privacy policy? If so, what is it?
- Do you think employers have the right to bug the phones?

Step 3: Conduct your interviews. Try to talk to both employers and employees. Start your interviews like this:

"Excuse me. I'm doing a brief survey for my English class on the topic of workplace privacy. Could I ask you a few questions?"

While you interview, take notes on the answers to your questions.

Step 4: Present a summary of your findings to the class.

UNIT 8: Warriors without Weapons

Follow the steps to research the topic.

Step 1: Use the Internet to research human rights groups such as Doctors Without Borders (www.doctorswithoutborders.org), Oxfam (www.oxfam.org), UNICEF (www.unicef.org), or Human Rights Watch (www.hrw.org) to learn about relief agencies that do not adhere to strict positions of neutrality.

Step 2: Organize your research into three parts:

- purpose and philosophy of the organization
- recent activities (for example, countries the organization is now working in, projects in those countries, new approaches to the work in the face of terrorism)
- volunteer opportunities and qualifications

Step 3: Compare this organization to the ICRC, and present your findings to the class. Support your oral presentation with a poster, handout, short video clip, audio recording, or photos.

UNIT 9: Boosting Brain Power through the Arts

Follow the steps to research the topic.

You will organize an experiment on "The Mozart Effect." The experiment will try to determine if listening to music by Mozart can increase the speed of performing simple math, logic, or spatial problems.

Step 1: Choose four to six people to participate (or divide the class into two groups). Divide the participants into two groups: Group A: control group, and Group B: test group. Explain to the participants the purpose of the experiment, and give a little background that you have learned in this unit.

Step 2: Direct the participant groups to go into two rooms. Group A sits in silence. Group B listens to Mozart. After 10 minutes, all participants do the problems. You can use these sample problems, or find or design your own:

1. Study the table of numbers below for 2 minutes. Then cover it up, and try to reproduce it yourself.

2	6	6	1
3	4	2	6
6	3	6	0
4	2	1	8

2. How many rectangles are there in the figure?

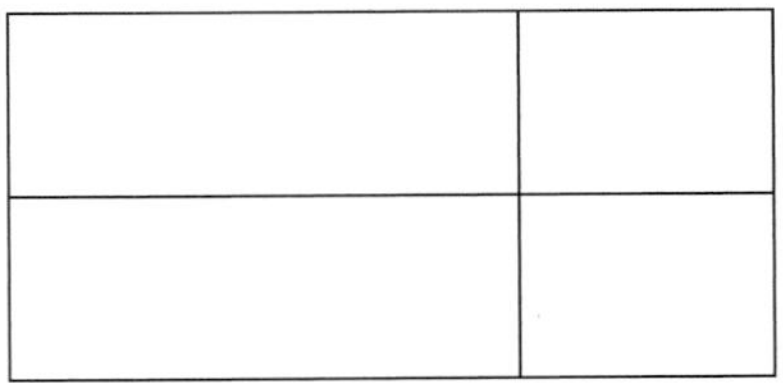

3. What is the minimum number of arrows that must be turned in some manner so that all arrows point in the same direction?

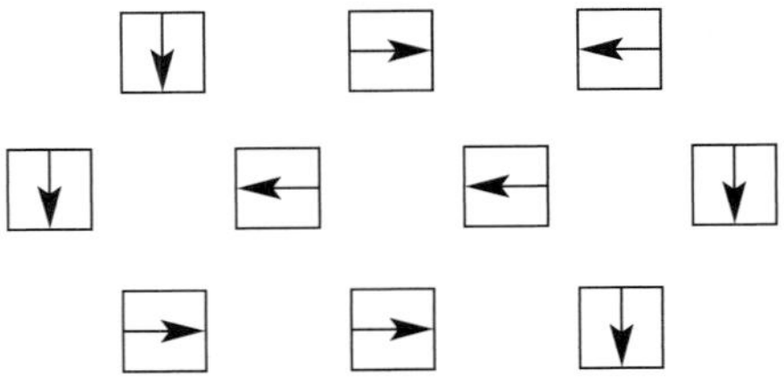

Step 3: Compare the two groups' problem-solving skills in terms of speed and accuracy.

Step 4: Report the results to the class. Then compare the results. Use the expressions of contrast and similarity and the passive voice to explain the process.

Step 5: Work in small groups, and discuss the answers to these questions:

- Did you see evidence of the Mozart effect? Why or why not?
- If you were to repeat the experiment, how would you do the experiment differently?

2. Answer: 9 3. Answer: 6

Complete one of these projects.

TOPIC 1

Choose a Microborrower

Imagine that you would like to lend money to a microentrepreneur who is posted on the Kiva.org website. Visit the Kiva.org website and click on the link, "see all businesses in need." Read about the various microborrowers and choose one to whom you would like to lend money. Create a 2–3 minute presentation about your new business partner, explaining the reasons for your choice.

TOPIC 2

Muhammad Yunus

Conduct research on Muhammad Yunus either on the Internet or by reading his autobiography, *Banker to the Poor,* in which he narrates the story of microlending. Present your findings to the class.

TOPIC 3

Celebrities Who Fight Poverty

There have been quite a few well-known celebrities who have become active in the fight against global poverty. Some of the most famous of these celebrities are Bono, Sir Richard Branson, actresses Angelina Jolie and Natalie Portman, Oprah Winfrey, and Haitian musician Wyclef Jean. Research the efforts to fight poverty by one of these celebrities and present your findings to the class.

TOPIC 4

Research a Microfinance Institution

Unitus is a non-profit organization that supports and helps other microfinance institutions. Visit the Unitus website (http://www.unitus.com) and look for the Client Success stories. Read about one of their clients, summarize and then present your findings to the class.

GRAMMAR BOOK REFERENCES

***NorthStar: Listening and Speaking Level 5*, Third Edition**	***Focus on Grammar Level 5*, Third Edition**	**Azar's *Understanding and Using English Grammar*, Third Edition**
Unit 1 Wish Statements—Expressing Unreality	**Unit 23** Conditionals; Other Ways to Express Unreality	**Chapter 20** Conditional Sentences and Wishes: 20-6, 20-10, 20-11
Unit 2 Modals—Degrees of Certainty	**Unit 6** Modals to Express Degrees of Certainty	**Chapter 10** Modals, Part 2: 10-1, 10-2, 10-3, 10-4, 10-5, 10-6
Unit 3 Adjective Clauses—Identifying and Nonidentifying	**Unit 11** Adjective Clauses: Review and Expansion **Unit 12** Adjective Clauses with Prepositions; Adjective Phrases	**Chapter 13** Adjective Clauses: 13-5, 13-6, 13-7, 13-8, 13-10
Unit 4 Adverb Clauses of Result	**Unit 18** Adverb Clauses	**Chapter 19** Connectives that Express Cause and Effect, Contrast, and Condition: 19-4
Unit 5 Spoken Discourse Connectors	**Unit 20** Connectors	**Chapter 19** Connectives that Express Cause and Effect, Contrast, and Condition: 19-2, 19-6, 19-7, 19-9
Unit 6 Count and Non-Count Nouns and Their Qualifiers	**Unit 7** Count and Non-Count Nouns **Unit 8** Definite and Indefinite Articles **Unit 9** Quantifiers	**Chapter 7** Nouns: 7-9, 7-10, 7-11

NorthStar: Listening and Speaking Level 5, Third Edition	*Focus on Grammar Level 5,* Third Edition	Azar's *Understanding and Using English Grammar,* Third Edition
Unit 7 Verb + Gerund or Infinitive—Two Forms, Two Meanings	**Unit 15** Gerunds **Unit 16** Infinitives	**Chapter 14** Gerunds and Infinitives, Part 1: 14-4, 14-7, 14-8, 14-9, 14-10
Unit 8 Direct and Indirect Speech	**Unit 22** Direct and Indirect Speech	**Chapter 12** Noun Clauses: 12-6, 12-7
Unit 9 The Passive Voice and the Passive Causative	**Unit 13** The Passive: Review and Expansion **Unit 14** The Passive to Describe Situations and to Report Opinions	**Chapter 11** The Passive: 11-1, 11-2, 11-7
Unit 10 Unreal Conditionals—Present, Past, and Mixed	**Unit 23** Conditionals; Other Ways to Express Unreality	**Chapter 20** Conditional Sentences and Wishes: 20-1, 20-2, 20-3, 20-4, 20-6, 20-7

AUDIOSCRIPT

UNIT 1: The Internet and Other Addictions

2A. LISTENING ONE: *Interview with an Internet Addiction Counselor*

Ira Flatow: Welcome back to *Talk of the Nation: Science Friday.* I'm Ira Flatow. We're talking this hour about how and why people might become addicted to things other than drugs . . . addicted to things like gambling, sex, even shopping. Of course, our high-tech society also offers new high-tech **addictions** like video games, online chat rooms. Jonathan Kandell is a counselor at the University of Maryland who **puts together** a **support group** for students who find themselves addicted to the Internet. Maybe you should listen carefully to this one if you are an Internet groupie. He joins me now from his office in College Park.

Welcome to the program.

Jonathan Kandell: Thank you very much.

LISTEN FOR MAIN IDEAS

Ira Flatow: Welcome back to *Talk of the Nation: Science Friday.* I'm Ira Flatow. We're talking this hour about how and why people might become addicted to things other than drugs . . . addicted to things like gambling, sex, even shopping. Of course, our high-tech society also offers new high-tech **addictions** like video games, online chat rooms. Jonathan Kandell is a counselor at the University of Maryland who **puts together** a **support group** for students who find themselves addicted to the Internet. Maybe you should listen carefully to this one if you are an Internet groupie. He joins me now from his office in College Park.

Welcome to the program.

Jonathan Kandell: Thank you very much.

IF: Is this a relatively new **addiction**?

JK: Well, for some people, I mean, some people have been involved with the Internet for years and uh . . . some of them may have been addicted for a while . . . with the widespread usage of the Internet now. . . . I mean . . . it's certainly growing especially on college campuses . . . we are seeing more and more of it.

IF: And how does it present itself? Does a student come to you and say, "Doc, you gotta help me. I'm addicted to the Internet"?

JK: Well, I've seen people who have been, but they haven't **presented with** that particular issue. They've presented with issues like relationship problems, or they're having problems maintaining their grades because they are spending so much time doing other things and when you find out what's really **going on** . . . they're spending a lot of time on the Net and they're not paying attention to their studies . . . they're not devoting the attention to the relationships. And, you know, these problems are coming out in other ways.

IF: Do other people **turn** their friends **in** . . . saying, "Doc, you gotta find out . . . this . . ."

JK: They haven't to this point. At this point, people still see computers as a very positive thing. And I mean, I agree. . . . I think there are many positive benefits for computers. But . . . uh . . . it is such a new idea that there is a **problematic** piece to it . . . that, um . . . there haven't been many people **turning** other people **in**.

IF: This is something I worry about . . . personally, myself. I'll share this with you for a free consultation. I mean . . . whenever I get a chance and have some time, I love to go **surfing** on the Net. I'll be on there sometimes, very surprisingly, I'll be on there one o'clock in the morning . . . I'll send somebody an e-mail message thinking they'll get it the next morning. And I'll get an immediate response back . . . you know.

What are the **symptoms**? How do I know when my Internet **compulsiveness** is **turning into** an Internet **addiction**?

JK: Uh . . . I'm not sure the exact amount of time is really the issue, I think when it becomes something that really begins to affect other areas of your life . . . like, for instance, your work performance or your school performance . . . or relationships with other people. Uh, one of the problems I see with the Internet, especially with the chat rooms, is that people start developing relationships over the Net and they are very different than relationships that you have on a face-to-face basis, and you start losing some of the skills that make relationships successful . . . so that's certainly a warning signal. I think if people are beginning to say something to you like, "You seem to be spending a lot of time online," that's probably a good indicator as well. . .

But, I think, a real important thing is to examine what's **going on** with you when you are not on the Net . . . I mean, if you are beginning to feel **anxious** or **depressed** or feeling **empty** and lonely . . . and you know you really look forward to those times when you can be online to be connected with other people in that way . . . then, I think, a serious issue is starting to happen.

IF: What about if you just stop giving up other things, like going out for a walk or something like that . . . is that a **symptom**?

JK: Uh, well, I mean, people have to make choices every day about the different activities that they're going to do. I think it's helpful to have some sort of balance in your life . . . I mean, if you can spend some time on the Internet and then also take a walk at a different time of the day. I think that's not an issue. In fact, that's one of the things that we suggest in the group is to somehow break the pattern . . . set an alarm clock or something. Go out and take a walk, and then come back before you get back online.

IF: You speak of the group, then, I'm assuming then some of the treatments you offer are group **therapy** sessions for these kids.

JK: Yes, this is a support group. And the group itself becomes a therapeutic tool . . . because people are getting out of their rooms, getting out of the isolation that they may find themselves in, and are dealing with other people face-to-face. They're talking about the issues that are **going on** with them. They're getting support from other people. Uh, they realize that it is not just them . . . that there are other people who are engaged in the same behaviors and facing the same problems, and also they can help each other strategize about what's the best way for them to break the pattern . . . to figure out other things to do. Uh, also we examine people's life situations . . . it's important to figure out what's **going on** in the person's life that's contributing to these particular behaviors. . . . Why is the person spending so much time? Are they avoiding something? What type of pain is going on in their life . . . that they're looking to find some **fulfillment** in this way?

LISTEN FOR DETAILS

(Repeat Listen for Main Ideas)

MAKE INFERENCES

Excerpt One

IF: Jonathan Kandell is a counselor at the University of Maryland who puts together a support group for students who find themselves addicted to the Internet. Maybe you should listen carefully to this one if you are an Internet groupie.

Excerpt Two

IF: Is this a relatively new addiction?

JK: Well, for some people, I mean, some people have been involved with the Internet for years and uh . . . some of them may have been addicted for a while . . . with the widespread usage of the Internet now . . . I mean . . . it's certainly growing, especially on college campuses . . . we are seeing more and more of it.

Excerpt Three

IF: And how does it present itself? Does a student come to you and say, "Doc, you gotta help me. I'm addicted to the Internet"?

2B. LISTENING TWO: *Time to Do Everything Except Think*

Warren Levinson: It's *Newsweek on Air.* I'm Warren Levinson of the Associated Press.

David Alpern: I'm David Alpern of *Newsweek.*

WL: David Brooks, you argue that we already live in an over-communicated world that will only become more so in the next tech era. What exactly do you mean by that?

David Brooks: The problem is that we've developed technology that gets us so much information that we've got cell phones ringing every second, we've got computers and laptops, we've got personal organizers and it's just—we're just being **bombarded with** communication and every advance and technology seems to create more and more communications at us. I do believe at the end of the day it **shapes** our personality because we are sort of **overwhelmed** by the information flow.

DA: Seriously though, just last week we reported on research suggesting that all the **multi-tasking** may actually make our brains work better and faster, producing as its been reported a world-wide increase in IQ up to 20 points and more in recent decades. Can you see any benefit in all these mental gymnastics we now have to **go through**?

DB: Yeah I, I, I don't think we're becoming a race of global idiots. Uh, but I think certain skills are **enhanced** and certain are not. You know the ability to make fast decisions, to answer a dozen e-mails in five minutes, uh to fill out maybe big SAT-type tests. Uh, that's **enhanced.** But creativity is something that happens slowly. It happens when your brain is just noodling around, just playing. When it **puts together** ideas which you hadn't thought of or maybe you have time, say, to read a book. You are a businessperson but you have time to read a book about history or time to read a book about a philosopher and something that happened long ago or something or some idea somebody thought of long ago. Actually, you know, it occurs to you that you can think of your own business in that way, and so it's this mixture of unrelated ideas, uh, that **feeds** your productivity, **feeds** your creativity, and if your mind is disciplined to answer every e-mail, then you don't have time for that playful noodling. You don't have time for those unexpected conjunctions, so I think maybe we're getting smarter in some senses but I think it's a, it is a threat to our creativity and to our reflection.

DA: So how wired or wirelessly are you tied into the new technology?

DB: A total addict. When I'm out there with my kids playing in our little league or something like that, I've got my cell phone in my pocket. I'm always wondering, "Gee, did I get a voicemail?", uh, and that's why I think I'm sort of driven to write about this because I do see the negative effects it having on my own brain patterns.

DA: Could be *Newsweek on Air* calling . . . David Brooks thanks a lot.

DB: Thank you.

UNIT 2: Honesty Is the Best Policy

2A. LISTENING ONE: *Interview with a Psychiatrist*

Dr. Goodwin: Lies are usually about the here and now. They're a short-term solution to an immediate problem, a way to avoid criticism or anger, to look good, to please another. I believe that what helps most people stay honest most of the time is an awareness of the long-term impact of lies, the slow, but **relentless erosion** of trust.

LISTEN FOR MAIN IDEAS

Part One

Dr. Goodwin: I'm Dr. Fred Goodwin. As you'll hear during this show, lying can be approached from a variety of perspectives: moral, legal, interpersonal. Let me offer the perspective of one psychiatrist. People who lie more or less regularly often tend to narcissism. Absorbed as they are with an **inflated** sense of themselves, they are tempted to lie because they believe they can do it so cleverly that they won't get caught. But beneath this confident **veneer** lies a **pervasive** sense of insecurity that fuels the need to lie. Lacking a core, a consistent sense of who one is, narcissists must constantly define and redefine themselves through the responses of those around them. In a way, to survive, the narcissist develops a **finely honed** intuitive focus on the moment, but ultimately cannot see beyond it. To do so requires that internal compass, that independent, stable sense of one's true self.

Part Two

Dr. Goodwin: But what does the narcissist's **preoccupation** with the moment have to do with lying? It is this: Lies are usually about the here and now. They're a short-term solution to an immediate problem, a way to avoid criticism or anger, to look good, to please another. I believe that what helps most people stay honest most of the time is an awareness of the long-term impact of lies, the slow, but **relentless erosion** of trust. It's as if the narcissist, with his inability to see beyond the moment, is ultimately trapped in his lies, confirming for others what he deep down believes to be true: there's nothing there.

Part Three

Dr. Goodwin: Dr. Paul Ekman is professor of psychology at the University of California Medical School, San Francisco, and director of the Human Interaction Laboratory.

Welcome to *The Infinite Mind,* Dr. Ekman.

Dr. Ekman: Thank you.

Dr. Goodwin: Nice to have you. Now start out with basics. Why don't you tell our listeners how do you define a lie? What is a lie?

Dr. Ekman: Well, a lie is a very particular kind of deception that lies meet two criteria. First, it's a deliberate choice to **mislead** another person. That one's pretty obvious. But the second, a little less obvious, is that you don't give any notification of the fact that you're going to do that. And in many situations in life, we either notify someone, like a magician does . . . a magician lies to us, a magician fools us, but we're notified.

Dr. Goodwin: Is there more to the definition than that?

Dr. Ekman: That's all it requires. There are many different ways to tell a lie. You can **conceal** information. You can falsify information. You can even sometimes tell the truth in a mocking fashion. I call it telling the truth falsely.

Part Four

Dr. Goodwin: Have you cataloged sort of why people tell lies?

Dr. Ekman: Yes. And there are nine different reasons. The most common one for both children and adults is to avoid punishment for something that you've done. You know, you . . . you tell the traffic cop, 'Gee, officer, I didn't think I was going over 55.'

The second is to get a reward that you couldn't get otherwise or you couldn't get as easily, so you cheat on an exam 'cause you're more certain that you're going to get a high mark, or you don't want to put in all the time studying and preparing for it.

The third is to protect another person from being punished. That's an altruistic lie. And, in fact, we disapprove. If one . . . if a brother tells on a sister, we say that's **tattling**. We expect kids to protect each other.

A fourth is to protect yourself from the threat of physical harm.

Another is to win the admiration of others. You know, it's—it is the name droppers. The father who says, 'Well, you know, the last time I saw George W., he said so-and-so and so-and-so.' It's . . . it's . . . it's trying to get people to admire you.

A very common one is getting out of an awkward social situation, even a **trivial** one, like the telephone salesman.

Another is to avoid embarrassment. You see that particularly in kids who make mistakes. Kids who wet their pants will lie about it because they're so embarrassed.

Another is to maintain privacy. This particularly occurs in adolescents who have overly **intrusive** parents.

And the last is to get power over other people. It's the greatest power and the most complete power in the world is to have somebody believe something that you've told them that you know is untrue. You've really got control over them. Most adolescents will do this once or twice or three times. They can now **put it over** the old man, or they can fool their mom now. But they won't continue to do it. But there are people who continue that as a lifelong pattern. So those are nine very different reasons why people lie.

Part Five

Dr. Ekman: You lie, because life itself is more important than telling the truth or lying. The rule of thumb I think people should follow in trying to decide, 'Should I tell this lie or not?' is, 'Do I care about a future relationship with this person? And if I do, how would they feel if they found out?' Because to lie is—to be caught lying is to destroy trust, and nobody knows the steps that you could take to ever re-establish trust. So it's a very high price. The loss of trust is a very high price to pay for being caught in a lie.

LISTEN FOR DETAILS

(Repeat Listen for Main Ideas)

MAKE INFERENCES

Excerpt One

Dr. Goodwin: I believe that what helps most people stay honest most of the time is an awareness of the long-term impact of lies, the slow, but relentless erosion of trust. It's as if the narcissist, with his inability to see beyond the moment, is ultimately trapped in his lies, confirming for others what he deep down believes to be true: there's nothing there.

Excerpt Two

Dr. Ekman: Well, a lie is a very particular kind of deception that lies meet two criteria. First, it's a deliberate choice to mislead another person. That one's pretty obvious. But the second, a little less obvious, is that you don't give any notification of the fact that you're going to do that. And in many situations in life, we either notify someone, like a magician does . . . a magician lies to us, a magician fools us, but we're notified.

Dr. Goodwin: Is there more to the definition than that?

Dr. Ekman: That's all it requires.

Excerpt Three

Dr. Ekman: The most common one for both children and adults is to avoid punishment for something that you've done. You know, you . . . you tell the traffic cop, 'Gee, officer, I didn't think I was going over 55.'

2B. LISTENING TWO: *Family Secrets*

Exercise 1

Part One

Pola Rapaport: Many years after my father died, I had found a small photograph of a young boy that resembled him enormously in my father's desk, which had remained un—undisturbed for all those years. The picture was signed 'Pierre' on the back, and I really didn't know what to do with it, even though it looked so much like my father and he had never mentioned having—certainly never mentioned having a child before. I knew he didn't have any other relatives other than us. That was over 10 years ago. When years later my mother got a letter from Romania signed with the name Pierre, which was the same name on the back of the picture, we started to **put the pieces** together, and I thought perhaps this is someone who's looking to find his lost family. And, in fact, after a short exchange of letters between me and this stranger, Pierre, in Bucharest, he finally acknowledged that his father was my father.

Interviewer: So that the photograph that you found in the drawer was in fact your long lost half-brother.

PR: That's who it was, I mean, the suspicion was right that he was our long lost brother or half-brother, living in Bucharest all that time. And then I had never been to Romania, but I had an opportunity to go. Actually, my husband was shooting a documentary there. So I kind of piggybacked and went along and I met Pierre for the first time. And it was an absolutely extraordinary experience to see him waiting for me at the airport with a little bouquet of flowers, and it was as though I were seeing my father reincarnated standing there because he resembles him almost identically.

Interviewer: He looks a lot like the photographs of your father, in the film.

PR: Yeah. It's really uncanny.

Interviewer: Your father had never told you or your sister anything about a son that he had had in Europe?

PR: No, he was really incredibly successful at keeping the secret from us.

Part Two

PR: My father was very secretive about the period in his life when he lived in Romania. In fact he was secretive about the period of his life when he lived in France prior to meeting my mother.

Sister: Daddy was a secretive person and people who . . . people who had to run from, you know, Gestapo persecution I think became secretive, as a matter of survival.

Part Three

Interviewer: So how did you as a filmmaker and as a person go into uncovering these secrets when you have a family legacy and teaching of, maybe this is not such a good thing to explore secrets. Was it scary for you? Was it elating for you? Did you have a feeling that you were trespassing on forbidden ground?

PR: Oh, all of those things, actually. But I—the feeling of trespassing was actually very elating; it was very exciting to get into this territory. I—I think I used to kind of **mull over** these things alone and come up with all kinds of images of what things could be and ideas of what things could be. And so actually to open it up and have a real situation where I could uncover these things that were forbidden to me was actually very exciting.

Interviewer: Do you think that there's any relationship between the family secrets and the experience of being lied to?

PR: You know, you can't blame people for lying. I think sometimes they're trying to go for a higher value, like not hurting someone else. But I must say, I think the truth is always best because, eventually it's going to come out, particularly—I—I mean, people are smart and children are really smart, and they know something isn't right when something isn't right. I think they know when something's being kept from them, on some level, often non-verbal with children. And, um, so eventually—sometimes the truth doesn't come out, but there's always going to be a hole in your experience, like an emptiness or some—something that's not right and out of order if this kind of secret—secret is kept in families.

Exercise 2

(Repeat Exercise 1)

3A. VOCABULARY

EXPAND

Exercise 1

Beatriz: Dr. Sanborn, I hate to have to tell you this, but I am concerned that Martin has **fudged** the results of his study.

Dr. Sanborn: You mean he has **manipulated** the data in order to get the result he wanted?

Beatriz: Yes, I am pretty sure that he is **bluffing** about the safety of his sweetener.

Dr. Sanborn: Come on, Beatriz. It's really hard to believe that Martin would lie about his work. He has always been an accurate, honest researcher.

Beatriz: Well, apparently his ambition is blinding him. I'm telling you, he's going down a **slippery slope** with this project.

Dr. Sanborn: I can't bear to hear that such a bright intelligent researcher would be **headed toward disaster**.

Beatriz: I know, but he's too afraid to **fess up** to the fact that his sweetener might pose a health risk.

Dr. Sanborn: Beatriz, I've known Martin for years. I can't believe he wouldn't tell me if his experiments were failing.

Beatriz: Well, trust me, Dr. Sanborn, Martin's project is definitely a **recipe for disaster**. His results will not be duplicated, I'm sure.

Dr. Sanborn: Thanks, Beatriz. I understand. If his project is a failure, our lab will lose funding. I'll speak to Martin tomorrow.

Exercise 2

Martin: Wow, Beatriz. I absolutely cannot believe the **whopper** you told Dr. Sanborn about my experiment. You're just jealous that I'm finally getting the results that'll make me famous.

Beatriz: Are you kidding? I didn't tell him a lie, and I am not envious of you. You should know me better than that.

Martin: I thought I did, Bea, but you are **two-faced**. I can't trust you now.

Beatriz: Martin, I'm not being **deceptive**. Whatever I told Dr. Sanborn, I would tell you directly. Look, I don't trust the results of your study. You are falsifying the data.

Martin: That's not true. The chubby mice have lost weight, and my sweetener is safe. I am being totally **up front** with you and everyone else about my results.

Beatriz: You can't really believe that! You're so preoccupied with success, you're not being honest.

Martin: My reputation does depend on this project, but I would never risk my career to **pull the wool over everyone's eyes**.

Beatriz: I'm sorry, Martin, but the facts show you *are* trying to trick us, despite our lab policy to "**relentlessly** pursue knowledge and truth."

3C. SPEAKING

PRONUNCIATION

Exercise 2

Anton: I think José's hair looks awful. I could've given him a better haircut with my eyes closed. Do you really think he looks good?

Molly: No, I agree, he looks terrible. He should've kept his hair long. But I couldn't tell him that.

Anton: No, but he didn't ask you what you thought. You volunteered the compliment. You shouldn't've said anything at all.

Molly: But he saw me staring at him. If I hadn't said anything, he would've thought I didn't like his haircut. He knew I'd noticed, so I told a white lie. What's the harm?

Anton: Well, first, you told a lie when you could've said nothing. But what's worse, now José thinks he looks good when he really doesn't.

Molly: But if I hadn't said anything, it would've been awkward. Anyway, when his hair grows, I'll tell him he looks even better.

UNIT 3: The Bold and the Bashful

2A. LISTENING ONE: *Americans Are Getting Shyer*

Philip Zimbardo: Virtually all the people that we have surveyed, certainly 75 percent of them, say shyness is undesirable, has **adverse** consequences. Shy people are less popular, they have fewer friends, they have lower self-esteem, they make less money, their life is more boring, they have less intimate . . . less intimacy, less sex, they have fewer leadership skills, less social support, they're more likely to be depressed and, as you get older, more likely to be lonely. That's a terrible **syndrome** of **negative** consequences.

LISTEN FOR MAIN IDEAS

Part One

Alex Chadwick: Do you find these days that it's more difficult meeting people? In social situations with strangers do you **wind up**

asking yourself, "Am I dressed wrong today or something?" Friends, take heart. A new study says it's not you at all. The problem is Americans are, generally speaking, more shy than many people would expect, and getting shyer all the time.

Philip Zimbardo is a professor of psychology at Stanford University who runs a shyness clinic in Palo Alto. He's the author of numerous studies on shyness. Good morning, Professor Zimbardo.

Philip Zimbardo: Good morning.

AC: Your earlier study showed shyness already **widespread**, but what about the newest figures?

PZ: Our research, which we've been conducting since 1972, focused on adults who were shy. Before our research started, of course, the interest was always in shy children and, to our amazement, we discovered that about 40 percent of all Americans label themselves as currently shy, and over the past ten years that figure has increased to about 48 percent. What that means is two out of every five people you meet **think of** themselves as shy, and now that figure is moving toward one out of two, which is a surprise, especially to foreigners, who think . . . **think of** Americans as **bold** and **outgoing** and not at all shy.

AC: Why is shyness so common, and why is it becoming even more common?

PZ: Well, shyness is a fascinating problem because at one level to be shy means to be **reticent**, to be **self-conscious**. It's a kind of social **phobia**, a fear of people, and it's very hard to avoid people, and there are just many things in a culture, our culture, which leads lots of people to be shy. We have a very competitive culture. We have a culture where people are constantly . . . at least feel they are being evaluated, where the . . . the whole notion of testing, of . . . of individual **merit** that starts in school, at work, really extends for many people to their social life.

But what's been happening recently is a whole series of social forces that are increasingly isolating people from normal day-to-day informal social contact, which is essential to be a social being, an **extrovert**, an **outgoing** person who can easily and comfortably relate to other people.

AC: A set of social factors, you say. What do you mean?

PZ: Well, first, the electronic revolution replaces people with computer chips wherever possible, so at every level where you replace bank tellers with ATM machines, you replace operators with direct dialing, you replace the gas station attendant with automatic gas fill-ups . . .

AC: So there's . . . there's just less opportunity for social interaction? People forget about . . .

PZ: Well, people don't forget, they don't learn . . . young people don't learn in the first place, they don't practice it, they don't see it practiced, as you have, so this gets really complicated because computers, computer games, video games, are things people can play alone. You don't need other people the way you used to in the past and, also, as families get smaller, as both parents work, we no longer have extended families, children don't see . . . don't have the opportunity to see their parents and relatives relating in a natural, easy, friendly way. So . . . so they just . . . we are losing the . . . the . . . the social lubrication that's essential for people to feel comfortable in the presence of each other.

Part Two

AC: Professor Zimbardo, when you say shy, when you say it's a problem, what kind of shyness do you mean? Many people feel some awkwardness in social situations, especially if they get attention from others, if they're the object of attention from others.

PZ: **Virtually** all the people that we have surveyed, certainly 75 percent of them, say shyness is undesirable, has **adverse** consequences. Shy people are less popular, they have fewer friends, they have lower self-esteem, they make less money, their life is more boring, they have less intimate . . . less intimacy, less sex, they have fewer leadership skills, less social support, they're more likely to be depressed and, as you get older, more likely to be lonely. That's a terrible **syndrome** of **negative** consequences.

AC: So this is not just a momentary shyness that . . . that . . . people feel; this is something that really **marks** their lives?

PZ: Yeah. The momentary shyness is something we call situational shyness. That is if . . . if you're on a blind date, if you're asked to perform in public, we are not really prepared. Or if your mother says, you know, "Play the piano for Aunt Tilly." Well, you have the feelings of shyness, the . . . the arousal, the **negative** thoughts, the . . . the physical tension, but that is situational. So you say to yourself, "Well, that's not me; that's that external situation which I have to avoid." It's when it becomes **chronic** and dispositional. You begin to see shyness as Quasimodo's hump, the thing you carry around with you that's always there and even . . . even if . . . if people in the world don't notice it, you know it's there ready to emerge.

AC: When . . . when you're at a cocktail party, or just in conversation with someone anywhere and you recognize that they're shy, what do you do to **draw them out** or try to make them more comfortable?

PZ: Essentially what we say, for example, to shy people is, "If you begin with the knowledge that maybe half the people out there are also shy, then when you're in a situation, do your best to find those other people, those **kindred souls**." And a great way to **break the ice** is to talk about how uncomfortable these situations make you feel, and you presume the other. Admitting your shyness is really an important first step because if you don't, people make **misattributions**. That is, if you don't perform in a situation where people expect you to perform, to smile, to be **outgoing**, to start a conversation, people assume you're dumb, you're unmotivated, you're boring, or you're not interested in them. You're bored or boring, and those are terrible **misattributions**, especially if you're attractive as a man, or beautiful as a woman, and shy. Then it's a double **handicap** because people then assume you are **aloof**, you are **condescending**, you think you're too good for them.

AC: Professor Zimbardo?

PZ: Yes?

AC: Are you shy?

PZ: No, not at all. In fact, I'm a firstborn from a big Sicilian family, so my job was making all the other kids feel comfortable, and so I . . . I am more like a Zorba the Greek-type person whose job in the world it is to make people feel comfortable, you know, at life's party.

AC: Professor Zimbardo, thank you very much.

PZ: It's been a joy, thank you.

AC: Stanford University psychologist Philip Zimbardo runs a shyness clinic at Palo Alto. He spoke to us from member station KQED in San Francisco. This is NPR's *Morning Edition;* I'm Alex Chadwick.

LISTEN FOR DETAILS

(Repeat Listen for Main Ideas)

MAKE INFERENCES

Excerpt One

AC: Do you find these days that it's more difficult meeting people? In social situations with strangers do you wind up asking yourself, "Am I dressed wrong today or something?" Friends, take heart.

Excerpt Two

PZ: Our research, which we've been conducting since 1972, focused on adults who were shy. Before our research started, of course, the interest was always in shy children, and to our amazement, we discovered that about 40 percent of all Americans label themselves as currently shy, and over the past 10 years that figure has increased to about 48 percent. What that means is two out of every five people you meet think of themselves as shy.

Excerpt Three

AC: Professor Zimbardo . . . Are you shy?

PZ: No, not at all. In fact, I'm a first born from a big Sicilian family, so my job was making all the other kids feel comfortable.

2B. LISTENING TWO: *The Pollyanna Syndrome*

Host: If you're the sort to divide people into two groups, consider the division between those who always see the bright side and those who'd rather wallow in their misery.

Julie Danis tackles the **Pollyanna syndrome** in today's "Tale from the Workplace."

Julie Danis: I'm Julie Danis with "Tales from the Workplace."

Arriving at the office after a visit to the eye doctor with no diagnosis for my blurred vision, I was in a **grouchy** mood. "No time to be cranky," a co-worker said, "we have a project due."

"Besides," she continued, "now you have a prescription to skip the mascara and rest your eyes, every two hours."

She'd done it again, I realized. She had made lemonade out of lemons. We all know people like this. They find the silver lining inside the darkest cloud . . . all the time . . . without fail . . . driving others to distraction with their "find the bright side" philosophy.

"Oh well," they say, "a stop-and-go commute is perfect for listening to language tapes while doing relaxation exercises, mais oui?"

They may emit an occasional, "Oh, no," when the computer crashes and the hold time on the 1-800-HELP line promises to be hours. But that is soon replaced by an, "Oh good, time to purge the files."

This optimistic **outlook** does have its **merits**. When you're snowed in with no hope of flying for 24 hours or more, take it as a sign you should catch up on some movies.

But don't get **carried away**. Nothing will take away the ache in your mouth or **fill the void** in your pocketbook from two root canals not covered by your company's health plan.

So, the next time someone says, "You can't cry over something that can't cry over you," **assert** yourself in the face of their sunny-side-up point of view. State firmly, "Yes I can, and I plan to do just that." Then go suck on some lemons and feel better in your own way. I'm Julie Danis with "Tales from the Workplace."

3C. SPEAKING

PRONUNCIATION

Exercise 2

1. "Philip," said the doctor, "doesn't suffer from shyness."
2. My sister who lives in California is a Pollyanna.
3. Suzanne's manager told me she's gotten over her shyness.
4. Zimbardo interviewed the students who had admitted they were shy.
5. Everything he said was based on research.
6. The therapy, which the clinic provides, gets people to be more outgoing.

UNIT 4: The Tipping Point

2A. LISTENING ONE: *The Tipping Point*

Malcolm Gladwell: I—I—you know in the book I **profile** them, they are these extraordinarily social people with a lot of energy who are **consumed by**, with kind of the task of getting to know people. Of meeting people, of knowing them, of keeping in touch with them. They're the people who write little notes. They're the people who keep in touch with you after they've left town. They're the people who make, you know, phone calls all day long. And these people—

LISTEN FOR MAIN IDEAS

Malcolm Gladwell: I think that same idea **holds** for **word-of-mouth epidemics**—that there is a small number of exceptional people who play a huge role in the **transmission** of **epidemic** ideas. I call them **mavens**, connectors, and salesmen.

Christopher Lydon: Say it again. . . . **Mavens**, connectors, and salesmen.

MG: **Mavens**, connectors, and salesmen. Connectors are um, the kind of people who know everybody. There are a handful of people in any group, in any social group who have extraordinary social ties. Well above . . . I mean if the average. . . . I do this names test in the book, which is . . . I have 350 names in the Manhattan, last names in the Manhattan phone book and you go down the list and every time you see a last name you know, you give yourself a point. Well, the average score is, most people score like 25, 30. There is in every group someone who scores 120 or 130. That kind of person is incredibly powerful in **generating word-of-mouth epidemics**. Because if they like something and **get a hold of** some idea, they can spread it five or six times, you know, further than anybody, than most of . . . than average person.

CL: Who are those people? What defines them?

MG: Well there are, I you know in the book I **profile** them, they are these extraordinarily social people with a lot of energy who are **consumed by**, with kind of the task of getting to know people. Of meeting people, of knowing them, of keeping in touch with them. They're the people who write little notes. They're the people who keep in touch with you after they've left town. They're the people who make, you know, phone calls all day long. And these people—

CL: I'm afraid I'm one of them.

MG: I think you might be one of them—they, you know, this is not typical behavior. This is behavior that's actually rare. Most of us don't do that, and you know I'm someone who is not that way. If I like, go to a movie, a new movie, and like it, I can't start a **word-of-mouth epidemic** because I simply don't know enough people. I can't get it outside of my own immediate circle of friends. Someone who has friends all over the place, they can and someone you know who is sort of relentlessly social, they can spread the news about a new restaurant or a new movie or something far and wide in a very very short time.

CL: These are the connectors. Who are the **mavens** and who are the salesmen?

MG: The **mavens** are people who have specialized knowledge. If you, if you examine why you make certain decisions, why do you shop somewhere, why do you go to a certain movie, why do you go to a certain restaurant, what you find is that you are relying on the same person over and over again for recommendations. Those people I call **mavens**. And **mavens**, I always give the example of this friend of mine Ariel who knows all about restaurants in lower Manhattan. If I want to know about the hot new restaurant I call Ariel. Well all of Ariel's friends call Ariel and if you go to restaurants in lower Manhattan and look around the room, you will see friends of Ariel. The restaurant market in Manhattan, which is an **epidemic** market, right?—restaurants come and go—is controlled by a group of Ariels. I don't think there's very many of them, I think there's probably you know, two dozen of them. If you knew who the Ariels were, you could, you know—that's an extraordinarily powerful piece of information if you're interested in restaurants in Manhattan. Well, that's true of lots of things. That's true of shopping and books and movies, and um, you know the Ariels of the world, the **mavens**, uh, and if you think about it if a **maven** gets together with a connector, than you can begin to see why a **word-of-mouth epidemic** might happen. Um, someone who knows everyone, in combination with someone who knows everything, is a really powerful connection.

CL: And then introduce the salesman.

MG: Well there's also, I think there's also a role played by people who are incredibly persuasive, and again, that's a very rare and unusual trait and—

CL: Leaves me out you see, I connect but I can't sell.

MG: You can't sell. Well—these are—they're separate categories. I have—I've met with this guy in the book, a guy I called Tom Gau—who I—who is known as one of the greatest salesmen in America today and tried to get at the **root** of what was, you know, why he's so persuasive and you know it's a really fascinating question, and—but you—you know when you meet someone like that you begin to realize as well, why do, why do trends happen? They happen because someone like this, who has this extraordinary natural ability to **win you over**, **gets a hold of** an idea, and when they **get a hold of** an idea, they can really make it go a long way.

LISTEN FOR DETAILS

(Repeat Listen for Main Ideas)

MAKE INFERENCES

Excerpt One

Malcolm Gladwell: I think that same idea holds for word-of-mouth epidemics—that there is a small number of exceptional people who play a huge role in the transmission of epidemic ideas. I call them mavens, connectors, and salesmen.

Christopher Lydon: Say it again. . . . Mavens, connectors, and salesmen.

Excerpt Two

MG: They're the people who keep in touch with you after they've left town. They're the people who make, you know, phone calls all day long. And these people—

CL: I'm afraid I'm one of them.

MG: I think you might be one of them—they, you know, this is not typical behavior. This is behavior that's actually rare.

Excerpt Three

MG: The restaurant market in Manhattan, which is an epidemic market, right?—restaurants come and go—is controlled by a group of Ariels. I don't think there's very many of them, I think there's probably you know, two dozen of them.

Excerpt Four

MG: Well there's also, I think there's also a role played by people who are incredibly persuasive, and again, that's a very rare and unusual trait and—

CL: Leaves me out you see, I connect but I can't sell.

MG: You can't sell. Well—these are—they're separate categories. I have—I've met with this guy in the book, a guy I called Tom Gau—who I—who is known as one of the greatest salesmen in America today. . . .

2B. LISTENING TWO: *Tipping Points in Fighting Crime*

Exercise 1

Todd Mundt: Let's talk about a social condition that you wrote about then, there are a few that I want to touch on but the first one is the one I mentioned in the introduction, crime in New York City. Crime was a problem for a very long time in New York City and it was rising and rising and rising and then it started dropping and, um, I suppose there could be a number of different reasons for it but I can't really find that anybody really knows exactly for sure what caused it.

Malcolm Gladwell: Crime is so—is such a fundamentally **contagious** thing that once we reached a kind of tipping point and once certain influential people in communities hard hit by crime stopped behaving in that way, it was **contagious**, and there was a kind of sea change that happens all at once.

TM: Maybe we can go into those little **triggers**, because I find this really interesting because we're talking about such a big change that takes place uh, being **triggered** by very small things, uh, what do you think some of those were?

MG: Well, I'm very impressed by this idea of "caught the broken windows theory" which is an idea George Kelling has put forth in New England. He's argued for some time that criminals and criminal behavior is acutely sensitive to environmental cues and he uses the example, the broken window—that if you—if there is a car sitting on the street with a broken window, it is an invitation to someone to **vandalize** the car. Why? Because a broken window on a car symbolizes the fact that no one cares about the car. No one's in charge, no one's watching, no one's . . . and if you think about it, it's actually a fundamentally different idea about crime than the kind of ideas that we've been carrying for the last 25 years. We have been told by conservatives over and over again that crime is the result of moral failure, of something deep and intrinsic within the hearts and souls and brains of criminals, that a criminal is by definition in the sort of conservative topology, someone who is insensitive to their environment, right? They just go out and commit crimes because that's who they are, they're criminals. Well, Kelling came along and said well no no, a criminal is like all of us, someone who is acutely sensitive to what's going on in the environment, and by making subtle changes in the environment, you can encourage and induce much more socially responsible behavior.

Well, in New York we had the perfect test case of that idea. It starts in the subway. You know, in the early '80s they decided to clean up the subway. Well, how did they do it? The subway was a complete **mess**, right? It was . . . crime rates were going through the roof. They bring in a man who is a big disciple of this idea, of "broken windows," and what does he do? Well, the first thing he does is he picks up all the litter. The second thing he does is he cleans up the graffiti, and the third thing he does is he says from now on, no one will ever jump a turnstile in a

New York City subway station again. He puts cops by the turnstiles and if someone jumps, he arrests them. Everybody said he was crazy, but you've got a subway system where people are killing, and robbing, and assaulting, and raping each other and what do you do? You go after the two kinds of criminality that, the only two kinds of criminality that in fact don't hurt anybody else, right? Turnstile jumping and graffiti, you know, littering and graffiti . . . but it turns out that those were tipping points. Once they put those three changes in place, the subway starts to come around really quite dramatically. It's because if you're on a subway that's clean and if you're walking into the subway and no one's allowed to jump the turnstile anymore, all of a sudden, everyone gets the message that someone's in charge, and somebody cares about this. It's not a space that permits this kind of criminal behavior.

3C. SPEAKING

PRODUCTION

Exercise 1

Announcer: Looking to do something good? Well, there's lots teenagers can do. Like saving the rare speckled Burmese bear cub.

Girl: Oh, isn't he cute and furry!

Guide: OK, be careful, Susie.

Girl: C'mere little fellow.

Guide: Don't feed him . . .

Girl: C'm

Bear: Roar!

Girl: (starts screaming)

Guide: Whoa!

Girl: He's got my arm!

Guide: Wow, that's gotta hurt.

Announcer: Or how about just saving something closer to home, like your neighborhood? Tutor. Mentor. Volunteer. Help change your community and change the way the world sees you. Click on weprevent.org or call 1-800-722-TEENS. A message from McGuff, the U.S. Department of Justice, the Crime Prevention Coalition of America and the Ad Council.

Exercise 2

(Repeat Exercise 1)

UNIT 5: Feng Shui: Ancient Wisdom Travels West

2A. LISTENING ONE: *Interview with a Feng Shui Expert*

Sedge Thomson: When you walk into a building, are you able to sort of immediately **sense** whether it has good feng shui or not . . . a good flow of the ch'i?

Kirsten Lagatree: Yes, and so are you. You know, anytime you walk into any room, you get a feeling about it, whether you feel good about being there or not so good. So everyone has experienced good feng shui. Anytime they've walked into anybody's home or even an office where suddenly they think, "Oh, this is pleasant. I feel good." You know, maybe their mood's a little peppier or maybe they're more relaxed . . . whatever. It's just a positive reaction that you get when you're **in the midst** of good feng shui.

LISTEN FOR MAIN IDEAS

Part One

Sedge Thomson: So, feng shui is exactly, what, a way of ordering buildings, rooms, corridors in your life to **keep out** evil spirits?

Kirsten Lagatree: Well, I wouldn't say to **keep out** evil spirits. That sounds so superstitious. But I would say, it's a system of arranging all the objects around you at home or at work in such a way that they are in harmony and balance with nature in the way that feng shui teaches us to do . . . then, therefore, you are in harmony and balance, and so is your life.

ST: Now this is something that's very important in Asia. In fact, you know, it's part of the architecture of buildings . . . how the staircases go up, where buildings are **aligned**, how people are . . . how live . . . what is your particular interest in it? You sound as if you have a Scandinavian background. I mean, is feng shui something important in Scandinavia?

KL: Well, there's—there's—a **huge digression** coming. My name is Scandinavian. I was named for a Norwegian opera singer. I identify as Irish, though. But so I don't know if there is any feng shui in Scandinavia. But their designs are so clean. I would suspect so. Yes, feng shui is **huge** in Asia, Taiwan, Singapore, Hong Kong. I believe it's practiced widely in mainland China, even though it's officially **frowned upon** as a superstition. But it's also **huge** here in the U.S., no less than the Donald. Donald Trump doesn't **make a move** without it. He would no more start working on a building project without a feng shui master than he would without, you know, if it was L.A., without . . . a seismologist to tell him that the building would stay up in an earthquake. Umm. . . . that's because . . . these observations that amount to feng shui have developed over thousands of years and they work— as Donald Trump says. I do love to **quote** Donald Trump, not that I've ever talked to him, but . . .

ST: A famous feng shui expert, as we all know. I know for instance that people in San Francisco, if a one-way street sign is put up pointing toward a house where there are some Chinese living, they can approach the city traffic sign department and have the sign removed . . . not necessarily pointed back in the opposite direction, but have the sign removed or at least not pointing at their house.

KL: You know, I didn't know that. But thanks, that's a great little **anecdote** for the rest of my book tour.

ST: Did you choose your home because of feng shui? How did you set it out?

KL: We didn't choose our home because of feng shui. . . . I arranged my office at home according to feng shui . . . and it's a real basic example that illustrates a couple of principles. I am lucky enough to have a great view out the window at the far end of my office. And I was going to put my desk facing out the window, and . . . uh . . . but I would've had my back to the door which is such . . . you know . . . it's not just old west saloons and feng shui, it's also a bad idea to sit with your back to the door. Anybody who comes into your office can surprise you. They surprise you with the things they have to say. You're constantly **off guard**. So I turned my desk, so that I still had the view at one hand and I had the door and the rest of the room at the other hand, and then I kind of put the other furniture in the office where it **worked around** that. I've got a better floor plan than I would've figured out for myself.

Part Two

ST: What's the role of mirrors?

KL: Well, mirrors in the bedroom. That's about the only room where mirrors are not wonderful. You don't want a mirror to reflect your bed in the bedroom because that could **scare the heck out of** you when you wake up at night. It also could frighten your spirit. You know, there's always a common **sense** and, uh, the **transcendent** explanation. So, it'll either scare your spirit, or if you prefer, it'll scare you. In every other room in the house, mirrors are terrific. They reflect ch'i, which is the basic principle of feng shui . . . this energy. It's like electricity. We can't see it, but boy is it there doing things. So, mirrors will reflect ch'i, help it **circulate** in a more healthy way, and they also say in the dining room or the kitchen they double your **abundance**. Suddenly, you have twice as much food, twice as many friends sitting at the dining room table.

ST: That is true. . . . Um . . . how did you develop your interest in feng shui?

KL: I came at this topic pretty **skeptically** as a journalist, **hard-bitten** journalist that I was. I did a piece for the *Los Angeles Times* a few years ago on feng shui as real estate phenomenon, because major deals **rise or fall** on good or bad feng shui. That was kind of that. And, so then, I really got more deeply into it, started to study it. I was still at the . . . you know . . . my friends would sort of lean in, look at me with one eyebrow up, and say, "Yeah, but do you believe this stuff?" And I would say, "Well, no, but don't **quote** me." Now, based on just simple things I've done and also lots and lots of people I talked to for the book, I'd have to say, it works and at the very least, it couldn't hurt.

ST: When you walk into a building, are you able to sort of immediately **sense** whether it has good feng shui or not . . . a good flow of the ch'i?

KL: Yes, and so are you. You know, anytime you walk into any room, you get a feeling about it, whether you feel good about being there or not so good. So everyone has experienced good feng shui. Anytime they've walked into anybody's home or even an office where suddenly they think, "Oh, this is pleasant. I feel good." You know, maybe their mood's a little peppier or maybe they're more relaxed . . . whatever. It's just a positive reaction that you get when you're **in the midst** of good feng shui.

LISTEN FOR DETAILS

(Repeat Listen for Main Ideas)

MAKE INFERENCES

Excerpt One

ST: So, feng shui is exactly, what, a way of ordering buildings, rooms, corridors in your life to keep out evil spirits?

KL: Well, I wouldn't say to keep out evil spirits. That sounds so superstitious.

Excerpt Two

KL: But it's also huge here in the U.S., no less than the Donald. Donald Trump doesn't make a move without it. He would no more start working on a building project without a feng shui master than he would without, you know, if it was L.A., without . . . a seismologist to tell him that the building would stay up in an earthquake. Umm . . . that's because . . . these observations that amount to feng shui have developed over thousands of years and they work—as Donald Trump says. I do love to quote Donald Trump, not that I've ever talked to him, but . . .

ST: A famous feng shui expert, as we all know.

Excerpt Three

KL: I really got more deeply into it, started to study it. I was still at the . . . you know . . . my friends would sort of lean in, look at me with one eyebrow up, and say, "Yeah, but do you believe this stuff?" And I would say, "Well, no, but don't quote me."

2B. LISTENING TWO: *Feng Shui in the Newsroom*

Steve Scher: Kirsten Lagatree is our guest. Her book is *Feng Shui: Arranging Your Home to Change Your Life—A Room by Room Guide to the Ancient Art—to the Ancient Chinese Art of Placement.* OK, so, I would like to walk into our newsroom, if we can, and have you just quickly kind of look at it and figure out what we can do for some of the people here who need a little help in their careers or their happiness. Any initial thoughts you have looking at this room?

Kirsten Lagatree: Umm . . . There are some very good things about this newsroom. For one thing, some of the writers are facing northeast. Northeast is the direction that governs mental ability, **acuteness** of thinking, **scholarly** success. So, those people in this newsroom, who are facing this, they not only get an extraordinarily peaceful and beautiful view out the window, they are facing in the direction that's going to make them **sharp**, and make their writing better.

SS: OK, so this is my desk, over here, scattered with a barrel of monkeys, and they're red, so that's good . . . I'm facing east here, right? I'm facing—yeah—east, almost to the southeast. Am I blocked up a little bit?

KL: Yeah, well, facing east, actually . . . when you face east you are facing the direction of growth, **vitality**, the color green. Health, **vitality**, youth: Those are the things that come with the direction. So maybe that's what makes you so **peppy**, Steve, and so young **at heart**. I'd like to say something about this southeast wall right here. That is your money corner. Southeast is the direction that **governs** money. You haven't done anything with this direction. You've got lots of equipment there . . . what you should have is the color purple, the number 4.

SS: And a fish tank.

KL: Well, one thing at a time. The color purple and the number 4 go with that one direction, with the southeast. I'm glad you mentioned a fish tank . . . water flow symbolizes cash flow. There's a lot in feng shui that does word play, both in the Chinese language and in the English language, and so, water flow equals cash flow. You walk in to some major corporate buildings nowadays, in New York or Los Angeles or Hong Kong, you are going to see fountains in the lobby. A lot of that. The fish that are in the tank . . . they symbolize **abundance**, as in "there are always more fish in the sea." What's your goal? You know . . . if your goal is to be a better writer, **talk somebody into** changing places with you here so that you can face northeast. If your goal is to become wealthy, do some enhancement there on your southeast wall, or do it at home. Say you want to get in a relationship in your life . . . at home, enhance a southwest wall with the color yellow and the number 2. The southwest corner **governs** marriage, partnerships, motherhood. You pay attention to what, umm, you know, what you can do to make something happen, and then you work with these outward symbols.

3C. SPEAKING

PRONUNCIATION

Exercise 1

So, this is the story of a true tragedy that occurred in Hong Kong, involving feng shui. Of course you've heard of Bruce Lee, the famous kung fu actor. Well, he decided to buy a house in a valley that got a lot of wind. And wind can destroy ch'i. Actually, people couldn't understand why he chose that area. He was wealthy and could have lived anywhere in Hong Kong. Anyway, he bought the house. And then, to change his feng shui, he put a mirror on a tree in his backyard. However, a storm destroyed the tree, and he never replaced it or the mirror. Now, doctors concluded that he died of a cerebral edema. But a lot of people believe that unfavorable feng shui also played a role.

UNIT 6: Spiritual Renewal

2A. LISTENING ONE: *The Religious Tradition of Fasting*

Duncan Moon: But while there are differences in approach and style, those who fast are most often hoping to increase spirituality and come closer to the **divine**. Dr. Diana Eck, professor of comparative religion at Harvard Divinity School, says **fasting** accomplishes this in part by breaking an attachment to material things.

LISTEN FOR MAIN IDEAS

Duncan Moon: **Fasting** is an ancient tradition. The three Abrahamic religions, Judaism, Christianity and Islam, all **trace it back** to the **prophets** of the Old Testament. For example, many believe the **prophet** Mohammed's first fast was probably Yom Kippur. Many Eastern religions trace their roots of **fasting** to ancient yogic and **ascetic** traditions. But while there are differences in approach and style, those who fast are most often hoping to increase spirituality and come closer to the **divine**. Dr. Diana Eck, professor of comparative religion at Harvard Divinity School, says **fasting** accomplishes this in part by breaking an attachment to material things.

Dr. Diana Eck: And of course the most repetitive attachment to earthly things is that that we **enact** every day by our desire for food. So there is a way in which breaking that, even in a symbolic way, speaks against the consumption, the materialism that is so pervasive in our world.

DM: Professor Barbara Patterson of Emory University is an Episcopal priest. She says **fasting** is similar to the discipline displayed by an athlete in a gym, although in the case of **fasting**, it's a spiritual gym.

Professor Barbara Patterson: There is a celebration itself in establishing a discipline for oneself and actually working, making decisions, forming the **will**, if you would say, intention—to be able to move through a time where there's a certain amount of stress that's not undoing but that gives you a sense of your capacities. It's very much a way of sharpening the heart's capacities.

DM: The Church of Jesus Christ of Latter Day Saints, the Mormons, fast the first Sunday of every month. They skip two meals and take the money they would have spent on those meals and give it to the poor. Mormon Bart Marcoy says **fasting** helps to **foster humility** and **gratitude**, allowing him to put aside his human competitiveness.

Moon: In Islam during the holy month of Ramadan, Muslims fast from sunrise to sunset, **refraining from** food, water, smoking, and sex. Dr. Ahbar Ahmed, a professor of Islamic studies at American University, says in this time of rapid change and fear, **fasting** is vital to spiritual **well-being**.

Dr. Ahbar Ahmed: Because if you do not withdraw during the day, then the **replenishment** of the soul is not being affected, and when that does not happen, then **over time** the individual begins to become exhausted, spiritually exhausted.

DM: Dr. Ahmed says the rhythm of life has become so **hectic**, so fast moving, that finding time to **pull back** from our daily lives, even temporarily, has become more difficult than ever. But he says that only means the need for it has never been greater, and that the ancient tradition of **fasting** is still necessary, even in the twenty-first century.

Duncan Moon, NPR News, Washington.

LISTEN FOR DETAILS

(Repeat Listen for Main Ideas)

MAKE INFERENCES

Excerpt One

DM: . . . Dr. Diana Eck, professor of comparative religion at Harvard Divinity School says fasting accomplishes this in part by breaking an attachment to material things.

Dr. Diana Eck: And, of course, the most repetitive attachment to earthly things is that that we enact every day by our desire for food. So there is a way in which breaking that, even in a symbolic way, speaks against the consumption, the materialism that is so pervasive in our world.

Excerpt Two

DM: Professor Barbara Patterson of Emory University is an Episcopal priest. She says fasting is similar to the discipline displayed by an athlete in a gym, although in the case of fasting, it's a spiritual gym.

Professor Barbara Patterson: There is a celebration itself in establishing a discipline for oneself and actually working, making decisions, forming the will, . . . It's very much a way of sharpening the heart's capacities.

Excerpt Three

DM: Dr. Ahbar Ahmed . . . says in this time of rapid change and fear, fasting is vital to spiritual well being.

Dr. Ahbar Ahmed: Because if you do not withdraw during the day, then the replenishment of the soul is not being affected, and when that does not happen, then over time the individual begins to become exhausted, spiritually exhausted.

2B. LISTENING TWO: *Describing Monastic Life*

Alex Beam: Was this an . . . Was this an . . . sort of an intellectual fact-finding journey or was this a spiritual **quest** for you?

Willam Claassen: It was a number of things. It was a . . . certainly it was a project that I took on as a journalist, as a writer. It was also a spiritual journey for me because it allowed me to continue my journey in, uh, monastic traditions, uh, and what I might find there and how that might apply to my life and what I could communicate about what I had witnessed in these various communities.

AB: I want to **draw you out** on the subject of the work of the monastery. Why don't you briefly talk about the work of that monastery which is in a sense the easiest to illustrate.

WC: Sure. Although Wat Tham Krabok is part of this forest monastic tradition, it was different in the sense that they were working on issues that were outside of the monastery. They had **taken on** efforts of working with AIDS patients and also providing assistance with Hmong villagers who were refugees out of Laos who had began gathering in that area where the monastery was located. So, actually, a great deal of their time was spent in this work, the AIDS work, and also the work with the refugees, which, uh, created a little different situation in terms of their daily schedule, in terms of how rigorous their chanting schedule was, in terms of the solitude of the community because there were a lot of people coming in, children as well as adults, as well as Westerners, coming in to view this program uh, uh, for the AIDS patients, also for drug addicts. They also worked in that area. So, there was a lot of movement in and out of the community which made it a different situation than I experienced in other forest monasteries.

AB: What um . . . were you ever . . . um . . . I am going to use a term—not totally flattering, but this **notion** of the monastic day tripper, the visitor. Were you . . . I know that at sometimes you were sort of greeted with a bit of suspicion. Isn't that fair to say?

WC: Oh, I think so. I mean, I talk in the book about a term that I learned on Mt. Athos—the two legged wolf, the idea of an individual being on pilgrimage, but really more interested in the uniqueness of what this community is . . . and sort of the temporary visitor, and there were certainly times when there was suspicion about my time in those communities.

AB: The two-legged wolf, um, obviously refers to sort of tourists who are kind of visiting the beaches in Thailand and the monks of Mt. Athos, kind of joy riders. But what specific impact have the two-legged wolves, had, say, on Mt. Athos?

WC: Well, on Mt. Athos, for example, at one time, there was maybe a seven or ten day period that men could make a pilgrimage on the peninsula because of the numbers of men that are wanting to be on Mt. Athos, they've reduced that period of time to four days. Actually, four days was five or six years ago, so they may have reduced it even further than that. But it creates a demand on the land, and it also creates a time demand on the part of the communities.

AB: You also visited another monastery that's well-known and from your description, too well-known to our listeners. That's the Monasterio de Santo Domingo in Spain which has gained international notoriety. Tell us why, please, and what impact that's had.

WC: Well, as you may remember, there was a very popular album of Gregorian chant called the Chant Album that was produced back in the early '90s and that was a recording made by the monks, Benedictine monks, at El Monasterio de Santo Domingo which is in Silos, Spain. Although they had been making recordings for the last 20 years, this particular recording happened to **catch on** internationally. So that's actually one of their cottage industries . . . uh . . . there at the monastery. This is one of the ways that they're able to survive, by making their recordings.

AB: But what impact . . . I mean . . . celebrity and going platinum isn't like the greatest thing that's ever happened to them, is it?

WC: No, I mean, it's one of many ways that they do make a living and they see it as an extension of their work, of their spirituality, of their hospitality, really, of sharing their music with the world.

AB: Did you every get a sense of—I mean—there must be some sort of excess revenues there. What does that particular monastery do with the **royalties** from the CD?

WC: All I know is that the money goes back into their work, the community work.

3C. SPEAKING

FUNCTION

Exercise 1

Mary Tilotson: Give me an idea William, of, as a guest—and your experiences were various enough that there's not going to be one schedule that applied to every monastery, but more or less how would the day start, when would it start, how would it unfold for you in retreat?

William Claassen: Well, I'll pull in an example first from Thailand where I spent time in a forest monastery in the northeast part of the country near the Laotian border. It's an old tradition . . . the forest monastic tradition in Thailand. We would wake up at 3:30 in the morning. We would gather as community to chant for approximately an hour and a half to two hours. We would chant, we would also sit meditation, we would also walk meditation. From there, each individual would return to their living space and focus on their meditation. They would then come back together again. In this tradition, the monks would go out and collect food in the morning. They would go out in the community. So, that was an important daily ritual to collect food for their one meal of the day. They would go out to collect the food in the various villages that surrounded the community, come back, deliver the food, the food would then be served to the community. Then there would be a separation of the members of the community to again return to their meditation. A little later there would be a work period, late in the morning and a work period in the afternoon. The community would come back together again for at least two more chanting sessions before the evening chant, but usually the evening chant would end about 8:30 or 9:00 and then the individuals were permitted to study, return to their living quarters to meditate. It was independent time.

UNIT 7: Workplace Privacy

2A. LISTENING ONE: *Interview on Workplace Surveillance*

Elaine Korry: And the practice is on the rise. According to the ACLU Workplace Rights Project, the number of **employees** being monitored has doubled in the last five years.

What's **driving** this increase? Partly, it's competition. If everyone else in an industry is **keeping tabs** on their workers, there's pressure to join in.

But, to a large extent, companies have **stepped up** monitoring simply because it could be done, cheaply and efficiently.

LISTEN FOR MAIN IDEAS

Part One

Scott Simon, host: Many **employees** can assume that they're being watched while they work during the day. The majority of U.S. companies keep watch on their workers with video cameras, tape recorders, computer **surveillance**.

Most **employers** insist that these are **legitimate** and even necessary business practices. But as NPR's Elaine Korry reports, many attorneys are arguing that **employees** do not give up their privacy rights when they show up for work.

Elaine Korry: If you send personal e-mail on your office computer, there's a good chance the boss is **keeping an eye on** you. In a new survey of more than 900 major U.S. companies, nearly two-thirds of them acknowledged using a range of **surveillance** methods to monitor their **employees**.

Eric Greenberg directed the survey for the American Management Association.

Eric Greenberg: Employees should know that any **employee** at any time may be under watch, and that any **employee's** communications, be they on the phone or via the Internet, may be **subject to** review.

EK: Greenberg issues that warning. But some **employers** do not. In what he calls the most worrisome finding of the survey, up to a quarter of the companies that monitor their workforce do it secretly.

And the practice is on the rise. According to the ACLU Workplace Rights Project, the number of **employees** being monitored has doubled in the last five years.

What's **driving** this increase? Partly, it's competition. If everyone else in an industry is **keeping tabs** on their workers, there's pressure to join in.

But, to a large extent, companies have **stepped up** monitoring simply because it could be done, cheaply and efficiently. Yet, Greenberg says even as **surveillance** becomes more widespread, there's nothing **sinister** about the practice itself.

EG: When you read data like this, there's a certain tendency to do a Big Brother metaphor . . . Big Brother is watching and whatever. But really, I think that's a **cheap shot**. What we're talking about for the most part are very **legitimate** forms of performance monitoring.

EK: Greenberg says **employers** have a right to know how equipment they provide is being used on the job, if rules are being obeyed, if **employees** are getting the job done. That helps explain why banks routinely tape customer service calls, and why the U.S. Postal Service is testing a satellite system to track how long it takes to get the mail delivered.

Part Two

EK: But Larry Finneran, with the National Association of Manufacturers, says companies are using technology to accomplish other important goals. Video cameras were recently installed in his building to **deter** theft. And the Association keeps a **log** of all phone calls so **employees** can pay the company for their personal calls.

According to Finneran, monitoring can be used for the workers' own protection.

Larry Finneran: If an **employee** is sending pornography from an **employer**'s computer, obviously the employer would be expected to go through there. If somebody complains about sexual harassment, that somebody's sending out **racial slurs** over the e-mail, the **employer** has a right to take action.

EK: In fact, the Chevron Corporation was sued by female **employees** who said they were sexually harassed through company e-mail.

That's all well and good, says Rebecca Locketz, the legal director of the ACLU's Workplace Rights Project. She **concedes** there are **legitimate** uses of monitoring programs. But too often, says Locketz, **surveillance** practices **demean** workers for no good reason.

Rebecca Locketz: You certainly do not need to monitor key strokes. When you give someone 50 reports to key into a computer, and you see that they have only completed 20 by day's end, you don't need to count key strokes. They only finished two-fifths.

EK: Locketz argues that **employees** should not have to leave their human **dignity at the workplace door**. And she says they're entitled to a few **safeguards** in this area.

First, the ACLU says **employees** should always be informed when they're monitored. And second . . .

RL: There should be no monitoring whatsoever in purely private areas.

Part Three

EK: Yet, so far there is only one state—Connecticut—that forbids **surveillance** in areas such as locker rooms or the **employee** lounge. In other states, **employers** do secretly videotape private places if they suspect theft or criminal activities such as drug dealing. There's only one federal statute, the 1986 Electronic Communications Privacy Act, that **safeguards employee** privacy. But according to Larry Finneran with the National Association of Manufacturers, the **scope** of the act is limited to **eavesdropping** on private telephone calls.

LF: There are specific rules. An **employer** listening for content of personal phone calls . . . an **employer** can . . . can limit duration of personal phone calls. An **employer** can say, "no personal phone calls." But under the Electronic Communications Privacy Act, an **employer** cannot listen for content. And that . . . they are already protected to that degree.

EK: Employee rights attorney Penny Nathan Cahn is involved in a case over this very issue. She says as companies continue to expand **employee** monitoring, workers are turning to the courts to protect their rights.

Penny Nathan Cahn: Then unless there is a substantial interest to be served by the **employer**, I don't think the juries are going to look at the . . . the **willy-nilly surveillance** and monitoring very sympathetically.

EK: There may even be good business reasons for companies to **think twice about** increased **surveillance**. Studies link electronic monitoring to higher levels of worker stress, which can lead to lower productivity.

I'm Elaine Korry reporting.

LISTEN FOR DETAILS

(Repeat Listen for Main Ideas)

MAKE INFERENCES

Excerpt One

Eric Greenberg: Employees should know that any employee at any time may be under watch, and that any employee's communications, be they on the phone or via the Internet, may be subject to review.

Excerpt Two

EG: When you read data like this, there's a certain tendency to do a Big Brother metaphor . . . Big Brother is watching and whatever. But really, I think that's a cheap shot. What we're talking about for the most part are very legitimate forms of performance monitoring.

Excerpt Three

Rebecca Locketz: You certainly do not need to monitor key strokes. When you give someone 50 reports to key into a computer, and you see that they have only completed 20 by day's end, you don't need to count key strokes. They only finished two-fifths.

Excerpt Four

RL: There should be no monitoring whatsoever in purely private areas.

2B. LISTENING TWO: *Managers and Employees Speak Out*

Speaker 1: Um, well, I own a small data-processing company in which I employ about eight to ten workers. And, uh, the point I want to make has to do with trust. Listen, I know it's possible to force people to be 100 percent efficient. But, um, but I think when you do that you lose **morale**, and confidence, and trust. I let my **employees** use our equipment, and our computers, and make personal phone calls, and, and whatever—whatever they need. They are more than welcome to decide what is right and wrong! Because, I think, I mean, you can't just run a company by just issuing orders to robots and watching them like Big Brother. Right? I think you have to trust people, and respect them, and give them a little freedom. And, also, as far as phone calls and all that go, I want my people to call home and check on their children, and know their children are OK, because if they do that, then they can refocus on the job . . . yeah! Right? . . and their work is better. So, as a result, um, I have **dedicated employees** who are willing to **go that extra mile** . . . and I can honestly say they show up to work smiling. So, I get more satisfaction and rewards by trusting my **employees** than by suspecting them of doing something wrong.

Speaker 2: Well, uh, I'm an attorney in a large law firm in Seattle. And, uh, well, at my work, in my firm, yeah, there's a capability, of course, of monitoring my performance. I put a lot of work onto a laptop, you know, I input a lot of my work onto computer systems with, well, limited security. And you know what? I'm not bothered by that in the least. I mean, to me, the real question is, if we're not doing anything wrong, what do we have to worry about, right? You see, I think **employers** have the right to **keep an eye on** what goes on in their businesses, just like home owners have the right to use video and audio **surveillance** to protect their own homes. I mean, you'd have to agree that when you're in the office, you're at work, you're not conducting your private life. You're conducting business. Uh, in some cases, such as lounge areas at work, yeah, there's a **fine line** there; but mostly I believe it's OK for, you know, an **employer** to actually listen and watch while you're working. They're just looking out for their own investment. You know, they're, they're safeguarding their businesses.

Speaker 3: Uh, well, I'm a chemist in a large pharmaceutical company. And, well, I'd like to say specifically that private communication that doesn't relate to my job shouldn't be an open book just because it happens to occur between nine and five. I mean, I've got a right to talk privately even on the job. Um, it's impossible to totally separate my job from my home. Let me just pose a question here. Um, isn't it a fact that we all take work home every once in a while? And every once in a while you've got to have a communication at work, on the phone, on your computer, or your e-mail that isn't work related. I mean, you know, if I were making 47 long-distance calls to Honolulu for no reason, sure . . . my boss would want to know why I'm running up all these long-distance phone calls. Maybe something **sinister** is going on. But . . . I mean, a handful of local phone calls that everybody has to make once in a while? I just don't get why an **employer** would or should object to that! I don't see why any employer has any **legitimate** reason to **bug** my phone to find out who I just called. . . . quite honestly, it's an invasion of my privacy, and that's just not fair.

Speaker 4: Uh, yeah, I . . . um, I run a video production company and employ—I don't know, somewhere around, like, 50 professionals and support staff. Um, so listen, the point I want to make is this . . . even though I trust my **employees**. . . I own the place. You know, the company's still mine. So, stuff on their desks, their, their work product certainly, and, you know, other stuff in the office . . . yeah, while it might be inappropriate for me to look at it or remove it, look, the fact of the matter is . . . it's not private stuff. I have a right, you know, I would say, I have a responsibility to know the materials that are in the workplace. I mean, no question, if it's a work product, you know, I've got to have access to that. Oh, one more thing I want to say . . . I could absolutely go into their computers after they leave and read anything that's business-related. You know, it . . . it's my right.

UNIT 8: Warriors without Weapons

2A. LISTENING ONE: *Warriors without Weapons*

Terry Gross: This is *Fresh Air,* I'm Terry Gross. Journalist Michael Ignatieff spent a year traveling to the sites of **volatile** regional wars. He wanted to learn how war is changing, and what that means for the safety of relief workers. In a recent *New Yorker* article called "Unarmed Warriors," he wrote about the international committee of the Red Cross, the new risks its unarmed members face in war zones, and the new controversies surrounding the group's position of neutrality. I asked him why he wanted to write about the Red Cross.

LISTEN FOR MAIN IDEAS

Part One

Terry Gross: This is *Fresh Air,* I'm Terry Gross. Journalist Michael Ignatieff spent a year traveling to the sites of **volatile** regional wars. He wanted to learn how war is changing, and what that means for the safety of relief workers. In a recent *New Yorker* article called "Unarmed Warriors," he wrote about the International Committee of the Red Cross, the new risks its unarmed members face in war zones, and the new controversies surrounding the group's position of neutrality. I asked him why he wanted to write about the Red Cross.

Michael Ignatieff: . . . As a group I was very **drawn to** them because I thought they could take me into the whole world of what involves people in that kind of humanitarian relief work. . . . From being interested in the Red Cross, I then became interested in the laws of war and came to see that the laws of war are a very different moral tradition than, say, the human rights tradition. And I began to see that there are two traditions at work out there in the humanitarian movement: One of them is, you know, international human rights, which most Americans can **identify with**, and then there's this very different tradition called the laws of war tradition, which is basically trying to make sure that if people are going to fight, conduct the fighting according to certain rules . . . and that's what the Red Cross is trying to do.

Part Two

TG: The international committee of the Red Cross is trying to **disseminate** information about the Geneva Conventions, about the International Laws of War. What are they trying to do? How are they trying to educate people who are fighting, about these **codes**?

MI: Well, I think first of all we need to back up a little and just understand what the **codes** are. They're these things called the Geneva Conventions, which were ratified by hundreds of countries and the basic document dates to 1864 and then it was revised in 1949. They're a bunch of rules that are quite simple . . . they simply say, "Don't fire on ambulances, don't shoot on non-combatants, don't torture prisoners, allow prisoners to communicate with their families, allow the Red Cross to visit you if you're a prisoner of war, **spare** civilians . . ."

I mean, they're very **house-and-garden** common rules, and in lots of combat situations they function more or less adequately. In the Gulf War, for example, when a hundred thousand Iraqi prisoners were taken, the United States subscribed to the Geneva Conventions, released them according to those conventions. That's . . . so it's a system that . . . it's easy to laugh at . . . people say, you know, "You can't wage a war that's civilized." Well, in fact, the Geneva Conventions have done a lot to civilize certain aspects of war, and so they have a lot of **legitimacy**. . . .

I think something very interesting's going on there . . . an attempt to say, "The standards of decency that ought to **prevail** in the world are not white, western European values; they're **human universals**, and if you look deeply enough into your own traditions of warrior culture, you will find them." And that's what the Red Cross is trying to do . . . they're just beginning that work, but they're putting out comic books that tell the story, they're running radio soap operas to tell the story. They're not just sitting there reading out the Geneva Conventions; they're trying to translate them into new languages, and it's one of the most interesting bits of work that's going on.

Part Three

MI: . . . Yes, I think what I'm trying to **get at** here is that . . . it's a sort of **counterintuitive** thought. One of the oldest moral traditions, that all human societies have, is the warrior tradition—the tradition of warrior's honor. The idea that a warrior has a very dangerous and therefore sacred responsibility; that is, his job is to protect the community and to engage in the infliction of death. Because that's a very dangerous and very serious task, men have to be trained for it, and they're trained not to simply **unleash** their aggression, but to control it and to discipline it, you know, and use it for the benefit of the community. And those traditions then mean that there are certain people you can kill and there are certain people it's wrong to kill. There's certain ways of waging war that are honorable, and certain ways of waging war that are dishonorable. Most modern militaries—most modern military forces attempt in some way or the other to **subscribe** to those very ancient **codes**; and I think we forget . . . partly because war has become so awful and so horrible and so **devastating**, we've come to **equate** war with pure **barbarism** and pure **savagery**. It seems to us to be a zone where morality cannot **prevail** at all. And so it's a rather **counterintuitive** thought that in fact the warrior's honor is one of the oldest moral traditions in the world, and the Red Cross is trying in a way to simply **institutionalize** that culture . . . remind people that in their own cultures they can find elements of a warrior's honor which should **restrain** their people.

LISTEN FOR DETAILS

(Repeat Listen for Main Ideas)

MAKE INFERENCES

Excerpt One

MI: And I began to see that there are two traditions at work out there in the humanitarian movement: One of them is, you know, international human rights, which most Americans can identify with, and then there's this very different tradition called the laws of war tradition, which is basically trying to make sure that if people are going to fight, conduct the fighting according to certain rules . . . and that's what the Red Cross is trying to do.

Excerpt Two

MI: So it's a system that . . . it's easy to laugh at . . . people say, you know, "You can't wage a war that's civilized."

Excerpt Three

MI: I think something very interesting's going on there . . . an attempt to say, "The standards of decency that ought to prevail in the world are not white, western European values; they're human universals, and if you look deeply enough into your own traditions of warrior culture, you will find them."

Excerpt Four

MI: And so it's a rather counterintuitive thought that in fact the warrior's honor is one of the oldest moral traditions in the world, and the Red Cross is trying in a way to simply institutionalize that culture . . . remind people that in their own cultures they can find elements of a warrior's honor which should restrain their people.

2B. LISTENING TWO: *Michael Ignatieff's Views on War*

Part One

Terry Gross: In your article about the Red Cross in the *New Yorker,* you wrote that witnessing the Red Cross, and traveling to all these war zones, challenged your views on antiwar culture. What do you mean by that?

Michael Ignatieff: Well, I'm a Canadian; I was very involved in the antiwar, anti-Vietnam protests that were centered in Toronto during the '60s because Toronto was an antiwar center because so many **draft evaders** and draft resisters ended up there. I grew up in the antiwar culture of my generation . . . I think what I discovered in the Red Cross's approach is an **alternative ethic**, which is that, you know, you cannot abolish war, you can't **do without war**.

Part Two

MI: And war in fact is a natural, necessary, and sometimes, dare I say it, even desirable way to solve certain social conflicts between ethnic groups. Oppressed groups sometimes can only use war to free themselves. Well, if that's the case, if we can't abolish war from human culture, then we'd better find some way to **tame** it.

Part Three

MI: And that's the ethic that the Red Cross **lives by**, and I think the simple rules that the Red Cross tries to enforce, which is: You don't shoot prisoners, you don't make war on noncombatants, you try and stay away from civilian targets, you don't. . . you kill people, you don't torture or degrade their bodies.

Part Four

MI: You know, just very very simple rules of humanity are an important addition to civilization. And there is no necessary reason . . . I suppose this is what I've learned . . . to **equate** war with barbarism. There's a distinction between war and barbarism. And we should keep to that distinction and struggle to **ensure** it, and that's what the Red Cross tries to do. And . . . I don't want to sound like a recruiting sergeant from the Red Cross; I'm critical of some of the things they do . . . but I did learn that from them. And I respect this morality.

TG: Michael Ignatieff, I want to thank you very much for talking with us.

MI: A pleasure.

3C. SPEAKING

PRONUNCIATION

Exercise 3

1. cot **2.** cap **3.** luck **4.** nut **5.** hot **6.** lag

3C. SPEAKING

PRODUCTION

Exercise 1

Ever give a gift that didn't go over real big—one that ended up in a closet the second you left the room? There is a gift that's guaranteed to be well received, because it will save someone's life. The gift is blood. And the need for it is desperate. Over 20,000 people must choose to give this gift every day. We need your help. Please give blood. There's a life to be saved right now. Call the American Red Cross at 1-800-GIVE LIFE. This public service message brought to you by the Advertising **Council** and the American Red Cross.

Exercise 2

(Repeat Exercise 1)

UNIT 9: Boosting Brain Power through the Arts

2A. LISTENING ONE: *Does Music Enhance Math Skills?*

Michelle Trudeau, reporter: Just how music **enhances** mathematical skills is unknown. It may be by the more general effect of increasing **self-esteem**, or maybe something **neurological** happens in the brain, or maybe, psychologist Andrea Halpern from Bucknell University suggests, these children are learning how to learn.

LISTEN FOR MAIN IDEAS

Part One

Linda Wertheimer: This is *All Things Considered.* I'm Linda Wertheimer.

Noah Adams: And I'm Noah Adams. Most schools offer music and art classes to give students a **well-rounded** education. New research indicates those classes may **do more for** students than just give them an appreciation of the arts. According to a study in tomorrow's issue of the journal *Nature,* studying music and art can significantly **advance** a child's reading skills and especially **boost** math **proficiency**. Michelle Trudeau reports.

Michelle Trudeau, reporter: A class of six-year-olds getting a special music lesson, part of a special arts program that researcher Martin Gardiner and his colleagues at the music school in Rhode Island designed for several elementary schools in the state.

Martin Gardiner: We started out wanting to see the impact of arts training in some first- and second-grade kids.

MT: So, some classrooms had an extra hour of this special arts **curriculum** incorporated into their normal school week.

MG: And other classrooms getting the standard **curriculum** in the arts, which was pretty standard for Rhode Island and rather representative of the country **as a whole**.

MT: The standard **curriculum**, say the researchers, gave students music lessons twice a month and art lessons twice a month. The typical music lesson tended to be somewhat passive, says Gardiner. Students listened to tapes and concerts and talked about music in class. In contrast, the special arts classes met twice weekly and got students actively involved as a way to teach them the basic **building blocks**.

MG: The kinds of skills that they are learning in these grades are . . . in music, they're learning to sing together properly, sing together on pitch, sing together in rhythm, sing together songs; and, in the visual arts, they're learning to draw shapes and deal with colors and forms, and so forth.

MT: A very interactive, experiential approach that took advantage of children's natural inclination to master enjoyable tasks and build upon **sequential** skills.

MG: And at the end of seven months, all the kids in the school took standardized tests, and we looked not only at how these teachers rated the kids on attitude and so forth, but also how the kids scored on their tests.

MT: And here's what the researchers found. First of all, those kids who'd entered the first grade toward the bottom of the class in reading and then received the special arts program for the year had now caught up to the average in reading.

MG: And that in itself is wonderful. But, in addition, they were now statistically ahead in learning math.

MT: Dramatically ahead in math, compared to the kids who had not received the special arts classes throughout the year. The researchers found also that the kids who continued their special arts classes for a second year continued to improve in math.

Part Two

MT: Psychologist Frances Rauscher, from the University of Wisconsin at Oshkosh, says this is an important study showing that a group of typical children, **regardless** of talent or parental involvement, can **reap benefits** from arts training that affects other academic areas, especially math.

Frances Rauscher: It's getting as close as is absolutely possible to the real world. You know, this . . . these are kids that already enrolled in schools that are just simply assigned to these different groups, this test group and this control group. And what they're **finding** is a strong effect in the improvement of mathematical ability as measured by school standards. So, this has real general . . . real world appeal.

MT: Rauscher's own recent research could help explain why arts education might have this additional benefit. In her study, a group of three-year-olds were given music lessons in preschool—piano and singing. Rauscher found they scored significantly higher on a particular IQ test that measures **abstract reasoning**—a skill, adds Rauscher, essential to mathematics.

FR: Training in the arts, and particularly training in music, **enhances** the ability for children to understand proportions and ratios, and that's obviously a skill that's very important for mathematical reasoning.

MT: Just how music **enhances** mathematical skills is unknown. It may be by the more general effect of increasing **self-esteem**, or maybe something **neurological** happens in the brain, or maybe, psychologist Andrea Halpern from Bucknell University suggests, these children are learning how to learn.

Andrea Halpern: In other words, you can learn skills, but you can also learn about how you learn things. And that seems to be a **hallmark** of the true mature learner, that they know how to learn things. And it's possible that these early **interventions** might be having some effect in children knowing how to **attack** new material.

MT: Whatever may be going on in the growing brains of children, both psychological and biological, these new **findings underscore** an increasing awareness among scientists and educators that a rich learning environment can significantly **enhance** children's intellectual development in unexpected ways.

I'm Michelle Trudeau reporting.

LISTEN FOR DETAILS

(Repeat Listen for Main Ideas)

MAKE INFERENCES

Excerpt One

MT: The standard curriculum, say the researchers, gave students music lessons twice a month and art lessons twice a month. The typical music lesson tended to be somewhat passive, says Gardiner. Students listened to tapes and concerts and talked about music in class. In contrast, the special arts classes met twice weekly and got students actively involved as a way to teach them the basic building blocks.

MG: The kinds of skills that they are learning in these grades are . . . in music, they're learning to sing together properly, sing together on pitch, sing together in rhythm, sing together songs; and, in the visual arts, they're learning to draw shapes and deal with colors and forms, and so forth.

Excerpt Two

MT: Rauscher's own recent research could help explain why arts education might have this additional benefit. In her study, a group of three-year-olds were given music lessons in preschool—piano and singing. Rauscher found they scored significantly higher on a particular IQ test that measures abstract reasoning—a skill, adds Rauscher, essential to mathematics.

FR: Training in the arts, and particularly training in music, enhances the ability for children to understand proportions and ratios, and that's obviously a skill that's very important for mathematical reasoning.

2B. LISTENING TWO: *Music, Art, and the Brain*

Part One

Warren Levinson: "Your Child's Brain" is the subject of this week's cover story in *Newsweek.* To discuss it we have science editor Sharon Begley. Thanks for joining us again, Sharon.

Sharon Begley: Hi, Warren.

WL: What parts of an infant's brain are already physically set at birth?

SB: Really the only things that a baby is born with are the circuits that do the things absolutely crucial for life . . . keeping the heart beating . . . breathing . . . controlling temperature . . . reflexes . . . things like that . . . and of course a baby can see and hear. A baby has the primary senses when he or she comes into the world. But the rest of it is still a "**work in progress**."

Part Two

WL: I was fascinated by some of the research on music and the relationship to other kinds of reasoning, particularly mathematics. I had always assumed that musical talent and mathematics kind of went together because they had something to do with each other . . . um . . . in terms of filling puzzles . . . and in terms of . . . you have mathematics involved in setting out the beats to various kinds of music.

SB: That's right. Yes . . . music itself is highly mathematical, and that made some, um, neuroscientists think that somehow the patterns of firing in neural cells were similar, as in mathematical abilities and logical thinking and spatial reasoning. So what they did is give two- and three-year-old little preschoolers lessons in singing and in piano, and after several weeks of this the children were much better at solving mazes on pieces of paper and copying geometric shapes, so it seems again that these circuits were sort of primed to be wired up, and music somehow did it.

WL: But it also turns out that they tend . . . the wiring for both of those things tend to be right next to each other . . .

SB: They're in the same part of the brain . . . this old right side of the brain that we've heard about for years . . . yeah.

Part Three

WL: I have to say, though, that in your reporting . . . there . . . as a father of children, there are, I get two reactions: One fills me with excitement that I really have a very significant role to play in how my children grow up to be able to solve things and to be able to live their lives, but the other reaction . . . and it's a little bigger . . . is sort of scary . . . the notion that so many **windows** are closed so early, that by the ages of three and seven, I may have already blown it in so many areas.

SB: Well, I feel the same way . . . mine are ten and seven . . . and I look at all these missed opportunities and think . . . Oh God . . . I should've been doing this or that . . . or whatever. Um, you know, I think we should not panic parents.

Part Four

SB: If you love your child . . . if you do very simple things . . . again, we are not talking about the crazy superbaby stuff from the 1980s. This is really paying attention to your child . . . playing the kind of games that your grandmother played with your parents . . . you know, "peek-a-boo" and "Where did the object go?" It's paying attention and trying, and you know, if you **blow up** at your kid . . . or whatever . . . you're not going to **scar** the kid for life. We're talking about repeated patterns of how you play with and interact with your child. But, uh, yeah, I felt the same way.

UNIT 10: Microfinance: Changing Lives $50 at a Time

2A. LISTENING ONE: *Microfinance*

Raj Shah: In very poor environments, you see improved height and weight outcomes, which are signs of basic human nutrition. You see improvements in school attendance and in paying school fees. One of the most important things I learned by visiting so many of these programs is wherever you go, anywhere around the world, you ask people what they do with the expanded income they've earned from their business activity—buy a sewing machine, make a little bit more money—what's the first thing they do with that money, and nine times out of ten it is pay school fees for their children and provide better opportunities for their children.

LISTEN FOR MAIN IDEAS

Part One

Ross Reynolds: There are obvious benefits to credit, but there are also **pitfalls**. You can get **overextended**, you don't own anything, the bank ends up owning it. In some ways, paying as you go might be a better idea. Is credit always a good thing, particularly for poor people?

Alex Counts: Well, see for poor people who don't have access to jobs and don't have a **safety net**, the only alternatives are to starve or to work for yourself. For most of the poor, they have so little money that their businesses are highly undercapitalized. So the option of doing the same things they're doing but having them at a more reasonable capital level, that's an option that people should have. They shouldn't, obviously, be forced to take it, but many of them are extremely happy to be able to take 60 or 70 dollars which triples the capital of their simple, rural business doing trading or a **cottage industry** of some kind, and that becomes then a pathway to break the poverty cycle.

RR: Tell us how 60 or 70 dollars can make a big difference.

AC: Well, again, just to take a very simple example that I saw many times when I was living in Bangladesh was a woman who knew how to raise chickens and she would sell the eggs and that was how she would meet her daily needs. But she never had enough capital to have more than three chickens at any given time and every so often they would be **wiped out** by disease. By taking 60 dollars she would be able to have 12 or 13 chickens and do it on a larger scale and generate enough income to send her child to school, to treat illness with modern medicine. And, again, this is a very small amount. Some of the women who do that ultimately end up four years later having a poultry farm of 500 chickens.

Part Two

RR: Raj, how big a part do you think these microloans and microfinancing can be to raise people out of poverty?

Raj Shah: Well, it clearly plays a very important role over time. As Alex points out, it's also not for everyone. What I thought it's important for your listeners to get a picture of is that the idea of moving someone from extreme poverty to moderate poverty, while that may not sound like a lot, actually means quite a bit to both that household and the children in those households, and so some of the most **compelling** data around impact has been what happens to the kids of women who are participating in these microcredit or microfinance programs. In very poor environments, you see improved height and weight outcomes, which are signs of basic human nutrition. You see improvements in school attendance and paying school fees. One of the most important things I learned by visiting so many of these programs is wherever you go, anywhere around the world, you ask people what they do with the expanded income they've earned from their business activity—buy a sewing machine, make a little bit more money—what's the first thing they do with that money, and nine times out of ten it is pay school fees for their children and provide better opportunities for their children. So it is important to get a **characterization** of what we mean when we say move from extreme poverty to moderate poverty—that can have very important outcomes for children and for the next generation. And then, as Alex points out, maybe a third to 40 percent of all clients who stick with the program for a significant period of time will move out of poverty in some **sustainable** manner, so it's an important tool, but its not the only tool.

Part Three

RR: Is there a zero sum here? I'm wondering whether money that goes into microfinancing is money that might go to another program that might help people in poverty and whether it **diminishes** some of these other programs. For example, if I go to Kiva.org, Matt, I could make a loan to someone or I could say, you know, I think I'd rather write a check to CARE or in some other way provide support to people in developing countries who are in deep poverty. Is it taking away from other services to open up this line, or is it. . . .

Matt Flannery: Well, the great thing, I think, about microfinance is that it is a **sustainable** way of helping people in poverty, so unlike other development aid programs it is a **gift that can keep on giving**. The poor can borrow and that loan can be recycled and another person can borrow it, so I think of it as a contribution that is more leveraged and can help more people over time and can go on **into perpetuity** and help one entrepreneur after another.

Part Four

RR: Alex, you mentioned the **backlash**. Do your critics have any good points?

AC: Well, of course. I'm, again, having interviewed hundreds if not thousands of microfinance clients, you don't, uh, there's no **overnight** success even for those who succeed; it does take years and these things are not . . . is not a **panacea** but what I think your listeners should keep in mind—there are really two things; one is a shift from extreme poverty to moderate poverty, while you might think it sounds like a failure—you've not crossed the poverty line—it's probably a bigger life change financially and socially than any of your listeners are ever going to have over the course of their entire lives.

RR: Give us an example of what that actually means.

AC: Well, what it means is being able to have to make choices every nine or 10 months out of the year about which two members of the five member family will eat as opposed to almost every month of the year having some minimal basic foodstuff for everyone in the family, or having to make choices of which one of three children will go to school or being able to send all three of them to school.

RR: Thanks to all of you. And doubtlessly, with the involvement of the organizations such as Kiva.org and the Bill and Melinda Gates Foundation, we're going to see microfinancing developing quite a bit more in the coming years. We'll check in on it and tell you how it is developing.

LISTEN FOR DETAILS

(Repeat Listen for Main Ideas)

MAKE INFERENCES

Excerpt One

RR: There are obvious benefits to credit, but there are also pitfalls. You can get overextended, you don't own anything, the bank ends up owning it. In some ways, paying as you go might be a better idea. Is credit always a good thing, particularly for poor people?

Excerpt Two

AC: Well, see for poor people who don't have access to jobs and don't have a safety net, the only alternatives are to starve or to work for yourself. For most of the poor, they have so little money that their businesses are highly undercapitalized. So the option of doing the same things they're doing but having them at a more reasonable capital level, that's an option that people should have.

Excerpt Three

RR: Is there a zero sum here? I'm wondering whether money that goes into microfinancing is money that might go to another program that might help people in poverty and whether it diminishes some of these other programs. For example, if I go to Kiva.org, Matt, I could make a loan to someone or I could say, you know, I think I'd rather write a check to CARE or in some other way provide support to people in developing countries who are in deep poverty.

Excerpt Four

AC: . . . there are really two things: one is a shift from extreme poverty to moderate poverty, while you might think it sounds like a failure—you've not crossed the poverty line—it's probably a bigger life change financially and socially than any of your listeners are ever going to have over the course of their entire lives.

RR: Give us an example of what that actually means.

Excerpt Five

AC: Well, again, just to take a very simple example that I saw many times when I was living in Bangladesh was a woman who knew how to raise chickens and she would sell the eggs and that was how she would meet her daily needs. But she never had enough capital to have more than three chickens at any given time and every so often they would be wiped out by disease. By taking 60 dollars she would be able to have 12 or 13 chickens and do it on a larger scale and generate enough income to send her child to school, to treat illness with modern medicine. And, again, this is a very small amount. Some of the women who do that ultimately end up four years later having a poultry farm of 500 chickens.

2B. LISTENING TWO: *Interview with a Microfinance Director*

Part One

Interviewer: Thank you for joining me today, Will.

Will Bullard: It's a pleasure.

Interviewer: I was wondering if you could tell me a specific story of one woman whose life was changed with the help of a microloan that she got from Adelante?

WB: I'll tell you about a client that I went and visited maybe four or five times. She was the client who had nine kids and, **the world over**, when you have a **malnourished** child, that child's hair is going to turn a reddish tint, and she had . . . her ninth child had that reddish tint hair and everyone in the village knows what that meant and so when Maria Jose went to the assembly in her village to ask to be allowed to join the assembly there, one of the major components of microcredit is that the women themselves get to decide, or have to decide, who they allow in their assembly and who they will not allow in because they are going to co-sign for her loan. And the women in this community voted not to allow her in because they felt that she was going to eat the loan—and that's a very literal term here—that you'll get your 50 dollars and you'll go out and have a good meal that you only can dream about, so they said no. But there was a very nice woman who was another client and who **had faith in** Maria Jose and she gave Maria Jose, I think, 25 dollars just kind of as a test loan, and Maria Jose went out and invested the 25 dollars in flour and some cooking supplies, made some little meat pies that she sold in front of the school and she paid her friend back and that was enough evidence that she could handle her money that she was then allowed into the assembly. She became a dynamic entrepreneur and she became very successful. She lived in a horrible little grass hut and then she built a concrete house that she moved all of her kids into; it's only a one-room house but it's a huge step up. She became the vice president of her Adelante assembly.

Part Two

Interviewer: It sounds like from that **anecdote** that woman got incredible benefits and was really able to change her life through the power of microloans, but you were saying that you think the real benefits are not **monetary**. Could you **elaborate** on what you mean by that?

WB: I'm not sure that many people are leaving poverty behind and the impact studies are kind of suggesting the same, that there are other benefits—non-monetary benefits as well as the woman I just mentioned. So she gets to that house because she's been able to sell meat in her village but then, you know, things are kind of stopped, how much further can you go? You don't have a third grade education. You don't have a big market in your community. To be quite honest with you, that woman I just told about, she had such confidence in herself—that **non-monetary** benefit—that she sold her bicycle that she had bought, and she did what a lot of people here do; she went to the North, she tried to get to the States. She didn't make it; she came back and **took a huge hit** in the process. It's a very complicated world down here.

Part Three

Interviewer: It sounds like the power of microloaning kind of hits a ceiling at a certain point. And you were saying how you think the next step would be to bring in business training—how would that work exactly?

WB: Women here do want a better life; they want to do better and they know that selling used clothing and they know that selling little meat pies and sweetbreads are only going to get them so far. It might not even be the majority, but a good percentage of them would do whatever they could to make more money, and to do that, like in any country in the world—developed or developing country, you need skills, you need training to advance. So surely there's a way to go to women and to say, "Well, your sweetbreads are good, but what if you sold this kind of sweetbread or this kind of cake?"—that would have a little bit higher margins, that other people aren't selling, or "You're selling things nicely but what if you targeted this particular **niche market** where the revenues are . . ." that's being neglected. And the whole **kicker** is there are only so many sandals, and so many plastic pots and so many things you can sell in a village after you meet that very small pie . . . what do you do? How do you grow that pie? How do you start producing things that add value? It's a sort of tricky thing.

Interviewer: Well, thank you so much for talking with me today.

WB: Thank you, Eric.

3A. VOCABULARY

REVIEW

Exercise 2

Greetings from La Ceiba, Honduras. First, I must tell you that this little speck on earth is just unbelievably gorgeous—beautiful, lush with breathtaking cloud formations hugging spectacular green mountains. Still, on the drive from the airport to my lodge I witnessed the pervasive poverty we see the world over: skinny malnourished children standing next to houses and shops still not rebuilt since Hurricane Mitch struck much of the country in 1988. Already the second poorest country in Latin America, Honduras took a hit and never recovered. To research my article, I set out to visit microfinance institutions as well as meet the microcredit client to whom I had lent money from my laptop in Mexico City, where I live.

Kiva.org is a non-profit microcredit organization that allows individuals with access to the Internet to fight global poverty in a sustainable way by making a direct personal loan to poor entrepreneurs anywhere in the world. On the Kiva website I came across the compelling photo and story of Julia Marta Mendez, a fascinating Honduran widow in her late thirties with six children to whom I had lent 50 dollars. I had faith in her and just knew she would stick with her goals and use the money well.

With this tiny loan, Julia opened a small shop in which she sold delicious coconut bread made from a unique family recipe. After three months, she was able to leverage the initial investment to expand her business to include other savory Honduran foodstuffs, such as baleadas, special Honduran tortillas. I wish there were time to elaborate on these specialties, describing their delicate aromas and flavors. And I wish you all could witness the non-monetary benefits of the loans—no challenge, no obstacle, nothing can diminish Julia's enthusiasm, sense of confidence, and hope for her future.

But here's the real kicker, which you might find difficult to believe! In spite of Julia's outstanding success so far, she worries that her business may already have hit a ceiling. A competing shop has opened next to hers, so she now feels she needs training in marketing and advertising to fuel future business growth. Indeed, I realize that money alone is not a total panacea. We all know that when it comes to alleviating poverty, there is no such thing as overnight success. Truly, one of the biggest pitfalls of microfinance is the need for business training. Listen again for tomorrow's story—an anecdote from my visit with Julia.

THE PHONETIC ALPHABET

Consonant Symbols

/b/	**b**e	/t/	**t**o
/d/	**d**o	/v/	**v**an
/f/	**f**ather	/w/	**w**ill
/g/	**g**et	/y/	**y**es
/h/	**h**e	/z/	**z**oo, bu**s**y
/k/	**k**eep, **c**an	/θ/	**th**anks
/l/	**l**et	/ð/	**th**en
/m/	**m**ay	/ʃ/	**sh**e
/n/	**n**o	/ʒ/	vi**s**ion, A**s**ia
/p/	**p**en	/tʃ/	**ch**ild
/r/	**r**ain	/dʒ/	**j**oin
/s/	**s**o, **c**ircle	/ŋ/	lo**ng**

Vowel Symbols

/ɑ/	f**a**r, h**o**t	/iy/	w**e**, m**ea**n, f**ee**t
/ɛ/	m**e**t, s**ai**d	/ey/	d**ay**, l**a**te, r**ai**n
/ɔ/	t**a**ll, b**ou**ght	/ow/	g**o**, l**ow**, c**oa**t
/ə/	s**o**n, **u**nder	/uw/	t**oo**, bl**ue**
/æ/	c**a**t	/ay/	t**i**me, b**uy**
/ɪ/	sh**i**p	/aw/	h**ou**se, n**ow**
/ʊ/	g**oo**d, c**ou**ld, p**u**t	/oy/	b**oy**, c**oi**n

REVIEWERS

For the comments and insights they graciously offered to help shape the direction of the Third Edition of *NorthStar,* the publisher would like to thank the following reviewers and institutions.

Gail August, Hostos Community College; **Anne Bachmann**, Clackamas Community College; **Aegina Barnes**, York College, CUNY; **Dr. Sabri Bebawi**, San Jose Community College; **Kristina Beckman**, John Jay College; **Jeff Bellucci**, Kaplan Boston; **Nathan Blesse**, Human International Academy; **Alan Brandman**, Queens College; **Laila Cadavona-Dellapasqua**, Kaplan; **Amy Cain**, Kaplan; **Nigel Caplan**, Michigan State University; **Alzira Carvalho**, Human International Academy, San Diego; **Chao-Hsun (Richard) Cheng**, Wenzao Ursuline College of Languages; **Mu-hua (Yolanda) Chi**, Wenzao Ursuline College of Languages; **Liane Cismowski**, Olympic High School; **Shauna Croft**, MESLS; **Misty Crooks**, Kaplan; **Amanda De Loera**, Kaplan English Programs; **Jennifer Dobbins**, New England School of English; **Luis Dominguez**, Angloamericano; **Luydmila Drgaushanskaya**, ASA College; **Dilip Dutt**, Roxbury Community College; **Christie Evenson**, Chung Dahm Institute; **Patricia Frenz-Belkin**, Hostos Community College, CUNY; **Christiane Galvani**, Texas Southern University; **Joanna Ghosh**, University of Pennsylvania; **Cristina Gomes**, Kaplan Test Prep; **Kristen Grinager**, Lincoln High School; **Janet Harclerode**, Santa Monica College; **Carrell Harden**, HCCS, Gulfton Campus; **Connie Harney**, Antelope Valley College; **Ann Hilborn**, ESL Consultant in Houston; **Barbara Hockman**, City College of San Francisco; **Margaret Hodgson**, NorQuest College; **Paul Hong**, Chung Dahm Institute; **Wonki Hong**, Chung Dahm Institute; **John House**, Iowa State University; **Polly Howlett**, Saint Michael's College; **Arthur Hui**, Fullerton College; **Nina Ito**, CSU, Long Beach; **Scott Jenison**, Antelope Valley College; **Hyunsook Jeong**, Keimyung University; **Mandy Kama**, Georgetown University; **Dale Kim**, Chung Dahm Institute; **Taeyoung Kim**, Keimyung University; **Woo-hyung Kim**, Keimyung University; **Young Kim**, Chung Dahm Institute; **Yu-kyung Kim**, Sunchon National University; **John Kostovich**, Miami Dade College; **Albert Kowun**, Fairfax, VA; **David Krise**, Michigan State University; **Cheri (Young Hee) Lee**, ReadingTownUSA English Language Institute; **Eun-Kyung Lee**, Chung Dahm Institute; **Sang Hyock Lee**, Keimyung University; **Debra Levitt**, SMC; **Karen Lewis**, Somerville, MA; **Chia-Hui Liu**, Wenzao Ursuline College of Languages; **Gennell Lockwood**, Seattle, WA; **Javier Lopez Anguiano**, Colegio Anglo Mexicano de Coyoacan; **Mary March**, Shoreline Community College; **Susan Matson**, ELS Language Centers; **Ralph McClain**, Embassy CES Boston; **Veronica McCormack**, Roxbury Community College; **Jennifer McCoy**, Kaplan; **Joseph McHugh**, Kaplan; **Cynthia McKeag Tsukamoto**, Oakton Community College; **Paola Medina**, Texas Southern University; **Christine Kyung-ah Moon**, Seoul, Korea; **Margaret Moore**, North Seattle Community College; **Michelle Moore**, Madison English as a Second Language School; **David Motta**, Miami University; **Suzanne Munro**, Clackamas Community College; **Elena Nehrbecki**, Hudson County CC; **Kim Newcomer**, University of Washington; **Melody Nightingale**, Santa Monica College; **Patrick Northover**, Kaplan Test and Prep; **Sarah Oettle**, Kaplan, Sacramento; **Shirley Ono**, Oakton Community College; **Maria Estela Ortiz Torres**, C. Anglo Mexicano de Coyoac'an; **Suzanne Overstreet**, West Valley College; **Linda Ozarow**, West Orange High School; **Ileana Porges-West**, Miami Dade College, Hialeah Campus; **Megan Power**, ILCSA; **Alison Robertson**, Cypress College; **Ma. Del Carmen Romero**, Universidad del Valle de Mexico; **Nina Rosen**, Santa Rosa Junior College; **Daniellah Salario**, Kaplan; **Joel Samuels**, Kaplan New York City; **Babi Sarapata**, Columbia University ALP; **Donna Schaeffer**, University of Washington; **Lynn Schneider**, City College of San Francisco; **Errol Selkirk**, New School University; **Amity Shook**, Chung Dahm Institute; **Lynn Stafford-Yilmaz**, Bellevue Community College; **Lynne Ruelaine Stokes**, Michigan State University; **Henna Suh**, Chung Dahm Institute; **Sheri Summers**, Kaplan Test Prep; **Martha Sutter**, Kent State University; **Becky Tarver Chase**, MESLS; **Lisa Waite-Trago**, Michigan State University; **Carol Troy**, Da-Yeh University; **Luci Tyrell**, Embassy CES Fort Lauderdale; **Yong-Hee Uhm**, Myongii University; **Debra Un**, New York University; **José Vazquez**, The University of Texas Pan American; **Hollyahna Vettori**, Santa Rosa Junior College; **Susan Vik**, Boston University; **Sandy Wagner**, Fort Lauderdale High School; **Joanne Wan**, ASC English; **Pat Wiggins**, Clackamas Community College; **Heather Williams**, University of Pennsylvania; **Carol Wilson-Duffy**, Michigan State University; **Kailin Yang**, Kaohsing Medical University; **Ellen Yaniv**, Boston University; **Samantha Young**, Kaplan Boston; **Yu-san Yu**, National Sun Yat-sen University; **Ann Zaaijer**, West Orange High School

CREDITS

Photo Credits: Page 1 The New Yorker Collection 2001 David Sipress from cartoonbank.com. All rights reserved; **Page 2** Jon Riley/Getty Images; **Page 8** Copyright 1995, Boston Globe. Distributed by Los Angeles Times Syndicate. Reprinted with permission; **Page 23** © 2008 Peter Steiner from cartoonbank.com. All rights reserved; **Page 33** Vincent Hazat/age fotostock; **Page 45** www.CartoonStock.com; **Page 46** Lisa Peardon/Getty Images; **Page 73** Courtesy of Hush Puppies; **Page 77** (1) Plush Studios/age fotostock, (2) GoGo Images/age fotostock, (3) Michael Newman/PhotoEdit; **Page 78** (4) John Lund/Sam Diephui/age fotostock, (5) Corbis/ZEFA RF/age fotostock, (6) Juice Images/age fotostock, (bottom) Gerard Rancinan/Sygma /Corbis; **Page 90** Geoffrey Clements/Corbis; **Page 99** The New Yorker Collection 1995 Donald Reilly from cartoonbank.com. All rights reserved; **Page 115** Warner Bros./Photofest; **Page 119** Marco Cristofori/zefa/Corbis; **Page 123** Tom Nebbia/Corbis; **Page 125** Chris Hellier/Corbis; **Page 132** AP/Wide World Photos; **Page 139** Dean Lewins/AP Images; **Page 143** Bob Krist/Corbis; **Page 147** Signe Wilkinson/Cartoonists & Writers Syndicate; **Page 148** Blend Images/Alamy; **Page 150** (top) Jose Luis Pelaez, Inc./age fotostock, (middle) Amos Morgan/age fotostock, (bottom) Kevin Peterson/age fotostock; **Page 168** recognitionsystems.ingersollrand.com; **Page 171** Copyright International Committee of the Red Cross; **Page 173** Patrick Robert/Sygma/Corbis; **Page 187** (top) Yannis Kontos/Corbis Sygma, (bottom) AFP/Getty Images; **Page 193** Erik S. Lesser/Getty Images; **Page 197** The New Yorker Collection 1997 Leo Cullum from cartoonbank.com. All rights reserved; **Page 202** Shutterstock; **Page 221** Cindy Charles/PhotoEdit; **Page 225** (left) www.unitus.com, (right) www.adelantefoundation.org; **Page 234** BjoernSigurdsoen/AFP /Getty Images; **Page 237** Nicholas Gill/Alamy; **Page 238** Francisco Gonzalez/age fotostock.

Listening Selections and Text Credits: Page 4, *Talk of the Nation: Science Friday,* interview with Jonathan Kandell, February 2, 1996. Reproduced with permission of Talk of the Nation; **Page 6,** "Time to Do Everything Except Think" from *Newsweek on Air,* April 30, 2001 © 2001, Newsweek Inc. and The Associated Press. All rights reserved. Used with permission; **Page 28 and 31,** excerpts from *The Infinite Mind,* "Lies, Lies, Lies" broadcast on May 1, 2007, copyright © 2007 Lichtenstein Creative Media, Inc. Used with permission; **Page 49** © NPR. The text and audio of the news report by NPR's Alex Chadwick was originally broadcast in 1995 and are used with permission of NPR. Any unauthorized duplication is strictly prohibited; **Page 53,** "The Pollyanna Syndrome: from Tales from the Workplace: Making Lemonade" by Julie Danis, courtesy of Marketplace®, Copyright 1996, American Public Media. Used by permission. All rights reserved; **Page 68,** *Left of Center* by Suzanne Vega and Stephen Addabbo © 1986 WB Music Corp. (ASCAP), Waifersongs Ltd. (ASCAP) and Famous Music Corporation (ASCAP). All Rights o/b/o Waifersongs Ltd. administered by WB Music Corp. Warner Bros. Publications U.S. Inc., Miami, FL 33014; **Page 75,** "The Tipping Point" from an interview with Malcolm Gladwell on *The Connection* on April 13, 2000. Reprinted by permission of WBUR 90.9FM (Boston's NPR News Station), online at www.wbur.org; **Page 78,** "Tipping Points in Fighting Crime" interview with Malcolm Gladwell by Todd Mundt. © 2001.

Reprinted by permission of Michigan Radio; **Page 103,** "Interview with a Feng Shui Expert" with Sedge Thomson interviewing Kirsten Lagatree on February 10, 1996, Reprinted by permission of West Coast Live; **Page 106,** "Feng Shui in the Newsroom" interview with Kirsten Lagatree and Steve Scher on KUOW Public Radio on February 6, 1996. Reprinted by permission of KUOW Public Radio; **Page 126,** The text and audio of the news report by NPR's Duncan Moon was originally broadcast on NPR's All Things Considered® on December 14, 2001 and are used with permission of NPR. Any unauthorized duplication is strictly prohibited; **Page 129,** "Describing Monastic Life by William Claassen from WAMY 88.5's "The Kojo Nnamdi Show" broadcast on Monday, June 18, 2001. Reprinted by permission of WAMU, American University Radio; **Page 151,** The text and audio of the news report by NPR's Elaine Korry was originally broadcast on NPR's Weekend Edition® on May 22, 1996, 2001 and are used with permission of NPR. Any unauthorized duplication is strictly prohibited; **Pages 174 and 179,** "Warriors without Weapons" and "Michael Ignatieff's Views on War" on *Fresh Air* with Terry Gross on March 31, 1997. Reprinted by permission of WHYY in Philadelphia, PA, USA; **Page 198,** Bora Kim, 14 years old, a student at the Ichimura Music School in Englewood Cliffs, NJ. The piece is Mozart's Sonata for Piano in F Major, 1st Movement, Allegro, K-332; **Page 201,** The text and audio of the news report by NPR's Michelle Trudeau was originally broadcast on NPR's All Things Considered(r) on May 22, 1996 and are used with permission of NPR. Any unauthorized duplication is strictly prohibited; **Page 206,** "Music, Art, and the Brain" from *Newsweek on Air,* March 3, 1996, © 1996, Newsweek, Inc. Reprinted with permission of Pars International. All rights reserved.; **Page 230,** "Microfinance" interview with Alex Counts, Raj Shah, and Matt Flannery by Ross Reynolds on KUOW Public Radio on July 17, 2006 on *Weekday.* Reprinted by permission of KUOW Public Radio.

Illustration Credits: Paul Hampson, **Pages 58, 59**.